Social Transformation and Chinese Experience

China's success in economic growth and its exploration in political reform in the past few decades have attracted attention from worldwide economic and political experts. This book studies China's transformation and experience from a sociological perspective, which broadens the research horizons and explores more complexity in contemporary China.

This book examines China's social structural transformation, especially its implications on resource allocation, and expounds on China's sociology academic history. In addition, it covers a broad range of issues including China's experience with reform and development, urbanization, social hierarchy change, social conflicts, social management, and mass consumption. Lastly, it investigates China's "urban village" as a byproduct of economic development and urbanization, which is rarely seen in other countries. These themes are key to understanding contemporary Chinese society, which makes this book a valuable reference for specialists on Chinese studies and those who are interested in contemporary China.

Peilin Li is a professor of sociology and vice president of Chinese Academy of Social Sciences. His research interests include social development, social structure, and social policies. He has published and edited hundreds of articles, books, and essay collections in Chinese, English, and French.

China Perspectives series

The *China Perspectives* series focuses on translating and publishing works by leading Chinese scholars writing about both global topics and China-related themes. It covers Humanities and Social Sciences, Education, Media, and Psychology, as well as many interdisciplinary themes.

This is the first time any of these books have been published in English for international readers. The series aims to put forward a Chinese perspective, give insights into cutting-edge academic thinking in China, and inspire researchers globally.

For more information, please visit https://www.routledge.com/series/CPH.

Social Transformation and Chinese Experience
Peilin Li

Forthcoming titles

China's Low Birth-Rate and the Development of Population
Zhigang Guo, Feng Wang, Yong Cai

The Living Conditions and Succor Mechanism of the Urban Underclass in China
Li Zhu, Feifei Mao

Contemporary China Social Structure and Hierarchy
Xueyi Lu

Contemporary China Social Construction and Development
Xueyi Lu

Social Transformation and Chinese Experience

Peilin Li

Routledge
Taylor & Francis Group
LONDON AND NEW YORK

中國社會科學出版社
CHINA SOCIAL SCIENCES PRESS

First published 2017 by Routledge
Translator: Yujie Chen

2 Park Square, Milton Park, Abingdon, Oxfordshire OX14 4RN
52 Vanderbilt Avenue, New York, NY 10017

Routledge is an imprint of the Taylor & Francis Group, an informa business

First issued in paperback 2020

British Library Cataloguing-in-Publication Data
A catalogue record for this book is available from the British Library

Library of Congress Cataloging-in-Publication Data
A catalog record for this book has been requested

ISBN: 978-1-138-89959-9 (hbk)
ISBN: 978-0-367-52286-5 (pbk)

Typeset in Times New Roman
by Apex CoVantage, LLC

Contents

Figures and tables

Figures

Tables

Acknowledgements

This book is a collection of evidence-based studies funded by the Innovation Program of the Chinese Academy of Social Sciences (CASS). It contains my experience regarding both the practices and the theoretical studies of China's social transformation.

Here I would like to express my sincere gratitude to Ms. Chen Yujie, the translator of this book, for her painstaking efforts devoted to the book; I also thank all of the colleagues at China Social Sciences Press for their professional and energetic support.

My particular thanks goes to the CASS Innovation Translation Fund for having the book published.

June 2016

1 Another invisible hand

The structural transformation of the society

More than ten years after China's economic reforms, China is at the new threshold of the structural transformations of the society. Transformations are evident in China's transition from a self-sufficient and semi-self-sufficient product economy to a planned commercial economy, in the emergence of an industrialized China from an agricultural society, in turning a predominantly rural society into an urban society, in the evolution from a closed and semiclosed society to an open society, and the list continues (Lu & Li, 1999). This chapter attempts to elaborate on the theories regarding the structural transformation of the society.

It is commonly accepted that there are two hands at play for allocating Chinese resources and boosting Chinese economic development. Namely, they are the visible hand of the state intervention and the invisible hand of the market regulation. In fact, since China is currently at the stage of structural transformation and Chinese economy is in an unbalanced state (broadly defined); there remains a third, invisible hand: the structural transformation of the society. When a society is at the stage of transformation, the structural transformation, in a sense, is an invisible and enormous power that by its own rules sets the trend and directions for social development and resource allocations. This type of invisible and enormous power cannot be exhausted by the categories of state intervention or market regulation. The power of socially structural transformation is a potential driving force for the development, even more so and more salient for the transition from the old social system to the new.

Conceptualize the social transformation

Social transformation is a holistic development

When people describe the modernization of a nation state, the terms "growth" and "development" are often used alternately. On most of the occasions, they are interchangeable. However, there are fundamental distinctions in these two concepts that represent two different outlooks on development.

Economic growth refers to an increase in the gross national product (GNP) or national income. Economic growth can simply mean an increase in the ratio of national product output and labor force to population growth. In the post-WWII era, the world has entered a relatively peaceful time of development. As a majority of countries shifted their focus to economic growth, an economic-centered perspective dominated the outlook on development. This is what we now call "traditional development strategy" – the one that is centered on quantitative growth in GNP or national income. Influential theories such as the Harrod-Domar model, Joan Robinson's growth model, vicious circle of poverty, and theory of the big push took shape in this period of time. The United Nations (UN) has set the basic objective for the least developed countries in the first United Nations Development Decade (1960–1970) to grow their GNP at a rate no less than 6 percent. The Pearson Report to the World Bank in 1969 and proposals for the Second United Nations Development Decade in 1970 (known as Tinbergen Report) were emblematic of the traditional development outlook. The traditional development outlook holds economic growth as the expressway to social development. The more the economy grows, it reasons, the more surpluses are available for distribution so that poverty can be eliminated. Moreover, after the collapse of colonialism, Western developed countries attempted to maintain their control over raw material supplies from their prior colonies, which were also commodity markets for the former. For this reason, Western developed countries strove to incorporate the Third World into the orbit of the capitalistic economy, with the hope that their economic prosperity would be a convincing demonstration of the developmental model. It was against this backdrop that the hype of "economic growth" became prominent in Western theories, news coverage, broadcasting, and political addresses in the decades of the 1950s and 1960s.

Unfortunately, capitalistic economies began to suffer from "stagnation" from the early 1970s. Developing countries suffered more from depletion of irreproducible resources, and environmental deterioration resulted from unbalanced economic growth. Decades of postwar experience have made it evident that economic growth alone would not eradicate poverty. On the contrary, uneven development has caused great inequalities in wealth, the drain of profits, heavy debts, a shortage of resources, environmental pollutions, and a widening gap between the urban and the rural, and so on. What is at stake are programs for social progress, including education for the mass population, social security, Medicare, ecological environment, and social justice. All these problems cast a long shadow over the once catchy buzzword "growth."

The dictum "growth without development" best summaries the aforementioned circumstances. The concept of social development has holistic registers, which comprise average people's daily lives, science and technology, education, social security, Medicare, and social order, in addition to economic growth, wherein structural transformation of the economic society is the essence of development.

Social transformation is a particular type of structural change

"Tradition" is one of the most excessively used terms in theories on social transformation. When people use the term, they use it in a derogatory way that associates tradition with backwater, underdeveloped, and static social structures – an antithesis to the modern society, which implies advancement, prosperity, and mobility.

Therefore, the binary between the tradition and the modern is problematic yet pervasive in the Western classical theories on modernization. It is seen in Henry Sumner Maine's descriptions "from status to contract," Herbert Spencer's categorization of "militant and industrial societies," Émile Durkheim's distinction between "mechanical and organic solidarity," Robert Redfield's characterizing of the relationship between folk and urban societies, Max Weber's conceptualization of premodern and modern societies, and Ulrich Beck's theories about religion and secular society. The dichotomy created between "tradition" and "modern" causes a plausible and insurmountable hurdle for traditional societies that have to overcome the hurdle before becoming modern societies.

The truth is that in all these theories, the definition of tradition is vague. Setting their own society as the ideal model of the modern society, Western theorists on modernization are inclined to conceive a traditional society that is opposite to theirs as if there is a clear-cut distinction between the traditional and the modern. Among the things that are often lumped into the category of tradition are noneconomic factors or nonmaterial cultural aspects such values, behavioral norms, social psychology, and religion. This mind-set faced formidable challenges from Eastern countries' road to modernity in the past 30 years. For instance, a few east and south Asian countries and regions have reached the level comparable to that of moderate or most economically developed countries. However, their national ethos, social relations, the means of organization and administration, and their cultures remain "traditional," which is called having "oriental characteristics." Meanwhile, scholars refuse to acknowledge some Latin American countries and oil-exporting countries as modern states despite the fact that they have modern urban areas, extravagant hotels, shops for luxury goods, and fairly high per capita income.

In short, what makes a country modern is not a clean break with its traditions but the structural transformation of the society. For tradition per se is a dynamic process that involves accommodations of the past, the contemporary, and the future. Classical modernization theorists' understandings of social structure is circumscribed by their narrow definitions of culture and bias derived from the Western development model, so parts of their conclusions belie their original intentions.

We argue that social transformation is a particular type of structural change with three folds of meaning. First, social transformation refers to not only the changes that have occurred to the economic structure but also changes to other social aspects. It needs to be understood as a holistic and comprehensive transition. Second, social transformation is particular to an interim stage – a transition from one to another in a continued structural transformation. As Hollis Chenery, a professor at Harvard University and a consultant to the World Bank put forward the concept of structural change, he wrote, "In describing the process of development we have tried to replace the notion of a dichotomy between less developed and developed countries with the concept of a transition from one state to the other" (Chenery & Syrquin, 1989, p.147). Third, social transformation is also an analytical concept for quantitative relations, illustrated by a series of variables regarding structural changes, which cannot be captured by macrodescriptions or abstract analysis. We will elaborate on this point in the following section.

Social transformation as an analytical concept for quantitative relationships

Indeed, the introduction of quantitative analysis into inspecting the changes of social structures symbolizes a resumption of emphasis on structural issues.

Human society has an ancient interest in being attentive to social structures and spatial arrangements. However, social science scholars had long treated social structures as being static before the theory of evolution was introduced. This led to the establishment of sociology-enabled scholars who connect the inquiries into the social structures to the social process. Namely, as they examined how society worked, they explored changes to social structures. Nonetheless, their focus then was to discover the universal laws behind the history. Adam Smith's theory of an "invisible hand" is undoubtedly one of the most significant contributions by the endeavor to discover the universal laws, which the former propelled as an excitant. Scholars' explorations into universal laws (e.g., the syllogism that explained structural transformations) have not gone beyond abstract analysis and empirical observations ever since.

It was not until the late 1960s and the early 1970s that scholars in the field of social science began to recognize the significance of social structures. One indication was the introduction of quantitative analysis into the explorations into socioeconomic structures. In *Modern Economic Growth: Rate, Structure, and Spread*, Simon Smith Kuznets, a Nobel Prize laureate in economics sciences, conducted a comparative study about the economic growth in many countries with regard to production, allocation of resources, income distribution, consumption, and external relations through analyzing massive amounts of historical and statistical data. The valuable part of the book is when Kuznets, despite being an economist, incorporated statistical analysis on noneconomic factors as much as possible (such as demographics, political structure, cultural characteristics, and social integration) (Kuznets, 1989). Another economics Nobel Prize winner, W. Arthur Lewis, along with his dual-sector model, demonstrated the attention to structural issues from another perspective. Lewis examined the relationship between a traditional "subsistence" sector and a modern "capitalistic" sector by exploring the economy of surplus labor (Lewis, 1954; 1958). The dual-sector model, invented by Lewis and based on structural analysis, has become one of the significant theoretical frameworks for investigations into how structures would change and transform in the developing countries, with special regard to the urban-rural relations, the labor mobility, and the structure for income distributions.

In fact, introducing quantitative analysis into the exploration of socioeconomic structures fills the gap in the dichotomy between the traditional and the modern since it allows us to detect the sequence and trajectories of changes that happened to varied aspects of socioeconomic structures. Hollis Chenery adopted a quantitative approach toward the long cycle of economic growth and connected structural transformations to the industrialization process in his theory. As early as the 1970s, Chenery and Syrquin took advantage of the World Bank's data regarding 100-odd countries that were at different levels of development over the 1050–70 period to examine the trajectory of the transformations to the economic structure.

They divided the development process into nine stages based on a per capita income ranging from $100 to $1,000. They tested 27 variables corresponding to 10 measured elements about the economy in order to discover structural changes associated with development among countries. The ten measured elements were classified in three broad categories: 1) accumulation – investment, government revenue, and education; 2) resource allocation processes – structure of domestic demand, production, and trade; and 3) demographic and distributional processes – labor force allocation, urbanization, birth and death rates, income distribution (Chenery & Syrquin, 1989, p.9).

Since the 1960s, sociologists also attempted to consider a quantitative index in their evaluations of the transformations of social structures. Those quantitative indicators for modern social structures are often defined as "tipping points" for the transformation of the social structure. Alex Inkeles, a sociology professor from Stanford University and his colleague David Smith, after surveying a massive number of people from six nations in Asia, Africa, and Latin America, identified ten characteristics to describe a modern state's structure. In addition to major economic characteristics, they also included literacy rate, percentage of college graduates, net growth rate of population, average life span, and so on (Inkeles & Smith, 1974). Their inclusion of those widely acknowledged social characteristics indicated a profound mutation in the outlook pertaining to social development.

From these various conceptualizations of social transformations, we argue that the social structure is the core of social transformations that needs to be understood as a holistic and comprehensive transition of the structure, rather than reaching individual goals of development. Specific contents enclosed in the social transformation are structural and institutional transitions, benefit adjustments, and attitudinal changes. In the process of social transformations, there are remarkable changes happening to people's behaviors, lifestyles, and values systems.

Characteristics of structural transformations of Chinese society

Instead of being unique to socialist countries, the structural transformation of the society is a transitional stage for the modernization process. As Chinese society has its own specificities regarding history, cultures, and resources, the structural transformation of the Chinese society reveals some variations in the development process.

Structural transformation in phase with institutional transition

It is a rare case in the modernization process that a country's structural transformation is so tightly associated with its economic reforms. There are many reasons for current structural transformations of the Chinese society, but undoubtedly, the immediate cause is economic reform.

First, economic reform and opening up has unleashed many new factors. For the economic system, the establishment of public ownership serving as its main body but allowing for the development of all types of ownership has replaced the prior centralized organizational system, bringing about profound changes to production management, circulation, distribution, the financial system, the fiscal and taxation system, price system, and foreign trade. China has set the norms accommodating the establishment of a commodity economy, which particularly includes market competition. Market expansion has enhanced the mobility of resources and stimulated new forms of economy, social organizations, and professional associations, making the social stratification based on professionalization inevitable. The new norms are not centered upon stifling disciplines and regulations but work toward reasonable mobility of resources. Moreover, China has introduced more than 20,000 advanced technologies since the opening up. Technologies play dominant roles in social transformations because technological inventions not only foster productivity but also transform people's everyday lives and behaviors. Look no further than how the widespread use of home appliances has transformed people's lives in the past dozens of years. Public mode of thought has also undergone tremendous changes with new ideas taking shape regarding commodities, benefits, time, legal rights, and social participation.

In a modern society with mass media, such as broadcasting, televisions, movies, advertising, newspapers, magazines, telephones, fax, and the Internet, these new factors grow, spread, and circulate, causing changes to almost every aspect of the society, either rapidly or slowly.

This is only one side of the story. On the other hand, institutional transitions have disrupted the old traditional system. Some of the society integrations have been obsolete for contemporary era. However, the new social structure has yet to be in place, therefore, old and new social systems with their correspondent institutions and norms coexist, while the alteration, contradiction, and conflict between the two are extremely intense and will continue for a long period of time. In addition, institutional reform is essentially a process of adjusting interest patterns from which some would benefit but others would be temporarily at cost. Some organizations and individuals would lose their hitherto power in the process of decentralization and the separation of power. With the rising of income levels, some people might experience relatively lower income because others are among those who get wealthy first. The imperfect new social system, which has engendered unfair distributions in the adjustment of interest patterns, would widen the gaps and worsen the conflicts of interest. Moreover, structural transformation is a transitional stage when a variety of structural factors are constantly changing with extreme level of mobility and instability. Unbalanced and inconsistent development might emerge between the urban and the rural, the economic and the social, the material and the spiritual, and among different regions and industries. Finally, a continuous strengthening of the split of functions, increasing social mobility, and diverse ways for social promotion all contribute to making individuals' identities and roles fluid and ambiguous. The "ambiguity" deprives individuals and organizations of their identifications with their social roles and norms, which leads to recurring conflicts between different roles. For instance, corporations' roles as subordinates to administrative departments often contradict their roles as market competitors. Workers at township and village enterprises often find their rural household registry in conflict with their occupational identities.

In short, when the structural transformation is in phase with the institutional transition, conflicts in structures, among different roles, and of interests, along with institutional frictions, are intertwined with one as a check to the other. This circumstance makes structural transformation more difficult and complicated. When handling these conflicts, people cannot take everything into consideration, and they are fearful of the repercussions.

Double engines of the state and the market

The state and the market have played different roles in China's social transformations, but the way in which these two forces jointly work together is unprecedented in the world's process of modernization. As we mentioned before, economic reform and opening up is the most immediate cause of the social transformations in China. The Communist Party of China (CPC) and the government took an initiative role in reforming economic structure. At the Third Plenary Session of the Eleventh Central Committee of the CPC in 1978, CPC shifted its focus on economic development by promulgating a series of reforms. At the thirteenth party congress in 1987, among a series of reforms was the establishment of a new order for a planned commodity economy. Economic reforms have been spearheading in experiments and pilot and promotional programs through all these years. From the perspective of the market, economic reforms were market oriented, which resulted in a salient expansion of the market's power. The market has become a major driving force for regulating supply and demand and allocating resources. The market has emerged as a comprehensive system instead of a single, separate factor weighing in on the economy and the society. The role played by the market has expanded to the entire economic realm when it comes to the commodity markets of consumer products, intermediate products, and basic products, and the factor markets of capital, labor force, land, technology, and information. Once set in motion, the market is an irresistible and irreversible force, independent of people's perceptions and wishes, for structural transformations.

We have found three factors that contribute to the conjoining of the state and market in transforming Chinese society. First, economic reforms speak for the public will and mind. Things taking shape in the public pursuit for life and development such as household responsibility systems and the township and village enterprises are extraordinary creations. Second, economic reforms are for the benefit of the majority. Although the reforms involve complex adjustment of benefits and inequality would widen, economic reforms have earned wide support from the public precisely because their standard living is improved in general thanks to the principle that ensures the benefits of the majority. Meanwhile, public economical and psychological principles bearing capacity for structural transformation are strengthened significantly. Third, following the tide of history, the state insists on exploring and accumulating experience in practice and adjusts policies accordingly. The state is proactive in rectifying errors and suspending the measures that run counter to the market. Government interventions, no longer as supra-economic measures, supplement the market.

The interactions between the state and the market have increasingly become the theme for discussions on countries' development (World Development Report, 1991, p.1). There are two popular threads in those discussions. The first one erects a binary between the state and the market, treating them as antithesis and mutually exclusive forces. Pro-market scholars often denounce government interventions as state coercions, and pro-government intervention scholars reprove full-scale market competitions as laissez-faire. Another closely related point of view holds that the modernization processes of the developed countries have proved the market as the solely reliable force for sustainable development. It reasons that the fewer interventions from government the better, and the government should only intervene in areas outside markets or when markets prove inadequate.

Competitive markets, without dispute, are effective ways to allocate resources for production in human history. However, markets do not operate in a vacuum but abide by laws and regulations implemented by the government. On the other hand, far from autonomously adjusting itself in every aspect in all fields, the market has flaws. The market cannot take the place of the government in many registers, including, but not limited to, infrastructure construction, investment in education, poverty reduction, population control, and environmental protections. In almost all nations on the planet, the government shoulders major responsibilities for the aforementioned aspects. Government interventions are necessary in China, not the lease because of the imperfection in markets and legal systems. It also has to do with specific circumstances in China. Disequilibrium economy intertwines with unequal development, compounded by social contradictions, to which the market has limited coordination capacity. Kinship and geographical proximity remain significant binding forces for social relationships. The universal contractual relationship based on "causes" that is the prerequisite for commodity economy has yet to come. China has chosen the path of gradual reform, wherein policy adjustments are constantly in need, and it takes time to optimize legal systems and institutions.

How to reconceptualize the role of the state is a new challenge for development theories. The key lies in the understanding of how governments should intervene, or, rather, how governments can intervene "effectively." Chinese economic reforms have confirmed that effective interventions allow for the maximum level of market autonomy. In other words, government functions must change before transforming the mechanism of the enterprises. Government interventions should operate at the macrolevel and take advantage of economic leverage such as taxation, finance, interest rates, and exchange rates, rather than interfering with the microeconomy. The government should play a more proactive role in areas that are unsuitable for enterprises or should not purely rely on the market. Those areas include but are not limited to welfare service, social security, education, research and development, medical care, environmental protections, removal of regional trade barriers, and control of income inequality and so on. Ultimately, it is up to the power of the government and the legal institutions to maintain social stability, crack down on crimes, build spiritual civilization, ensure fair competitions, and establish new orders for the socialistic commodity economy.

Double-movement of urbanization

According to China's fourth national census, the urban population accounted for 26.23 percent in 1990, which is a percentage not only far below that of high-income countries (more than 75 percent) and middle-income countries (50–60 percent) but also lower than the average of low-income countries (35 percent in 1988). It seemed inconsistent with the rapid pace of professionalization and urbanization since economic reforms. However, this type of inconsistency represents a unique characteristic in China's path to urbanization – namely, a double movement of urban expansion and rural urbanization.

Urbanization across the world follows certain paths, which can be roughly divided into three stages. In the first stage, the rural population leaves villages and gradually concentrates in the cities. As the number of cities grows and the urban population increases, urban areas expand rapidly, which contributes to the economies of agglomeration in cities. The second stage is characterized by the development of suburbia and urban agglomerations. Fleeing from the overcrowding, pollution, noise, and expensive housing that were rampant in the cities, the rich and middle class move to the suburbs. As a result, suburban areas begin to flourish, linking surrounding suburbs and neighboring cities to form urban agglomerations such as the greater Los Angeles area in the United States and the Tokyo-Yokohama Metropolitan area in Japan. The third stage is defined by so-called counterurbanization. In this stage, the urban population build their second family houses in rural areas one after another to lead peaceful lives and enjoy fresh and clean air, which result in a revival of village life. However, most residents in rural areas do not engage in agriculture. One common thread running through the aforementioned stages is the urban areas expanding and radiating toward the rural.

Urbanization in China, however, is unique because it goes beyond urban expansion to the rural and is marked by rural urbanization. To put it metaphorically, urbanization in China is like "encircling the cities from the rural areas" (Mendras, 1991, pp. 301–308). Economic reforms have stimulated the rapid growth of township and village enterprises, which absorb a great majority of rural labor surplus. Thus labor flows out of agriculture instead of the rural areas. This is what is called "leaving the land without leaving the home and entering the factory but not the city." This explains the asynchrony between the decreased rate of the agricultural labor force and the increased rate of the urban population. In census, the agricultural population speaks of residential but not occupational status. In relatively developed regions, economies in many nominal "villages" and "counties" are not dominated by agriculture, and more than 80 percent of the labor force is in nonagricultural sectors. They still live in "rural" areas but have an urban living. From another perspective, township is among the fastest growing unit in rural areas since economic reforms facilitated urbanization on varied scales. The proportion of the population in towns has climbed from 30 percent of the urban population in the early 1980s to the current 50 percent or so. Township development can be attributed to the economic support from township and village enterprises and a variety of professionalization, socialization, and concentration of nonagricultural industries in rural areas. In short, township is at the center of the networks of rural society; therefore, the development of township is first and foremost an embedded part of rural development. In addition, a number of cities in China spring from rural-urban areas, and it is particularly true for those towns that were elevated to the municipal level in recent years. In rural-urban areas, the rural areas are not suburbs. In contrast, the rural society network absorbs the city by becoming the center for rural development. For those workers who leave the land and the home by joining in the seasonal or year-round labor force in construction or tertiary industries, their "roots" – their "families" in the traditional Chinese context – remain in the rural areas. According to the census and on the household register, they are still "farmers."

Three major reasons lead to the double movement in China's urbanization process. First, Chinese economic reforms started from the rural areas. Ever since the economic reforms, the most massive and remarkable structural transformations took place in the rural areas. The rural develops faster than the urban, with more flexibility and diversity. Second, barriers that divide the rural and the urban persist (e.g., the household registration system that limits labor mobility, food and non-staple-food supply system for the urban population, housing, education, medical care, employment, social security, and labor protection system). Consequently, urbanization in the rural areas manifests in their own structural transformations. Third, as the burden of population has mounted, urban areas have limited capacity to expand before the urban infrastructure (e.g., transportation, water and energy system, and housing) and service facilities are set in a better place.

Chinese urbanization with its unique double movement offers an alternative mode of urbanization for countries that have urban-rural dual structures. Thanks to this type of urbanization, China has mitigated the problems of country decay and social unrest that often accompany massive outflows of the rural population in a short period of time. The pressure of the urban population has been reduced, and the village life starts to flourish. The downside, however, is that the rural areas have taken the bulk of sacrifice in terms of environmental pollutions. Because urban centers are scattered and the rural and the urban are relatively separated from each other, the urban agglomeration economic effect is discounted, which limits rural surplus labor transfer significantly.

Unbalanced development in structural transformation

Unbalanced development needs to be distinguished from the concept of economic disequilibrium. As the former refers to the unbalanced state that different regions are in, in their development, particularly related to the unbalance in structural transformations, the latter, an economic concept relative to Walrasian equilibrium, refers to a particular situation of equilibrium that is achieved by imperfect markets and price mechanisms that are inadequate to adjust demand and supply. Both unbalanced development and economic disequilibrium are prominent in China. They are interweaved, but in comparison, unbalanced development poses more daunting challenges for Chinese structural transformation.

Unbalanced development in China is first and foremost evident in differences among regions. With China's vast territory and drastic differences in natural conditions, development has shown a "gradient pattern" among the eastern, middle, and western regions, wherein the eastern region is affluent, but the west is poor. After economic reforms, southeastern coastal regions spearheaded opening up, building special economic zones, costal open cities, and economic technical development areas. The level of opening up roughly follows the geographical lines along the gradient pattern of development. In the past decade, coastal regions have developed more rapidly than the hinterland and considerably faster than the western regions, which has widened the gap between the two and reinforced the existent gradient pattern of development for that matter.

Unbalanced development is also salient in the disparities between the rural and the urban. The existence of urban-rural barriers and relative isolation of the rural from the urban reflects an urban-rural dualism in China. Although economic reforms have brought tremendous changes to the rural areas and dramatic improvement to farmers' lives, the dualistic urban-rural structure has survived the impact from the labor mobility to nonagricultural industries and to the cities. Indeed, the gap between the two has the tendency to widen in certain aspects. With the rapid growth of non-agricultural industries, agriculture becomes increasingly unprofitable, and thus the disparity between urban household income and that of rural household income is intensified. The regions that are dominated by agriculture are almost always under-developed economically. Since poverty-stricken agricultural regions rely heavily on the labor force, yet lack sufficient social security, population grows faster than in other regions, which in turn has exacerbated the unbalanced development.

Industrial structures are crippled. Since the early 1980s, economic trends were shifting from capital-intensive to technology-intensive industries in the developed countries, because the profitability in technology-intensive industries is much higher than average. Despite its leading position in some of the new high-tech innovations, when it comes to the field of application, labor-intensive industries with an overwhelming majority of low-tech, labor-intensive sectors and sporadic high-tech ones still dominate the Chinese economy. This is emblematic of the unbalanced development. In more than 10,000 achievements annually in science and technology, about 20 percent to 30 percent of them were applied to economic development.

Unbalanced development also includes the disparity between economic growth and social development. Social progress lags behind economic growth – the main achievement of economic reforms. As compared to economic growth, improvements in technology, education, and social security are inadequate for the structural transformations. While the repercussions might be dormant at the beginning of reforms, as China deepens its economic reforms, profound problems caused by social development lagging behind the economic growth will emerge.

Last, but not least, with a tremendous population, natural resources per capita will always be in short. Structural transformations, constrained by these formidable conditions, will take longer. The burden of population has become a particularly daunting challenge for structural transformations, which might alter the normal path of the process. Scholars cannot afford to overlook the population burden for any exploration and analysis of social development problems in China.

The driving forces for structural transformations

Structural transformations are becoming the third force, on top of government intervention and market regulation, for social transition. In fact, more and more people start to realize that development by essence means successful transformations of the social structure. Once the transformations are set in motion, they will engender remarkable benefits and impacts. They form tremendous, irreversible driving forces and intangible tensions.

Structural transformation is irreversible

Decades of township and village enterprises (TVEs) development are emblematic of the fact that structural transformation is irreversible. Township and village enterprises are the peculiar outgrowth of Chinese industrialization in the circumstance where the rural and the urban are in relative isolation. At the incipient stage, TVEs have been called "wild child," as the word "wild" indicates its vitality. TVEs are so robust that people describe their development as "the unexpected booming." While TVEs were of little significance a decade or so ago, they are now one of the mainstays of the national economy. However, the attitude toward TVEs used to be different. In particular, there has been a persistent discrimination against them. They were once deemed as the root of all evil. TVEs were accused of "competing with the state-owned enterprises for natural resources," "causing the imbalance between the aggregate demand and the supply," "undermining socialism," "eroding the leaders of the Party and the government," "degrading social conduct," and so on. For this matter, TVEs have been cut and punished first as a warning for others in a number of places. Nonetheless, in 1990, the total output value of TVEs was 846.16 billion RMB, and they turned in 41 billion taxation to the state, with an annual increase rate of 13.9 percent and 19.0 percent, respectively, despite a sluggish market, a widespread deficiency in economic performance, and a shrunken market for themselves (statistics showed that the number employed by TVEs has been reduced by 10 million). In 1991, the total output value of TVEs reached 1,161.18 billion RMB, growing by more than 100 billion every year over several consecutive years. The pace of development is irreversible because TVEs have played a vital role in invigorating the rural economy (59.2 percent of the rural gross social production value). TVEs are the mainstay for developing agricultural pillar industries (they have provided 8.65 billion RMB to subsidize the develop agriculture via industrialization and 16.28 billion RMB to support rural constructions). TVEs are the channel for workforce shifting (by absorbing 22.3 percent of rural labor force). TVEs contribute to increasing state revenue (15.2 percent of the state tax revenue). TVEs serve as the solid foundation for increasing the quality of rural lives by earning foreign exchange through export (about one-fifth of the amount nationwide). Meanwhile, TVEs are one of the major suppliers of auxiliary products for urban industries and social commodities.[1] In a word, the development of TVEs has become an indispensable part of the structural transformations of the society.

Another example of irreversible transformation is the development of the tertiary industry. One of the most significant conditions for structural transformation is a rising proportion of the tertiary industry. At present, the tertiary industry accounts for more than 60 percent of GNP in the developed countries, about 50 percent of that in the middle-income countries, and 35 percent to 40 percent of that in the low-income countries, respectively. In China, the tertiary industry constitutes less than 30 percent of GNP (26.8 percent in 1991). At the end of the 1980s, many people have accused "the popularity of doing business" and "commerce by all" of causing buying sprees and then skyrocketing inflation. Even today, many people still believe that the tertiary industry does not produce value, but only channels industrial profits into the circulation and other domains, which have brought windfalls for small business owners and profiteers. This thought is biased for three reasons. First, the tertiary industry includes such a wide industry that the concept per se is a general one. It mainly consists of three industries: 1) heavy-weight economic sectors that include finance, insurance, postal service, trade, aviation, and railway; 2) services that are closely related to consumers' daily lives, including commerce, catering, housing, public transportation, entertainment, education, medical and health industry, and broadcasting and publishing industries; and 3) newly emerged service industries – consulting, information, technological service, and tourism. Having not directly produced value, these industries, however, facilitate in value realizations – an indispensable part for value creation. The second reason concerns the employment rate and the weight of the tertiary industry. In the developed countries and the majority of the developing countries, employment in the tertiary industry would either outnumber or be equivalent to the proportion of the industry in the GNP. However, in China, the tertiary industry, hiring 18.8 percent of the labor force, contributes 26.8 percent of the GNP (all figures are from 1991). There are 100 million surplus laborers in the rural areas and millions of job-waiting people in the cities. The development of the tertiary industry would benefit the citizens and the state alike. But in the first year of the eighth five-year plan, the tertiary industry grew only at 5.3 percent, which was slower than what was planned – ten-year planning and the eighth five-year plan set the increasing rate at 9 percent, 3.5 percent, and 6.5 percent for the tertiary industry, agriculture, and industry, respectively – and lower than the increased rate of GNP (7 percent) and the actual industrial growth (14.2 percent). Third, as China is developing from a society of sufficient food and clothing to well-off, remarkable changes have happened to the consumption structure, which becomes more diverse. Moreover, when the economy evolves from products based to commodity based and the market starts to play increasingly important roles, industries such as finance, insurance, information, real estate, and technological services are even more significant for substantial development of the tertiary industry. In short, the tertiary industry develops in accordance with the trends of the times.

Another controversy related to the development of the tertiary industry is farmers migrating to cities looking for employment. At a conservative estimate, there are hundreds of millions of such farmers and even more during the slack season. These farmers are being referred to, derogatorily, as an "aimlessly drifting population," as they often are accused of causing "heavy traffic," "urban over-load," or even "increasing crime rate." As a matter of fact, the "aimlessly drifting population" is not aimless. They are following the trend of transformation from the rural society to the urban society, from agriculture-based society to industrial society. They have distinct purposes and directions. These migrant workers do the dirty hard work that urbanites disdain but that fosters market growth. It is one thing to urge that migrant workers need to be regulated and better supervised, and it is completely another to judge the labor flow. One must not confuse the two.

To summarize, the development of the TVEs and the tertiary industry, farm-ers migrating to cities to make ends meet, and so on are parts of the irreversible trend of structural transformation, which is independent of subjective wills and opinions. They must break down the barriers and clear the way for their own development. Places where the trend is followed and the development of those industries is incorporated into the overall planning are flourishing. Conversely, if the society puts all of its energy into "stopping" the trend, it will be less prepared for the impact the structural transformation might have on the society. If so, struc-tural transformation would escalate social conflicts or even lead to social unrest.

The pressure imposed by structural transformations

As we know, the demand for reforming state-owned enterprises (SOEs) is widely popular. There indeed are some breakthroughs. For instance, state-owned com-mercial enterprises in some regions implemented "four decontrols" – decontrolling price, salaries, scope of business, and employment system. State-owned indus-trial enterprises were marketed and design the pilot shareholding systems in self-reforming with breakthroughs in the systems of property rights, of the organization and personnel, of labor and employment, and the payroll distribution. After a few years of explorations, obviously state-owned enterprises were able to take steps toward reforming because of the mounting pressure.

Nonetheless, where does the pressure come from? An immediate answer is that it comes from government interventions. Party and state leaders reiterated the significance of reinvigorating large and medium enterprises. During his southern tour, Deng Xiaoping urged again that economic reforms be sped up and that open-ing up occurs. The State Department has issued a series of measures for deepening the enterprise reforms. The National Development and Reform Commission has listed the priorities for enterprise reforms. The list continues. It seems that the force that rendered enterprises "being marketed" is first and foremost the govern-ment. An alternative explanation to enterprise reforms is that the pressure comes from the market. Recent years have witnessed the formation and perfection of our markets for consumption, production factors, and labor. As the gap between the state-fixed price and the market price has been narrowed significantly, the capac-ity for effective supply is enhanced. While the monopoly enjoyed by SOEs in a shortage economy is disappearing, the market that was once dominated by sellers is now buyers oriented. Particularly under the circumstances of a slack market and credit squeeze, the reasoning goes, because economic benefits of SOEs continue to decline, there are no other options left but reform. The two aforementioned answers are plausible. However, one should also notice that on one hand, SOEs reforming their systems is concurrent with functional transformation of the government. That means what should not be regulated by the government in the first place is left to the enterprises at their own discretion. At the same time, the responsibilities that should not be shouldered by enterprises are shifted to the government and the society. Consequently, the government and the enterprises are facing the pressure to reform to the same degree. On the other hand, the market does not exist on its own. Without enterprises' active participation, the market falls short to adjust autonomously. In addition, even the enterprises that have a ready market and effective economic benefits still face the pressure to reform. Along this line, the pressure to reform has another source – namely, the structural transformation of economic society.

In China's transition from a rural society to an urban society, a massive amount of surplus labor force in the countryside has followed the trend of transition, circumventing the barriers and participating in the constructions of TVEs. TVEs take advantage of the cheap labor force and their resourcefulness accumulated by surviving in the crevice. TVEs thus have thrived and become strong competitors against state-owned enterprises, which are obviously under pressure. Although SOEs have better facilities and more advanced technologies, they take initiatives in reforming the employment system and hiring large quantity of contractual workers from rural areas. The reason is that when labor-intensive enterprises still dominate the market, the cost of labor management is not as low as one would imagine. The cost would be even higher if one considers the growing costs of benefits, nonproductive expenditures, and low productivity. SOEs' reactions reflect the pressure caused by structural transformations.

Three types of foreign-invested enterprises benefit from China's development from a closed and a semiclosed society to an open society. They soon become another potential competitor against SOEs, which puts more pressure on the latter for reforms. However, the foreign-invested enterprises derive their competitiveness from technological advancement, product quality, and export orientation instead of cheap labor or resourcefulness accumulated by surviving in the crevice. Foreign-invested enterprises and being attentive to both the international market and the potentially enormous domestic market have gained a firm foothold in the most advantageous regions in China. The Chinese business world is forced to "learn a lesson from the painful experience" that SOEs "changed all of a sudden" once they became "joint ventured."

All of the aforementioned analyses are about salient reality, which falls short of approving the potential characteristic of the pressure caused by structural transformation. We need to look beyond the hot spot issue such as SOEs reform and turn to the silent reforms in rural areas. Some local governments try to incorporate the efforts to servicize agricultural production into the administrative orbits. They solicit capital from farmers via social pooling to establish funds for agricultural organizations, which in turn provide service for farmers at a low or no cost. However, not all farmers are embracing these measures, because they feel the contributions they have made to "the pool" are worth more than "the service" they have received. However, agricultural service-provision organizations have become the economic entity in places where they are more improved, and farmers welcome them. The economic entities they have become relate to famers and their families via commodity exchange. Taking advantage of the scale economy of the agricultural service provision, the economic entities reduce the cost of labor and alleviate the financial burdens for otherwise scattered agricultural business. At first glance, it appears the difference lies in the directions to which funds move. However, what essentially sets the service-provision model apart is that it corresponds to the tide of structural transformations that demand that the social organization move from the ethical to the contractual and economic organization move from the administration to the market. Consequently, the latter must point to a more promising development prospect.

The unusual meaning of the structural transformation for China

In the analysis of structural transformations so far, scholars tend to focus on the correlations between the income increase and the structural transformation – namely, what fundamental changes would occur to the economic structure as the economy and income grows. More often than not, scholars are prudent enough to avoid concluding any causal relations between economic growth and structural transformation. Nonetheless, there is one presumption, by accident or design, in the scholarship: economic growth is the true cause of structural transformation, and the latter is treated as the natural outgrowth of the former. Our analysis indicates that the structural transformation is not only the product of economic growth but also a driving force for social reforms. It makes structural development irreversible and imposes invisible pressure for reforms, which affects the behavioral patterns in microeconomic fields. We are interested in structural transformation, not only because it is powerful but also because it has unusual meanings for developing countries such as China.

First, if we draw a comparison between the developed countries and developing countries, we will find that the economic growth in the developed countries can be largely attributed to technological advancement instead of investment in capital, raw materials, and labor. Compared to other factors, progress in science and technology made up about 5 percent of the economic growth in the developed countries at the beginning of the twentieth century. The number rose to 40 percent at midcentury and more than 60 percent in the 1970s, and it continued to climb to the present level of 70 percent to 80 percent in some developed countries. In China, during the three decades spanning from 1952 to 1982, progress in science and technology only accounted for 19 percent of the economic growth. Its contribution has seen a significant increase in recent years but remained at about 30 percent. Although one of the keys to boosting productivity lies in the advancement level of science and technology, in the developing countries, such as China, rather than in the developed countries, production factors such as fluidity, labor force transfer, and resources reallocation become more significant to economic growth. From this perspective, structural transformations are particularly important.

Second, our analysis also shows that the meaning of structural transformation is different for economic growth and social development in different countries. Generally speaking, it varies in accordance with the level of development. Many renowned economist prove this in their long periodic quantitative analyses about structural transformations in modernization. In other words, the process of modernization can be divided into different phases, with each phase being dominated by specific and particularly significant growing factors. The less developed the country is, the more important the structural transformation is, and the more powerful and effective is the force unleashed by structural transformations for the country.

Third, in the developed countries, because they already accomplished structural transformation during modernization, mature markets have left relatively little room for resource reallocations and structural shifts. However, China is currently at the stage of structural and system transformations. The old system collapsed, but the new one has not yet been established. The structural imbalance and the disequilibrium in production factors market are remarkable. This precisely means that there is much more room for structural shifts. In the circumstances of double imbalances, structural transformations would propel the economy even more.

Fourth, developing countries are facing issues of development strategy changes or adjustment. Namely, they need to move away from the pursuit of sheer output growth to all-round structural transformations, away from focusing purely on economic growth rate to seeking better effects and results of economic growth, away from the inward-oriented economy (import substitution) to the outward-oriented economy (export orientation). In this period, countries with different strategies would experience different pace and order of structural transformations. Emerging industrial countries' experiences have taught us that the structural transformation and utilization of advanced science and technology are two major factors that speed up their economic growth. At present, Chinese structures of industries, employment, and urban-rural relation are shifting rapidly. If the national strategy gave priority to the needs of structural transformations, the boosting force would have become more palpable.

From the aforementioned analysis, we argue that it is necessary to examine the characteristics and the rules of structural transformations of the Chinese society and to put the social problems, tensions, conflicts, and contentions within this context. By doing so, we gain a new research perspective that raises our consciousness, stops blindness, and helps avoid inevitable errors. Moreover, it deepens our understanding of Deng Xiaopeng's theory of constructing socialism with Chinese characteristics, with great guidance for reform and opening up and modernization.

Note

This chapter was originally published in *Social Science in China*, 1992, issue 5.

1 Unless otherwise indicated, all statistics in the chapter are from the *China Statistical Yearbook*.

References

Chenery, H. B., & Syrquin, M. (1989). *Patterns of Development, 1950–1970* (X. Li, Trans.). Beijing: China Financial & Economics Publishing House.

Inkeles, A., & Smith, D. H. (1974). *Becoming Modern: Individual Changes in Six Developing Countries*. Cambridge, MA: Harvard University Press.

Kuznets, S. (1989). *Modern Economic Growth: Rate, Structure, and Spread* (R. Dai & C. Yi, Trans.). Beijing: Beijing Economics Institute Press.

Lewis, W. A. (1954/1958). *Economic Development with Unlimited Supplies of Labor* (1954) and *Unlimited Labor: Further Notes* (1958) (W. Shi, Trans.). Beijing: Beijing Economics Institute Press.

Lu, X., & Li, P. (Eds.). (1999). *Reports on Social Development*. Liaoning: People's Publishing House.

Mendras, H. (1991). *La Fin Des Paysans* (P. Li, Trans.). Beijing: China Social Science Press.

World Development Report. (1991). Beijing: China Financial & Economic Publishing House.

2 The implications of Chinese structural transformations for resource allocation

In my article "Another Invisible Hand: The Structural Transformations of the Society," published in *Social Science in China* (1992, Issue 5), I argued that the structural transformations of the society function as "another invisible hand," differing from market adjustment and government interventions. This invisible hand would trigger forces for reform and innovation, which would affect resource allocation and development trends. In early 1994, I published "Reconsider Another Invisible Hand" in *Social Science in China* (1994, Issue 1) and appropriated normative and ethical systems to strengthen my theoretical and logical groundwork. Specifically, I elaborated on the point that the fundamental fabrics in the social structure (e.g., family structure, enterprise organization, and informal rules and regulations for social relations) are peculiar forms for resource allocation. They are shaped by an array of historical, cultural, and noneconomic factors, not merely by the rule of "self-interest" or "profits maximization." The existence of another invisible "hand" indicates the need to revisit some of the implicit assumptions and premises in the economics. In this chapter, we attempt to theorize Chinese reform of the economic system. We do not conceal our theoretical goals, to wit, that we need establish a new theoretical framework to explain Chinese economic system reforms and development – the one that challenges the methodological individualism that dominates contemporary Western economic theories.

The limitations of methodological individualism

One of the significant premises in the free-market theory of modern economics is that individuals pursue their own "self-interest" under "natural order." The pursuit of self-interest, however, would lead to unintended social benefits. This premise can be traced back to Adam Smith, a Scottish classical economist. He writes, "By pursuing his own interest he frequently promotes that of the society more effectually than when he really intends to promote it" (Smith, 1981, pp. 25–27).[1] As economic agents compete with each other, in the pursuit of their own interests, the reasoning goes, the cost of production will be reduced and the output maximized. The economic rule that builds upon the "individual-based" actions presumes a hypothesis of "profit maximization." This is reasonable if one promotes the rationality of an individual's "self-interest" in his/her economic activities, which is common in the methodological individualism.

Meanwhile, political theories after Jean-Jacques Rousseau center on the "social contract" and sociology after Émile Durkheim takes on the theme of "social order." Rousseau believed that the "social contract" was achieved by the human pursuit of social equality. The social contract limits individuals "intemperate desires" and requires individuals to obey "the General Will constructed by their entry into the social contract." By doing so, they have gained social freedom – a "superior" freedom (Rousseau, 1982, p.30).[2] Durkheim, however, maintained that the "social order" is a "social fact" that exists in its own right, independent of individuals' actions. Social facts, either in forms of laws or norms, are endowed with a coercive power that exercises control over the individual when social interests are harmed. Consequently, "the determining cause of a social fact must be sought among the antecedent social facts and not among the states of the individual consciousness" (Durkheim, 1956, pp. 3–13, 110).[3] American sociologies Robert K. Merton built on Durkheim's thoughts and pointed out that "some social structures exert a definitive pressure upon certain persons in the society to engage in non-conforming rather than conforming conduct" (Merton, 1968, p.186).[4] These theories reject the hypothesis of "self-interest equals public good." Their proposition is, however, that for the society to function properly (call it sociological principle of profit maximization), self-interest must be constrained. A social order thus emerges from negotiations of collective interests in the real world.

The aforementioned propositions coming from different disciplines with different logics have remarkable "theoretical contradictions." Dismissing either one of them would be imprudent when it comes to explaining the contradictions.

It is not our intention to ethicize the debate, so it is necessary to distinguish methodological individualism from egoism in ethics. While the former rests upon the premise that "self-interest equals public good," the latter means benefiting oneself at the expense of others, or as the ancient Chinese saying has it, "too stingy to donate a penny to benefit the world." According to French sociologist Raymond Boudon, the opposite concept of methodological individualism is holism, but economists who emphasize individualism often advocate laissez-faire (Boudon, 1985, p.644).[5] However, the debate cannot be devoid of ethics because any economic order must have its ethical rationality that matches certain social values.

Methodological individualism was introduced as a methodology for modern social science by German sociologist Max Weber. After Austrian-British philosopher Karl Popper's expansion and Friedrich von Hayek's controversial endorsement, methodological individualism has become an influential methodological precept in social science. Popper put forth what is called the principle of "liberal razor," viz. "[the] state is a necessary evil: its powers are not to be multiplied beyond what is necessary" (Popper, 1986, p.499).[6] Hayek (1989, pp. 4–11) believes that "[social phenomena] are accessible to us only because we can understand what other people tell us and can be understood only by interpreting other people's intentions and plans." He also calls the understanding of the society as being independent of individuals as "false rationalistic individualism," which stands in sharp contrast to "true individualism" on two points. On one hand, it presumes individuals to reach agreement with each in a formal social contract, but on the other hand, it presumes the social process is subject to individual human reason.[7] Hayek's thoughts on methodology became widely accepted, particularly after he received the Nobel Prize in economic science with Gunnar Myrdal in 1974. However, his theories are biased in a couple of aspects. First, he politicized the issue in question by claiming false rationalistic individualism is the source of socialism or collectivism. Second, he made simplistic and inappropriate connections between complex debates over philosophical ontology by stating, "Individualism is a necessary result of philosophical nominalism, while the collectivist theories have their roots in realism." Third, he based his position along national lines. He vehemently attacked rational traditions from European continent, particularly those from France, such as Descartes's rationalism, "the Encyclopedists" Rousseau, and the physiocratic school. But he raved about "true individualism of the British thinkers" who shared an economic tradition (Hayek, 1989, pp. 4–11).[8]

Our question is whether methodological individualism has limited applicability to explain what is facing Chinese's structural transformation and economic development given that China is a "family-oriented" or "collectivism" society. In other words, Western scholars who attempted to apply methodological individualism to examine issues along with China's rapid economic growth often found themselves baffled by the phenomena such as "the expansion of familial altruism," TVEs' progress despite "the absence of privatization," and "the collaborations between the local government and enterprises."

When it comes to examining the structural transformations and economic development of the Chinese society since the reform and the opening up, methodological individualism neglects some variables as follows:

- Methodological individualism accepts "natural order" as either a given fact or treats economic order as the "natural result" of free choices made within the market. Therefore, it neglects the roles played by interest conflicts and negotiations among individuals and groups, self-imposed altruism promoted by ethics, and coercive altruism imposed by laws.
- There is no "sole god" in economic activities. Organizational structure represents a force for resource allocation, other than the market adjustment and government intervention. Neither market transactions nor government orders could dominate the organization from within.
- Altruism plays a role in allocating resources in an array of markets. As Gary S. Becker points out, altruism can not only "induce efficient behavior where selfishness fails, but also . . . can significantly change behavior even when altruism is weak." He goes on to say, "[Even] if altruism were confined to the family, it would still direct the allocation of a large fraction of all resources" (Becker, 1987, pp. 217, 227).[9] In China, however, the role played by family in allocating resources is more significant than the role of the market in the developed countries.
- Individualists fail to explain why countless individual behaviors with varied motivations and purposes integrate into a common trend for structural transformation. They assume that individual's freedom to pursue their own

interests would be beneficial for the society at large, so benefits of the whole would offset individual and partial failures. However, they fail to recognize the intermediary role played by family, organization, and informal rules as to connect individual behaviors to the social structure, which could never be the natural result of individual motivations.

- Individualists claim that they have discovered a system that allows self-interest to transfer freely and autonomously to public good by subjectively precluding the possibility that interest conflicts in real life might damage the social structure and thus reduce overall welfare. In this manner, as they attack "necessary law," they offer yet another false "necessity."
- Outlook changes regarding social development attach richer meanings to the latter than economic growth. When individualists extend the economic principle of "profit maximization" to examine other social realms (group life, political operation, legal proceedings, etc.), their definition of "welfare" does not cover many conditions that promise human sustainable living and development.

Indeed, methodological individualism has invaluable insights that one cannot afford to ignore. I want to address two points. First, it acknowledges the individual's creativity when driven by his/her motivations. It also stresses the legitimacy of the individual as an independent agent of interest, which throws off the moral bonds imposed upon the pursuit of self-interests. Second, as far as "order" and "structure" are concerned, individualism insists that market order is based on individual's voluntary transactions. Thus it overcomes the drawbacks in methodological holism that often dislodge individual from social interactions. As James M. Buchanan (1989, p.74) writes, "order," as the result of the "process" from which it emerges, does not and cannot be independent of "process."[10] However, the limitations of methodological individualism cannot be eliminated or concealed by the fact that it overcomes the drawbacks in holism.

Group consciousness and group life norms

Group is the fundamental form for human survival and living. From family, tribe, and community to society, certain group forms are necessary conditions for humans to "maximize welfare," whether in the primitive, barbaric, or civilized age. Certain individuals may live all alone or as recluses, but human beings cannot survive and develop without any group forms. As a fictional abstract model, Robinson Crusoe economics in the cultural island is not without theoretical contributions. However, the idea that economic activities would still exist without group life is doomed to be disappointed as one puts a feather in a vacuum only to discover it would not flow.

Under certain circumstance, when individual interest matches group interests, individual pursuit of self-interest is a form of "objective altruism" – meaning what benefits the group and society benefits individuals. For instance, when people push a heavy-loaded cart to climb a slope, everyone wants to put forth less strength than others; meanwhile, they also realize the danger of death if the cart slides down outweighs the exertion of their strength. Between death and exertion of strength, everyone would pick the latter. In this case, the group interest is their own interest. This rather simplistic example sheds light on individual behaviors in human confrontation against nature and among group antagonism.

More often than not, nonetheless, group interest is unlikely in accordance with every single individual's interest. Chances are that group interest, as the general social welfare, matches with the interest of part of the group. Classical economists are optimistic about solving this dilemma, as they believe that under the auspices of the market's "natural law" every social member's pursuit of his or her own interest will contribute to society's overall benefits. This strikes an analogy to Darwin's mechanism of natural selection – survival of the fittest – in that classical economists assume that individuals who fail to make their interest part of the group interest would be compensated, so there is no conflict between the two at the end of the day. This premise derives from ethical demands.

In group life, there is almost always a mechanism to protect the vulnerable. This is both the necessary condition for a healthy group life and the foundation for group ethical norms. Ethics are internal and informal rules, which require "self-disciplinary altruism," or "the surrender of self-interest." "Self-disciplinary altruism" is a mechanism to reduce the cost of supervision and rule enforcement for group life. Many researches have shown that altruism is more "effective" than egoism when it comes to familial production, distribution, and consumption (Buchanan, 1989, pp. 196–221).[11] The effectiveness is also evident in the wide success of small family businesses as the base for capital accumulation. It is not saying that self-disciplinary altruism is widely effective in economic activities. Egoism or extended egoism is far more pervasive in business transactions. As the family system reorients from extended family to nuclear family, many of the functions that used to belong to the family are replaced by more efficient and modern organizations, such as banks, schools, and social insurance companies, whose efficiency and effectiveness do not rely on self-disciplinary altruism. However, it by no means declares the death of the "effectiveness" of self-disciplinary altruism outside of the family. A number of Chinese township and village enterprises (TVEs) have adopted familial management styles at their fledgling stage. Despite its drawbacks, familial management has "effectively" reduced the cost of supervision and rule enforcement.

However, the power of self-discipline as an ethical obligation is fragile in the market competition. Mandatory altruism is essential for group life in modern society, with no exception to economics, because how to possess scarce resources is the key game in economic activities and market competitions when group life is constantly threatened by resource scarcity. Without mandatory altruism or when mandatory altruism fails, excessive or lawless competition would result in fierce conflicts among individuals and groups, or even blood feuds and national wars in unusual cases. Throughout the history, blood feuds and wars were frequently supplementary means to market competition in order to possess resources. In fact, any economic order, including those "natural orders" shaped by the pursuit of self-interest, is based on mandatory altruism. When scholars conduct "pure economic analysis," they often treat this order as a given invariable rather than a function taking shape in the economic process.

The so-called mandatory altruism by no means refers to "ideal altruism" encouraged by ethics or asks individuals to "give up their own interests," or "put others before themselves," or "serves their objective needs by doing others subjective favors" in competitions. It only demands that when pursuing self-interest individual do no harm to public good. Methodological individualism's premise is that self-interest is in accordance with public good, which is a false proposition in reality. Manufacturing counterfeit and inferior products is a case in point. From the individual's or enterprise's point of view, manufacturers of counterfeit and inferior products are obviously motivated by the chase for "maximum profits" out of their concerns to "reduce the cost and increase profit" when the market is on the "normal" terms. If it were unprofitable in the eyes of manufactures who at the same time are constrained by formal accounting system, there would be little incentives for manufacturing counterfeit and inferior products. However, manufacturers of counterfeit and inferior products only "externalize the internal cost" of production, partially, onto consumers and other manufacturers. From the perspective of society, another party's loss might be still lower than the high profit gained by manufacturers of counterfeit and inferior products, which does not run counter to "profit maximization," but their existence is extremely detrimental to the economy. For the example they set will impede the market's competition mechanism and raise the cost to maintain a fair competition environment. In this sense, mandatory altruism is a mechanism for cost reduction. When we talk about market economy, it connotes the rule of law in economy. Another typical example is tax evaders. In any market economy, if they follow the rule of "profit maximization," market agents have the tendency to evade taxes because it is a palpable and effective means to increase profits. It is extraordinarily difficult or even theoretically impossible for any government to prevent tax evasion because the money spent on inspection, investigation, and evidence collection, and the huge number of tax inspectors is likely to be far more than the tax recovered. After all, it remains an open question of whether paying a higher price to increase tax fits the goal of enhancing social welfare. In other words, along with the reasoning of methodological individualism, tax evasion is not necessarily detrimental to profit maximization for the overall economy. Nevertheless, any market economy country does not hesitate to spend money on establishing a rigorous tax system (this does not concern the justification of the tax rate), as one of the most popular Western proverb puts it, "There are only two things certain in life: death and taxes." The establishment of high-cost tax and an inspection system are made possible by understanding that the cost of such a mandatory altruism can be offset by the deterrence resulting from punishing tax evaders and the maintenance of a fair order for competition.

Economic life is also group life, of which the proper function relies upon group consciousness and group-life norms. If group consciousness is based on "self-disciplinary altruism," then "group-life norms" center on "mandatory altruism." Under certain circumstances, mandatory altruism may turn out to be violent, but in modern society, it is enforced by law.

Social interactions and the shifts of social networks

There are many forms of social interactions, such as friction, conflict, compromise, and collaboration. In economic life, the most basic form of social interaction is trade. Resource scarcity makes every competitor on the market trade the resource in his/her hands for whatever he/she wants. The need for exchange is the driving force for setting up trading rules. Some economists consider market transaction as following established rules. However, in the "everyday economy," enormous trading activities happen that defy the established practice, which tend to alter the trading rules in a meaningful manner. Trading rules are similar to game rules, which emerge from playing the game and are revised as the game develops, not entirely springing from rational designs. No matter how perfect the rational design is, it is impossible to delineate the rationalized curve of hundreds of millions of people's impulse for survival and development. China's dramatic economic development has forcefully demonstrated that politicians and scholars tend to underestimate the "unexpected" outcome and creativity unleased by the impulse for development. It would be too utopian to believe that orders are brought by countless people's "free and autonomous" pursuit of self-interest.

Economic life is only part of human social life. People's motivations and behaviors for pursuing interests cannot be summarized by chasing profit or money. Modern psychological studies indicate that human needs range from survival, safety, self-esteem, and honor to self-fulfillment and self-development, which represent themselves as an ascending curve. To satisfy those needs, humans utilize all the original resources they have (knowledge, physical strength, technological skills, social networks, beauty, etc.) for instrumental compensations, such as money, wealth, power, and social status, which in turn are used for greater benefits and gratification. Money and wealth are the more sought-after goals, not only because they are closely related to the progress of living conditions but also because they have common exchange value. However, this is a universal rule. In other words, social networks (social game theory) take shape in the exchange of social resources, but the value of many social resources cannot be measured by monetary unit. As a result, some particular exchange forms rely on support, gifts, laudation, and so on.

When a system changes, an outside system is a wide realm where social "everyday life" is most vigorous. That's not because there are no rules for an outside system. On the contrary, an outside system is where new rules spring up, although those rules often appear "unofficial." We call them "latent social networks." Latent social networks become stable social relations after repetition, trial, and social choice. This is the inevitable interim process for the new system to come into being.

Social networks emerge and take shape in the social interactions among individuals and groups, but social interactions are not always "reciprocal" social exchanges. In addition, "exchange," the most common relationship in an economy, is not what all social interactions are about. Interest friction and conflict among groups are significant forces for shifts in social networks that lead to structural and system changes, and in the "everyday life" realm, this kind of interaction is more common than reciprocal exchange. Interest friction and conflict among groups often result from those of individuals, but individual interactions are trivial with regard to affecting social structures and systems unless they can lead to collective, class, or organizational actions. "The tide of migrant workers" is emblematic of this form of interest friction and conflict. Migrant workers move from the rural areas to the cities seeking higher payment for the same quantity of labor they otherwise exert, as well as more opportunities and higher living standards in the cities. Their outside system entrepreneurial practices have facilitated the creation of "urban village life," which also invited public complaints – traffic congestion, sanitary situation, and social order and management are all getting worse. Urbanites consider these "unilateral loss of interest" instead of the price they pay for the increase of accessory service and the multiplication of commodity supplies. The accumulation of public complaints would intensify friction and conflict, which might lead to three scenarios depending on each side's power and the intensity of the conflict. The first scenario is that the current urban system reinforces its tolerance of friction and conflict by incorporating migrant workers indiscriminately into the system. The second scenario is that the current urban system strengthens and imposes restrictions on migrant workers, and limits the scale and scope of their movement. The third scenario is that "the tide of migrant workers" becomes an unstoppable "torrent" that far exceeds the absorbing capacity of the urban system. This scenario calls for fundamental system innovations. Consequently, system innovations do not come out of theorists' rational design in the lab. Instead, they are "the result of compromises" made by individuals and groups in their search for the most possible solution for interest frictions and conflict.

"Regional protectionism" is another form of friction and conflict. Abiding by an executive order, a bank in region A suspends the loans for an enterprise from region B, as it is behind in paying its debt. The local people's procuratorate in region B also abides by an executive order and detains a concerning manager from an enterprise based in region A because the latter fails to pay off the debt as per the contract. People in the developed regions believe that the developmental and income gaps among regions are normal. That capital, technology, labor, and other social resources flow into developed regions is in line with the rule of market competition, because they will yield higher growth rates and greater profit margins, and ultimately faster development of overall social welfare. However, people in the underdeveloped regions believe that the widening development and income gaps originate from unequal starting points for competition. Namely, discrimination in policy priority and the state's initial financial support have transferred the profits from the underdeveloped regions to the high income of the developed regions. Thus it is the underdeveloped region that pays the price for the development of the developed regions and the overall economy. Because this type of friction and conflict becomes organizational movement, it is even more influential on the structural transformations of the society and thus more difficult to rein in via mandatory measures. However, no matter how intensified the friction and conflict turn to be, and regardless of the form and the length of the intensification, the ultimate outcome would be a rationally possible compromise in the restraint of "group-life norms." This compromise must be based on "interest transfer" from both parties and can only be institutionalized after being intermediated by social networks.

In society, where "equal distribution" takes a practical form, equally shared overall welfare is impossible for all social members. Those who have more advantages in the society take the lion's share. In other words, as the overall welfare grows, some people get the lion's share but others suffer from a loss of or a decrease in relative terms in their profit gains. "Pareto optimality" is a goal – an approachable yet unreachable goal. Interest friction and conflict among individuals and groups are inevitable in social life and especially so during the stage of structural transformations. Thus we need first to realize that those frictions and conflicts are likely to bring about meaningful changes to social rules, including economic rules. As far as social accounting is concerned, we also need to take into consideration the social cost caused by the intensification of friction and conflict. How to maximize social welfare is an issue of social accounting not merely of economic accounting.

Interest transfer via compromise is a form of mandatory altruism, but interest transfer via violence is not unheard of. In group life, social order, including economic order, is unlikely the natural outgrowth of individuals' pursuit of self-interest. Nor can it be built as an ideal system in which everyone's impulse would benefit the overall welfare, since one man's source of benefits is another man's cause of interest conflict or cheap passion.

Resource allocation under the corporate system

When Adam Smith demonstrated how "an invisible hand" leads to "maximize the profits," he stressed that it is under a "natural order." The theoretical development thereafter has stopped focusing on the "natural order." Instead, the focus has been put on how to effectively propel an individual's pursuit of self-interest. This approach, by accident or design, treats the "natural order" as a given or fixed condition, rather than a specific historical outgrowth of social exchange and a function that is contingent on economic growth and social development. In many of the purely economic analyses of "profit maximization" or economic "optimality," an individual's pursuit of self-interest is presumed to occur in a sealed system without "externality." Within this sealed system, economists have two additional hypotheses for the possible outcomes. The first one is called "Pareto optimality" – everyone benefits from voluntarily reciprocal exchange and no one gets hurt. For another, some people profit from fierce competitions at the cost of others. Profit gains are impossible unless certain people lose, but partial loss would be made up by the growth of overall benefits. This is called competitive equilibrium, a hypothetically optimal situation for competition. The second hypothesis in part acknowledges the "externality" of an individual's pursuit of self-interest, but it relies on the assumption that the externality can be incorporated into the internal calculation of cost benefit and yield favorable results.

It is possible and necessary to examine economic behaviors as theoretical abstractions, but in reality, no economic activities can be isolated from the entire social and group life. A great majority of social behaviors happen in an open system with clear "external effect." When brick works use waste residue from steel mills to manufacture construction materials, it is considered a "positive externality," as the former makes money and meanwhile helps with waste disposal. It is the same as bees coming to the beekeepers' orchards to gather honey "voluntarily" and meanwhile pollinate plants "voluntarily." In this sense, the individual's subjective pursuit of self-interest begets "objective" altruism. Just as smoking (we put aside the question that smoking is harmful for the health and consider it as an individual's profit-seeking behavior) that harms others yet frees smokers from indemnity is a demonstration of "negative externality," factories that discharge sulfur dioxide for environment pollution are not held accountable. Individualistic profit-seeking behaviors benefit an individual at others' expense. The economic accounting excludes or neglects the costs and benefits of these two types of "externality." However, when it comes to measuring social progress and human welfare, if we take into account not only economic growth but also broader social development, then the accounting of "social optimality" (at least "suboptimum," or "reasonable situation" if not optimality) must cover the costs and benefits caused by "externality" engendered by social behaviors. Otherwise, economic accounting becomes meaningless, since all the costs caused by negative externality of social behaviors (including economic behaviors) are paid through social welfare, which is not included in the economic accounting and tax, and tax rates are not based on social accounting.

Indeed, social structure per se is not without mechanisms that would overcome the "negative externality" of social behaviors. Family, enterprise, and "latent social networks" that are composed by informal systems are all part of internal mechanisms. When the market fails or weakens, these mechanisms – as basic resource allocation units or group-life norms – play the role of containing the "negative externality." Under certain circumstances, ethic norms from family production units, organizational systems from market participant enterprises, and "rules" of the latent social networks that govern the lowest tier of social class are all effective means to seek "collaborative" benefits, reduce the costs of social frictions, and overcome negative externality. This kind of structural power emerges from long-term "processes" of social lives. It is "another invisible hand" that guides an individual's pursuit of self-interest toward doing no harm to others and interest frictions and conflicts toward meaningful compromise and collaboration. By doing so, this invisible hand takes the place of market regulation and government intervention in a good part of people's everyday lives.

With the development of modern society, the rise of the legal person gradually undermines the effect the natural person has on social structural changes. As the corporate system composed of legal relationships gradually becomes the main entity in the social structure, corporate organizations such as corporations, schools, banks, and welfare institutions have taken over many of the functions that used to belong to the family, including production, distribution, consumption, education, saving, investment, and insurance. This change also renders the isomorphism derived from "the integration of family and nation," as well as the political analysis that compares "the governance of a large nation" to "cooking small fishes" irrelevant.

The legal person being an independent subject and abstract legal entity appears strange to the natural person in that it separates legal relations from personal relations. Corporate resources and interests are not equivalent to the resources and interests of natural persons who make up the corporation. Corporate behaviors are not a simple assembly of natural persons' behaviors. The goal of a legal person can be completely different from that of its members. The assumption that "the pursuit of self-interest automatically promotes the social interest" falls short of examining the internal relations of legal persons. What corresponds to the development and perfection of the legal person is a set of modern, micro-power systems concerned with stimulation, rewards, control, supervision, checks and balances, and punishment. In modern society, corporates hold a great majority of the social resources becoming independent players in the resource allocations. There is no market or government within the corporate organization. This additional "invisible hand" becomes increasingly institutionalized, and its power is of the utmost importance upon the structural transformations of the society.

China is currently at the crossroad of two transformations, one with the social structure and the other the economic system. On one hand, traditional ethics and social relations alternate with newly emerged legal contractual relations playing their roles in the evolution from rural society to urban society. Because of logical inconsistence and counterproductive "effectiveness," there are "ruptures" and "vacuums" in the social norms. On the other hand, as the highly centralized planned economy shifts to a market economy, the two systems remain at work. Their coexistence often leads to institutional friction and conflict, which cripples market regulation as a lever without a pivot or an encaged bird. Meanwhile, government intervention, under the pressure that "local policies trump central government policies" is often forced to seek a "soft landing." In this case, structural power jointly combined by restructured family relations, innovated enterprise organizations, and shifted social networks becomes "another invisible hand" promoting more sound resource allocation and the social development process.

Scholars have designed plenty of theoretical models and frameworks to explain market competition and government intervention, but we have little knowledge about the mechanism of "another invisible hand." In particular, the special role it plays in the structural economic transformation is under addressed in the overwhelming examinations of traditions.

Institutional factors in the rapid growth of Chinese economy

When it comes to explaining the rapid growth of Chinese economy in the past decades, Western scholars tend to adopt two approaches. They tend to adopt the analytic model for the East Asian economy because there are many commonalities in the development of East Asian countries, such as high savings, high investment rates, export-oriented economy, rich human resources, political stability, value of education, and shared cultural background and historical roots. However, there are also some flaws in this model. First, people are completely baffled when this model traces back to cultural characteristics such as Confucianism, preference for savings, management capacity, and even the use of Chinese characters and chopsticks for insights. But their conclusions are not convincing for lack of empirical evidence, which at best repeats what Max Weber did to attribute capitalism's roots to the Protestants' ethic. Ever since Fernand Braudel revealed the living world, the market economy, and capitalism from "the everyday life" from the 15th to 18th centuries, people increasingly cast doubt on the methodology based on isomorphic comparison. Second, there are a series of challenges in the application of the liberal economic model. In East Asian countries and regions, with the exception of Hong Kong, the governments play different roles than their counterparts in the West. Enterprise organizations are different as well. The challenge is particularly daunting when it comes to explaining the drastic contrast between East Asian and Latin American economic growth. Third, the analytic model for the East Asian economy does not take the institutional variables into account, although China's rapid economic growth in the past ten years has everything to do with the economic reform. This last characteristic is absent in the development process in other East Asian countries and regions.

Consequently, Western scholars who stress system analysis are inclined to compare China with countries in East Europe and the Soviet Union, putting them in the model of "institutional reform." These countries used to have the same institution – socialistic planned economy – and institutional reforms have occupied social lives in the past ten years or so; therefore, differences in reform results can be plausibly explained by the different means of reforms. However, the same group of scholars does not seem to pay enough attention to the differences in the political system, among whom some believe they are not substantial. They even hold that the Chinese underclass economy is more "capitalistic" and "liberal" because there has never been an "autocratic economy" established in China that is as tight and centralized as in the Soviet Union. They focus on the procedural variations in the institutional reforms: one starts from political reforms but the other starts from economic reforms; the central conflict for one is in the big cities to begin with, but for the other, the reform takes its shape in the vast rural regions; one initially takes on the problem of ownership, but the other first considers decentralization of power and the transfer of profits; one takes a sudden break in its institutions, but the other takes a steady approach toward institutional adjustment; one is going through a surgical "shock therapy," but the other follows a traditional Chinese medical treatment with the purpose of relaxing the muscles, stimulating the blood circulation, and fending off a fever and chill, and the list continues. This analytic approach has its own shortcomings too. The most common factors for economic growth are easily neglected, such as investment, technology, industrial structure, and trade. This approach also treats reform "procedures" purely as the result of rational designs, which in fact are the necessary outgrowth of interactions among social structures and a variety of social forces, not historical choices by accident.

The last shortcoming is to dismiss the differences in the development and cultural backgrounds provisionally.

Along this line, besides the most general factors that contribute to all economic growth, what else is at work, particularly in China's rapid economic growth in the past decade? How on earth does economic reform promote social development? How can China's rapid growth experience shed new light on current modernization theories? The author argues that the most luminous institutional factors can be summarized as follows:

- It is crucial for the system to be flexible. Flexibility can unleash tremendous power derived from numerous people's deep-down desires for survival and development, as well as the creativity that would have been underestimated otherwise. On the other hand, it leaves sufficient leeway for institutional adjustment, which allows for enough time and practice for amendments and reparations to the rational design.
- As agriculture is seasonal and follows natural growth cycles, it is the least suitable production department to be "organized" in the same way as industries. Mechanization does not change these fundamental agricultural features. Henceforth the agricultural supply and service system that is centered upon agricultural intermediary organization will be based on family operations. Family will remain a cost-effective economic entity for agricultural resource allocations. When the population far outnumbers the farmland, the main channel for farmers to raise their income is through plurality rather than the scale economy.
- It is important to take advantage of developing countries' structural flexibility and the high returns in investment. When institutional reforms can coordinate with social structural transformations, structural transformations in industries, employment, and the rural-urban relations will yield relatively high profits, which in return will impose spontaneous pressure on institutional reforms. In this way, institutional reform becomes an inevitable trend.
- As family operations, varied enterprises, and all kinds of informal rules have mushroomed from the institutional reforms with dual systems coexisting, they have played an irreplaceable role in allocating resources becoming "another invisible hand" to enliven the economy and promote sustainable development. This demonstrates the powerful "self-organizing" capacity that an old society might have.
- Decentralization of power and the transfer of profits have materialized the goal of leaving wealth with the people. The individual income tax accounts for 80 percent of GNP, increasing from 60 percent at the end of the 1970s. Capital gains thus garner stronger and wider public support.
- The price of institutional reform is payable by installments. Reform and development are easy to start but increasingly difficult thereafter, from the rural to the urban, from nonsystem to in-system. Although interests accompany installments, they can be compensated shortly and thoroughly by continuous gains from institutional reforms.

- Do not set a fixed model for reforms. It is crucial to value spontaneous innovations from the grassroots, the enterprises, and the local governments, and meanwhile to supplement with planned "pilot projects" and the introduction of advanced managerial techniques. The cost of institutional reforms and repetitive innovations will be significantly reduced by applying the experience from the pilot projects.
- Government's collaboration with enterprises, especially given that the interests of the local government and the local enterprises overlap, enables the government to take full consideration of enterprises' interests and to make compromises when needed.
- Material gains need to be at the center of reforms, which allow for "practical benefits" for a majority of the population. The principle of material gains also means coordination among different levels in policy implementations, rather than enforcing an ideal plan based on rational designs.
- Lastly, it is crucial to maintain policy consistency in reforms. During institutional reforms, the cost for inconsistent policies would be much higher than for institutional low efficiency.

The rise of the Chinese economy must have varied repercussions across the world. For some, if the Chinese economy maintains its rapid growth rate, the population living in the newly industrialized countries would increase by hundreds of millions from the 1950s. The whole world is going to change dramatically – from a world where a majority of the population (three-quarters) lives in poor, agricultural societies to a world where half of the population lives in relatively prosperous industrial societies. For others, in the face of the prospect that China with one-fifth of the world's labor force would become industrialized, the advanced countries must either facilitate industrial upgrading and transform themselves into the world market for industrial products or be prepared for fierce international competitions and carry out trade protectionism when it is necessary. There are still others who have warned of a shocking prophecy – the world order will move from fighting for resources, conflicts among religions, ethnic and racial purging, war between nation states, and ideological confrontation to "the clash of civilizations." Either way, human history will continue and will not revolve around one axis.

Notes

This chapter was originally published by *Social Science in China*, 1995, issue 1.

1 Adam Smith, *An Inquiry into the Nature and Causes of the Wealth of Nations*. Commercial Press, 1981, p.25 and p.27.
2 Jean Jacques Rousseau, *Of the Social Contract*, translated by He Zhaowu. Commercial Press, 1982, p.30.
3 Émile Durkheim, *Les Règles de la méthodesociologique*. Paris: P. U. F., 1956, pp. 3–13 and pp. 110.
4 Italics in original. Robert K. Merton, *Social Theory and Social Structure*. New York: Free Press, 1968, p.186.

5 Raymond Boudon, "L'individualisme methodologique," *Encyclopaedia Uiversalis Symposium*. Les Enjeux, Paris: Encyclo. Uni. France S.A., 1985, p.644.
6 Karl Popper, *Conjectures and Refutations: The Growth of Scientific Knowledge*, translated by Fu Jizhong et al. Shanghai Translation Publishing House, 1986, p.499.
7 Friedrich von Hayek, *Individualism and Economic Order*, translated by Jia Chen and Wen Yueran. Beijing: Beijing Institute of Economics Press, 1989, pp. 4–11.
8 Ibid.
9 Gary Becker, *A Treatise on the Family*, translated by Peng Songxiong. Huaxia Publishing House, 1987, p.217 and p.227.
10 James M. Buchanan, *Liberty, Market and State*, translated by Wu Jianliang et al. Beijing: Beijing Institute of Economics Press, 1989, p.74.
11 Ibid, pp. 196–221.

References

Becker, G. (1987). *A Treatise on the Family* (S. Peng, Trans.). Beijing: Huaxia Publishing House.

Boudon, R. (1985). "L'individualisme methodologique." In *Encyclopaedia Uiversalis Symposium*. Les Enjeux, Paris: Encyclo. Uni. France S. A.

Buchanan, J. M. (1989). *Liberty, Market and State* (J. Wu, Trans.). Beijing: Beijing Institute of Economics Press.

Durkheim, E. (1956). *Les Règles de la méthodesociologique*. Paris: P. U. F.

Hayek, F. (1989). *Individualism and Economic Order* (J. Chen & Y. Wen, Trans.). Beijing: Beijing Institute of Economics Press.

Merton, R. K. (1968). *Social Theory and Social Structure*. New York: Free Press.

Popper, K. (1986). *Conjectures and Refutations: The Growth of Scientific Knowledge* (J. Fu, Trans.). Shanghai: Shanghai Translation Publishing House.

Rousseau, J. J. (1982). *Of the Social Contract* (Z. He, Trans.). Shanghai: Commercial Press.

Smith, A. (1981). *An Inquiry into the Nature and Causes of the Wealth of Nations*. Shanghai: Commercial Press.

3 Searching for modernization

Enlightenment, evolution, and reformation

Enlightenment and the dissemination of the Western learnings: the birth of sociology

Social thoughts and sociological thoughts

In the Western world, scholars commonly attribute the foundation of sociology discipline to French Auguste Comte because he coined the term "sociology," a combination of Latin and Greek, in order to distinguish from the concept of "socio-physics," a concept that Comte believed had been pirated by social statisticians. In volumes four, five, and six (particularly volume four) from Comte's six-volume *The Course in Positive Philosophy*, published from the 1830s to the 1840s, he first introduced the idea that sociology is a new discipline. But Comte's ideas are generally classified under the category of social philosophy in the West. This means his ideas about sociology are hardly separated from philosophy – its parent discipline. The research subjects and methodology in sociology have not been specialized enough to distinguish them from other disciplines. Sociology as a discipline starts from Émile Durkheim. As he set up a sociology course at the university, published *The Rules of Sociological Method* in 1985, and established the journal *L'Année Sociologique*, Durkheim made sociology an official academic discipline in the educational system separated from its parent discipline, philosophy. There are some controversies regarding the establishment and the history of the sociology discipline,[1] but the scope is very limited, for the record is in black and white.

The foundation of sociology in China, however, is an open question, or rather, a controversial question. To clarify this question, we need first to distinguish social thoughts from sociological thinking. To institutionalize academic thoughts as a discipline is a rather recent phenomenon and an outgrowth of specialization of academic researches. Sages and saints in the ancient and classical periods were encyclopedic intellectuals with broad knowledge about the past and the contemporary, about a wide array of fields. They were considered grandmasters of ideas. Although they may have been more specialized in one or another field that today falls under arts and humanities, social science, or natural science, they were hardly specialists as we understand today. This phenomenon occurred to the East and the West alike. Aristotle from ancient Greece is canonized as the founding father of many disciplines. His writings span philosophy and natural science, such as *Meta-physics* and *Physics*, to arts and humanities and social science, including *Ethics* and *Politics*. His work also covers thoughts in philosophy, physics, biology, psychology, logics, ethics, political science, and economics. There is no wonder why he is regarded as the founder of many scientific disciplines. Taking nature and the human society as a holistic research subject and combining them into a unitary knowledge system is the common tendency and characteristic among all Western scholars prior to the modern times, not the least for those grandmasters of ideas who perceive it as their lifetime pursuit.

Specialization of academic disciplines was not finished in the West until the Enlightenment in the eighteenth century. An array of intellectuals such as Voltaire, Montesquieu, Diderot, and Rousseau were thinkers, but we can hardly consider them as political scientists, economists, or jurists, because their ideas were not specialized enough. Knowledge for them was universally applied to explain everything. People do not consider Montesquieu a specialized legal scholar based on his publication, *The Spirit of the Laws*. Instead, he is often perceived as a litterateur, political theorist, or legal historian. British renowned economist John Maynard Keynes (1953, p.13) even calls "Montesquieu the greatest French economist whom only Adam Smith is comparable to," in the French preface to his book *The General Theory of Employment, Interest, and Money*. People cannot tell if Keynes genuinely believed the originality of Montesquieu's economic thoughts or if he only meant to ridicule the absence of great economic thinkers in France. It seems more likely to be the former from the perspective of the English gentlemen who tended not to believe that tea-drinking English scholars would make such an international joke in the translation of their works. However, jean-wearing French professors frown at the praise from an Englishman, believing that is a "controversial pun." Western Enlightenment thinkers start from dismantling the past knowledge system, especially metaphysics. They believe that the pursuit of a metasystem knowledge becomes the obstacle and constraint to rationality instead of its motivation. What the Enlightenment thinkers attack is how the knowledge is built upon self-explanatory theorems and then evolves into a static system. With the liberal spirit, they create new knowledge systems based on induction. They would not be able to see that a clear path of seventeenth-century Western thoughts developed from René Descartes to Nicolas Malebranche, from Baruch Spinoza to Gottfried Wilhelm Leibniz, and from Francis Bacon and Thomas Hobbes to John Locke, but they all had the systematic spirit (esprit systematique) to establish a new system of encyclopedic knowledge, which is the key to understanding their intellectual pursuit and thinking inclination (Cassirer, 1988). In other words, what Enlightenment thinkers accomplished is a revolution in mental epistemology or conception about knowledge, but they did not complete specialization and institutionalization processes of knowledge. To borrow Thomas Kuhn's ideas about the scientific "paradigm," we can argue that this is also a "historical limitation" that failed to bring forth a "paradigm shift" in conceptions.

During the times when grandmasters of ideas have universal and integral knowledge systems, each and every one of them must have their own social thought. In the classical period, as great thinkers could not make a name by winning honorable and practical titles such as the Nobel Prize or other international awards, they could only be awarded a philosopher laureate, if not a knighthood. As far as philosopher is concerned, social thought appeared as a servant maid, a backdrop, and an extension, and suffixed to his philosophical thinking. In the textbook or biographies, authors almost always assessed the philosophical and political thought before moving on to the social thought concerning ethics, education, and history. Consequently, when it comes to the historiography of social thought, scholars often traced back to the first grandmaster of ideas in history. However, for sociological thought, it has to begin with Comte, the same as the history of economic thought has to begin with Adam Smith. At most, the history would include the "herald of ideas," but the history of different disciplines is impossible to trace back universally to Aristotle. Just as encyclopedic system of knowledge differs from a disciplinary system of knowledge, social thought is fundamentally different from sociological thought. The length of time needed to institutionalize a field of knowledge varies from discipline to discipline. Philosophy is perhaps one of the earliest established disciplines. Economics as a discipline is one generation earlier than sociology. Adam Smith had been a well-published academic and died when Comte was merely learning how to read. Political science has to wait a rather long time for its establishment as a discipline.

Chinese social thoughts can trace its history back to the ancient Hundred Schools of Thought. When does Chinese sociological thought come into being? When does sociology become an academic discipline in China? Who is the Chinese Comte? And who is the Chinese Durkheim? If not because of the introduction of Western thoughts and the cultural communication between China and the West, would the institutionalization of academic knowledge in China follow the same path it took? In other words, given the excessive humanistic orientation in the classical Chinese knowledge system, is it possible for that system to evolve naturally into a modern consciousness for specialization? Everything has its own standard and benchmark. However, what is the modern consciousness for specialization? The consciousness for specialization is not merely to coin new terms, create new concepts, or propose an unheard of "ology." In his groundbreaking *The Order of Things*, Michel Foucault (1966), the well-known French modern structuralist who is more often than not considered a great "postmodern" deconstructionist by Chinese scholars, divides the historical development of Western episteme from the Renaissance to the nineteenth century into three phases. The episteme in the sixteenth-century Renaissance is characterized by "resemblance and similitude," the classical episteme in the seventeenth and eighteenth centuries is characterized by "ordering," and the modern episteme since the nineteenth century is characterized by the search for "causal relations" and exploration of the hidden universal rules. Not all modern humans have a modern conscience, and the modern conscience does entirely originate from the modern age. The significant transition in academic consciousness from the perspective that sees God as the ultimate cause for every single phenomenon to the pursuit of universal laws in specific fields of knowledge takes centuries of efforts from generations of scholars. When Sir Isaac Newton sought to uncover the god's force behind a variety of phenomena from the fall of apples to the movement of planets, he arrived at "the universal law of gravity." In Comte de Buffon's exploration of the universal law in botany, he devoted himself to examining the biological taxonomy and the law of "organic molecules" for the formation and transformation of species. As Adam Smith was interested in the secret of wealth, he found "an invisible hand" that inadvertently directs individuals' pursuit of self-interests to improve public welfare. Comte put his efforts in pursuing laws in human society that are comparable to those in other fields. He realized that the development principle of "order" and "progress" governs the social history evolving from theology to metaphysics and then to empirical science.

There is no lack of the exploratory spirit for the universal law in the classical period in China. The theories of yin and yang and five elements are the manifestations of this spirit. However, the premature refinement of the theory is too sacred and canonized to allow for innovations for alternative ways of thinking. Meanwhile, the systematic spirit that accompanies the construction of this knowledge system did not survive its era and failed to transform into the inquiry into the universal causal relations in individual disciplines. Individual discipline, be it philosophy, alchemy, medicine or chemistry, continues to rely on the hypothesis of oneness that is derived from the theories of yin and yang and five elements to explain specific phenomena and technologies in specialized fields. Therefore, in China, the *Compendium of Materia Medica (Bencao Gangmu)* written by Li Shizhen appeared as early as 1578 and contains meticulous and comprehensive taxonomies of plants and animals. *The Exploitation of the Works of Nature (Tiangong Kaiwu)* published by Song Yingxing in 1637 is an encyclopedia that covers a wide range of production techniques and manufacturing methods. Due to the absence of the spirit to examine the causal relations in individual disciplines, no molecular biology derives from *Compendium of Materia Medica*, and no modern physics and chemistry evolve from *The Exploitation of the Works of Nature*. Along this line, well-developed Chinese philosophical, ethical, and historical thoughts can hardly give rise to sociology. The inquiry into the universal causal relations in individual disciplines represents the emergence of modern specialization consciousness. The emergence of modern specialization consciousness in China results from the dissemination of Western learnings and cultural integration between China and the West, although there were extensive knowledge and profound scholarship, as well as systematic social thoughts, that were full of wisdom in ancient China.

How can the emergence of Chinese sociological thought also be attributed to cultural integration, besides the dissemination of Western learnings? The reason is that China's enlightenment trend of empiricism emerged toward the end of the nineteenth century and the beginning of the twentieth century, which coincided with the empirical trend in sociology. When demonstrating the empirical characteristic of sociology, Comte pointed out that empiricism means concrete, useful, confirmative, and accurate knowledge taking the place of delusive theology and metaphysics. He self-righteously declared that because of him the study of social phenomena has turned into an empirical science. Liang Qichao (1985), in his speech titled *Chinese Academic History of the Recent 300 Years*, traced the origin of pragmatic thinking in the Chinese academe way back in history. He considers that Chinese academic mentality in the recent 300 years is a revolt against the neo-Confucianism of the prior 600 years.

> Our age is characterized by the tendency toward objective examinations and the sickness of subjective reflections. It is a common tendency in all branches of academics. It is a shame that objective examinations are restricted to the written world which significantly undermines its effectiveness. One offshoot is to advocate for practice yet reject theories. There are ebbs and flows for this offshoot but it has never dominated the field. In short, the approach that the past 300-year of academic exploration has represented, and I agree – is distinctive and progressive compared to that of the prior age. It is a pity that the spirit failed to complete its bloom. It is our responsibility to expand on this accomplishment and create a more tangible and magnificent era. It is also the modest significance of my speech.
>
> (Liang, 1985, p.91)[2]

Liang is not alone. As Jiang Baili (Fangzheng) wrote in the preface to Liang's *Introduction to the Learning of the Qing Dynasty*, "The academic spirit in the Qing Dynasty when the subjective deduction gave way to objective induction is synchronous with European Renaissance spirit." He went on to say,

> Current political situation has slightly altered, and thus well-versed scholars are contentious about cultural undertakings. But the social convention that is subject to the economic circumstance regards academics as the detrimental force, on which utilitarianism thrives. The priority is given to money and the second place is given to social status. In the eyes of the public, intellectuals are too pedant to be practical. Others believe that metaphysics remains. Government by people, society, reform, constitutional revolution are all terms. Is there any difference among them? Is there any similarity? I can only wish that contemporary intellectuals would take the effort to rectify this condition.
>
> (Liang, 1985, pp. 89–90)[3]

This reflects an academic turn to empiricism and the correspondent pragmatism in the society. Many scholars have summarized the trend of Chinese thoughts from the sixteenth century to the 1840s as "humanistic pragmatism" or "pragmatism of Ming and Qing Dynasty" (Chen, Xin, & Ge, 1989).

Indeed, the process of the dissemination of Western learnings and cultural integration is never a cultural tour that is brimming with romance and poetic atmosphere, but a resolution to succeed stimulated by external power and humiliation. There are numerous analyses of the process, but Liang Qichao's description perhaps touches the soul of his peers and reflects what they actually experienced:

It turns out that for all ethnicities China has contacted in the past thousands of years—except for Indians—are inferior peoples, so one tends to believe that only Chinese are knowledgeable people. 'Western learnings' was established after the introduction of Christianity. They include astronomy, cartography, and most importantly, cannons manufacturing techniques. This explains why Emmanuel Diaz Jeune and Franciscus Sambiaso were treated with honorable welcome in late Ming Dynasty and so were Ferdinandus Verbiest and Thomas Pereyra in early Qing Dynasty. Among others, that peacetime offered little incentives to learn how to make cannons resulted in a halt in the spread of Western learnings. This line of reasoning also explained the motivation and the roadmap of Western learnings under the reign of Xianfeng and Tong-zhi Emperors. After the loss of Hong Kong and Summer Palace being burnt down, but also having been impressed by Westerners' "hard ships and fierce cannons," the Qing court found it necessary to become self-reliant. Jiangnan Manufacturing Bureau in Shanghai and Fujian (Mawei) Arsenal were founded thanks to Qing court, but they also suggested the influence of Western learnings. The hassles in dealing with international affairs convinced the Qing court to have its own talents with foreign language abilities, so it built the School of Combined Learning (*Tongwen Guan*) near Zongli Yamen and the School of Foreign Languages and Literature (*Guangfangyan Guan*) near Shanghai Manufacturing Bureau. Meanwhile, the Qing court sent selected children under ten to the United States to learn English. This is what the first wave of Western learnings looked like. It is self-evident that to promote Western learnings along this line failed to make any impact on the academics. After the foundation of Jiangnan Manufacturing Bureau, however, a couple of dedicated scholars have translated dozens of scientific books and a few books about international laws and politics. Since then, Chinese started to acknowledge the knowledge hidden behind Westerners' "hard ships and fierce cannons." Consequently, the "conceptions of Western learnings" have gradually transformed among Chinese academics.

(Liang, 1985, p.91)[4]

Later on, in the "Introduction to Chinese Evolution in the Past 50 Years," an article written for the fiftieth anniversary of *Shen Bao* in 1922, Liang Qichao divided the awakening and the progress of Chinese scholarship into three phases. The first phase is characterized by "the sense of utensils inadequacy" of which the Self-Strengthening Movement is the best representative. The second phase is characterized by "the sense of institutional inadequacy," which is reflected in the "Hundred Days of Reform" after the disgraceful fiasco in the First Sino-Japanese War. And the third phase is characterized by "the sense of cultural inadequacy." Liang (1936b) argues that the seeds for the third phase were planted by the endeavors in the second phase during which "Yan Fu's translations that have introduced major thoughts in the nineteenth century to China have great academic significance but few Chinese could have appreciated it." Consequently, "the dissemination of Western learnings" is the outgrowth of "the spread of Western utensils" and "the dissemination of Western institutions." All three phases fit the same causal-relational logic.

The study of groups and sociology

The majority of Chinese scholars know that sociology was initially called "qun study" ("groups study") in China as symbolized by Yan Fu's translating *The Study of Sociology*, written by Herbert Spencer in 1873, into *Qunxue yiyan* in 1897. However, there is no knowing whether Yan Fu translated sociology to "the study of groups" because he wanted to capture the implication of sociology by following the translation principles of faithfulness, expressiveness, and elegance or because "qun study" was an established field in China, and he simply borrowed the term. If there has been "qun study" in China, then is its reference the same as what Spencer understood as "sociology?" If there is no such field as "qun study" in China prior to Yan's translation of Spencer, then why did Yan choose "qun study" over "sociology" as the translated term for sociology? After all, Japanese translation used sociology, and Yan was aware that the Japanese translated society into *shehui* (society). When he explained what "qun study" means, he often used the concept of "society."

According to the historical materials I have collected, before Yan's coinage of the term, there was no research field in China called "qun study" and no one had used the term. To put it in another way, before Yan introduced "qun study" into China, researchers were thinking about "groups" (social thought) but there was no "qun study" thinking (sociological thought). Yan is well aware of this. In a letter to Liang Qichao, Yan complained about the sweetness and bitterness of translation, but he also pointed out that as for *jixue* (economics) "the rationale existed in China but no discipline existed." His explanation is applicable to the study of groups:

> The name of jixue concerns with the origin of economics. It includes the name and incorporates the logos of the term . . . In ancient China, there were book-keepers (*jixiang*). When intellectuals were summoned by the Emperor, they would accompany each other in the trip to the capital (*jixie*). There were also terms like national strategy (*guoji*), family economics (*jiaji*), and livelihood (*shengji*). I thought that there was no better term than *ji* to capture the depth and scope of the original name . . . The principle of jixue such as everyday food and drinks is inseparable from living, but it takes two hundred years to develop a discipline from it. Therefore, there is no doubt that the rationale existed in China but no discipline existed. China has been civilized for two thousand years, there should already have proper terms for essential knowledge about everyday life, but I am afraid that jixue is not alone in the need for proper names.
>
> (Yan, 1996, p.525)

As early as 1894, Yan Fu was among the first to use the term "qun study." Around 1881 (the seventh and eighth year of Guangxu), at the age of 28,[5] Yan read *The Study of Sociology* by Herbert Spencer. After graduating from the naval academy –

the one near the Fujian Arsenal that is set up by Zuo Zongtang, one of the leaders of the Self-Strengthening Movement – Yan was sent off to study at the Old Royal Naval College, Greenwich, in 1877. Before graduation, Yan was summoned by Li Hongzhang and became the general coach at the Beiyang Fleet. During the nine years from 1885 to 1894, while working at the Beiyang Fleet, Yan failed the official civil examinations four times. It was not until after he failed the provincial examinations in 1894 that Yan got plenty of time to spend on translating. He started to translate works such as Alexander Michie's *Missionaries in China* and Thomas Henry Huxley's *Evolution and Ethics* after 1894. Yan may have started translating works of sociology and political science prior to or during his translating *Evolution and Ethics*, but his translations were not published then. In the note written for "Evolution and Ethics Prolegomena XIII," Yan wrote,

> Humanity begins with communities and groups, of which the principle is of the ultimate significance. There are no more articulate works on the study of groups than Herbert Spencer's *Social Statics: The Man Versus the State* and Bagehot Walter's *Physics and Politics*, both of which I have translated.
>
> (Yan, 1996, pp. 321–2)

This note reveals that, while he translated *Evolution and Ethics* during 1894 and 1896, Yan also translated other sociological works and started to use the term "qun study." I could not find the translated versions of these two books. Neither could I find any publication records. In addition, Yan attempted to translate an anonymous work from French with a tentative title *Introduction to National Economics*.[6] He only translated about 3,000 words, and the time of his translation was unclear. However, it should be one of his earlier translations, which occurred during or before 1894. There are two notes regarding the incomplete translated version, both of which have to do with qun study. One says, "Guided by qun study, there are many individual subjects, such as chemistry, law, economics, political science, religion, and linguistics." Another one says,

> Qun study is called Sociology in the West. It is originated from French philosopher Comte. As far as theories about ethics are concerned, sometimes some of them are radical or extreme, but it is better to be inclusive and use one term to cover them all without discriminations. I call it qun study.
>
> (Yan, 1986, p.847)

However, "no discipline existed" in China that was called sociology, so why did Yan not choose the same translated term of sociology as it was used by Japanese academics? American sinologist Benjamin I. Schwartz argues that Yan rejected the Japanese translation of sociology and preferred the term "qun" (groups) because he thought "qun" better described what "society" meant – namely, a term describing social collectivity rather than social structure. Yan's philosophy of translation concerns "maximum use of the allusive categories of ancient Chinese philosophic thought in rendering Western concepts. Ironically enough, however, most of his own neologisms were to perish in the struggle for existence with the Japanese creation" (Schwartz, 1964/1995, p.88). However, Yan's creation of "qun study" does not merely reflect his preference of allusive categories of ancient Chinese philosophic thought. Yan is first and foremost influenced by ancient Chinese philosopher Xunzi's thought. In his translation of Spencer, he explains "qun study" by frequently referring to Xunzi. For instance, in *On the Origin of Strength*, Yan mentions that Xunzi says, "What distinguishes human from animals is that humans form various groups." Again in the afterword to "The Study of Sociology," Yan (1996b, p.127) refers to Xunzi's saying that groups are concerned with human livelihood. Yan choose the term "qun" as used by Xunzi because the meaning of "qun" is close to what society implies, for one. But more importantly, in his search for the feasible path for national wealth and power, Yan found that this translation satisfied the urgent need of pragmatism. Ideas expressed in chapters from *Xunzi* such as "On the Wealth of the Nation," "On the Power of the Nation," "On the Regulations of the King" "On the Model of Conduct," "On the Military Affairs" and "On the Gentleman" fit Yan's goals. In particular, Xunzi's argument in "On the Regulations of the King" concerning the making of a powerful nation correspond to Yan's thought in this regard and his understanding of Spencer's works. Xunzi points out in "On the Regulations of the King" that humans can form groups although they are "divided" by social hierarchies. The society still works because of "*yi*" – a sense of duty and justice that ensures social order. With "division" and "yi," human beings can form a powerful society.

> Fire and water possess vital breath (qi) but without life. Grass and trees have life but no intelligence. Human beings not only have vital breath, life, and awareness, but the sense of duty and justice. For this reason, they are the noblest beings on the planet. Oxen far surpass humans in physical abilities, and horses far surpass humans in speed, but humans can use animals. Why? That is because they can organize themselves into social groups. Why can human for groups? My answer is by division. Why is it possible to organize human by division? My answer is yi. If the society were divided by this sense of duty and justice, it would lead to social concord and unity that give human strength to overcome the nature and build shelters for living. Nature has four seasons that give life to everything, precisely because the year is equally divided. Therefore, human beings are unlikely not to form groups. Grouping without proper divisions by the principle of justice result in strife, disorder, fragmentation, and weakness which eventually would make humanity not be able to triumph, losing their shelters and neglecting their ritual principles. Family is abided by filial piety; brothers are bounded by respect; subjects should be obedient and the ruler should pay attention to what is just. A ruler must be good at organizing groups. If groups were formed properly and reasonably, everything and animals would thrive and enjoy their lives.
>
> (Xunzi, 1979, p.127)

Yan Fu was influenced by Xunzi's ideas when it came to his translation of *Evolution and Ethics*, which occurred before he translated *The Study of Sociology*. His translation of *Evolution and Ethics* is half original meanings and half his own interpretations. In this significantly and selectively shortened version, languages discussing qun are everywhere, and some of chapter titles are simply paraphrased into "Adept in Organizing Groups" and "Governing Groups" and so on. As a matter of fact, what Yan truly valued was Spencer's work. He considered his translation of *Evolution and Ethics* as preparation for translating Spenser's work. For the latter "is tens of thousands of words, and is full of complex sentences and ideas, and thus it mustn't be a hasty translation" (Yan, 1986, p.1327). *Evolution and Ethics* in Yan's eyes was a work that applied biological principle in human morality and ethics – a theory concerned with "protecting groups." It appears like a prologue to Spencer's study of sociology. For this reason, Yan chose to translate Huxley's *Evolution and Ethics* instead of the then groundbreaking biological publication *On the Origin of Species* by Charles Darwin. Yan's goal was sociobiology rather than biology.

Yan also translated sociology into "qun study" because he believed that he had discovered ideas in Spencer's work that dovetailed with traditional Confucian aspirations for connecting knowledge with statecraft – namely, the notions concerning knowledge acquisition through studying the natural phenomena, self-cultivation, family and state governing, and the qualities of the "inner sage" and the "outer ruler." The only difference is that Spencer developed a specialized field of study from those ideas. In the afterword to "The Study of Sociology," Yan pointed out that "the book combines the distillations of thought from *Daxue* and *Zhongyong* yet offers substantial contents advocating studying social phenomena to acquire knowledge for governance and peace." In *On the Origin of Strength*, Yan expressed this understanding more explicitly when he talked about Spencer's "qun study":

> What is "qun study?" . . . Everything about human beings, from children-bearing and raising and social divisions and exchanges to activities concerning military, justice, rites, and music, relies upon human nature to form social groups. So Xipengsai (Spencer) established a discipline named as qun study. His treatise, along with his elaborations, coincides with ideas about morality, self-cultivation, family regulation, governance, and peace from *Daxue*. But *Daxue* only alludes to these ideas falling short to elaborate on them. Xipengsai (Spencer)'s book is erudite and subtle full of complex ideas and profound meanings. One theory explains one phenomenon, analogous to the principle of physics. It uses well-documented and extensive evidence from human life to investigate the cause and effect.
>
> (Yan, 1996b, p.8)[7]

For Western pioneers of sociology such as Comte and Spence, sociology was the "queen science": a comprehensive discipline that encompasses all other disciplines, or at least the aggregate of social science and humanity. Each discipline is organized by a unitary principle and into the all-encompassing universe of sociology. This is almost the same as the ideas of acquiring knowledge through studying natural phenomena and connecting knowledge with statecraft. That is to say, the study of "evolution" is for the same purpose as "the study of groups (qun study)" in "governing groups." There is no misunderstanding of that. Yan makes it explicit that "qun" is a broader concept than what people understand as "society." Yan (1996b, p.525) says,

> qun (group) is what people are naturally born into. There are varied ways to form groups guided by laws and regulations. Groups exist in society, business, industry, politics, and education. The most significant group is the formation of a nation. I have studies the six categories of Chinese characters and scriptures and found that our ancient wisdom in line with Western learnings.

However, there are alternative understandings to Yan's. Almost during the same time when Yan Fu was translating *The Study of Sociology*, Tan Sitong was writing his book titled *Renxue* (A Study of Benevolence). As Yan Fu published *On the Origin of Strength* in *Zhibao*, a newspaper based in Tianjing, from March 4 to 9 in 1895, which immediately stirred tremendous repercussions, the chance is slim that Tan Sitong who kept up with current affairs would have missed the first-sight love Yan had expressed for Spencer's "qun study." However, because of his limited knowledge about foreign languages, although Tan had all scriptures from Confucianism, Taoism, and Buddhism at his fingertips, he failed to capture what Yan was trying to convey in the name "qun study" as the Chinese version of sociology. Having drawn inspiration from Buddhist sutras, *Book of Changes, Zhuang Zi*, Confucian, Western learnings, and mathematics, Tan Sitong advocated circulation (*tong*) as the ontological body for *ren*, with a possible hidden agenda to pave the way for reform. In *Renxue*, Tan used both "qun study" and "sociology," but by referring to those terms, he meant either an array of disciplines or all kinds of Western social science disciplines – a way of usage that cannot be more divergent from what Yan Fu meant. In the preface to *Renxue*, Tang wrote,

> Traps in the world are as countless as the realm of vanity is borderless. [We] must first and foremost break out the trap of wealth, and then of study subjects like textology and poetry and prose, and then of **global qun study**, and then of the rule of the king, and then of moral human relations, and then of the Heaven, and then of **all kinds of religions across the world**, and then of Buddhist doctrine.
>
> (Tan, 1994, p.6, bold used for emphasis)

In Mr. Jia Runguo's annotation to *Renxue* in 1993, he included a note for the previous quotation specifying "qun study: sociology." This would be gilding the lily, because what Tan meant by "qun study" obviously differs from the sociology in Comte or Spencer's words, meaning "a variety of disciplines" or "all kinds of scholarship." The "global qun study" that Tan aspired to break out was the trap of a variety of disciplines rather than that of sociology. After all, Yan's advocacy of "qun study" facilitated reform, so there is no way that reformers must break out of it. Tan's use of "qun study" to mean "a variety of disciplines" was made even more explicit in the twenty-seventh item from the "Discursive and Definitive Boundaries of Renxue": "Without a good command of physics and chemistry, there is no way to master four disciplines of astronomy, the earth (geography), the body (physiology), the mind (psychology). This how to get started with **qun study** and **qunjiao**" (Tan, 1994, pp. 9–10).[8] At the twenty-fifth item in the same chapter, Tan also used the term "sociology," which is perhaps the earliest record of the term in China.[9] However, his usage of the term meant all kinds of Western social science disciplines:

> A student of renxue must grasp *The Hua-yen Sutra* and sutras from the schools of Zen and Dharma Characteristics from Buddhist scriptures; *New Testament*, mathematics, natural science, **sociology** from Western learnings; *Book of Changes, the Spring and Autumn Annals, the Analects of Confucius, Book of Rites, Mengzi, Zhuangzi, Mozi*, and *The Book of History* as well as works of Tao Yuanming, Zhou Maoshu, Zhang Hengliang, Lu Zijing, Wang Yangming, Wang Chuanshan, and Huang Lizhou from Chinese learnings.
>
> (Tan, 1994, p.9, bold used for emphasis)

By no means would Tan Sitong have been unaware of different disciplinary categories. In a prior publication titled *Letter to Yuan Zheng: Depression and Grief with Our Country*, Tan elaborated on the classification of Western disciplines.

> Westerners divide studies about the Earth into three branches of letters, matter, and politics . . . . One can never master knowledge about mathematics, calendar, meteorology, electricity, water, fire, light, sound, voyage and cartography and others unless he grasps the laws of letters. One can never master knowledge about chemistry, mines, forms, metals and stones, animals and plants unless he grasps the law of matter. One can never master the knowledge about politics, history, literature, military, law, business, agriculture, diplomacy, republic, tax, manufacturing and others unless he grasps the law of politics.

He continued, "For Westerners study of tables is called statistics," and "tables can be used to categorize all kinds of disciplines" (Tan, 1994, p.189). Therefore, in Tan's discipline classifications, "qun study" was not a discipline but a generic term for a variety of disciplines. Tan also understood "qun study" as popular knowledge. The proof lies in *Ten Essays on Governance at Zhuangfei Lou* published by Tan in 1898, the ninth chapter of which is titled "Qun Study." The entire chapter discusses how to organize associations in varied industries and from all walks of life (e.g., school association, peasant association, labor union, business association) in order to reach the goal of "reform without in the name of reform." It is thus clear that for Tan, who had no direct contact with Yan Fu, "qun study" was a very vague concept. However, ideas expressed in *Renxue* – such as "what rules China in the last 2,000 years remains the same as the ruling of Qin Dynasty – all despotism" and "making connections between China and the West, between the ruler and the ruled, between men and women, and between me and the world" – are so mind-boggling and inspiring that Liang Qichao used to exclaim before Yan Fu that Tan was "a weird genius."[10]

The emergence of "qun study" in China results from the dissemination of Western learnings along with the conflict and integration of Chinese and Western cultures. After its introduction, qun study was absorbed into Chinese cultural, discursive, and conceptual system, becoming a seed to change the system in question.

Social evolution: evolution, reform, and preservation of qun

Evolution and the transformation of society: in the search of laws for social evolution

To claim Liang Qichao is China's Comte is perhaps an overstatement, as Liang did not establish such a systematic social theory as Comte did. However, Liang's contribution to the foundation of qun study, his meaningful pursuit of causal relations in social changes, and his attempt to classify modern disciplines qualified him as the most significant founder for Chinese sociology. Moreover, what Liang's depth of knowledge and eminent intellectual position far exceeded for China what Comte was for Britain, France, or the West in general.

When it comes to "qun study," Liang Qichao was a pupil of Kang Youwei, and at the same time deeply influenced by Yan Fu and Tan Sitong. Where Liang learned social Darwinism from Spencer and Huxley through Yan, he deepened his understanding of *the Book of Changes* through Tan. In the preface to *A Discussion on Qun*, Liang talked about the source of his thoughts on reform and the preservation of qun:

> I ask Sir Nanhai (Kang Youwei) what is the rule for governing all under the Heaven? Sir answers, "[The principle of] institutional flexibility that centers on human-orientation would enable one to rule even for tens of thousands of years. In the *On Changing Institutions*, I have touched on this topic. I attempted to elaborate on this point by looking for illustrative examples from a wide range of literature and teachings only to find them inadequate. *Evolution and Ethics* translated by Yan Fu and *Renxue* written by Tan Sitong from Liuyang have shed light on my mind . . . With my teacher's thought in mind and borrowing insights from these two books, I write *A Discussion on Qun* – ten sections and a hundred and 20 chapters – to make my modest contribution to expanding on this topic."
>
> (Liang, 1936b)

At about the age of 25 in 1882, Kang Youwei failed the provincial civil service exams in Shuntian. On his way back home, he passed Shanghai and was exposed to Western thought: "Realizing that Westerners are well-trained in academics." Around 1886, he dismantled the shackle of outdated Chinese theories by expanding his theory from learning from "geometrical theorems" to building his own "universal laws" (Kang, 1988, pp. 58–83). In this way, Kang began thinking of "natural evolution" and "human changes" abiding by the same rules, and, most importantly, he believed that the most significant rule governing natural evolution and human changes had its parallel in the profound meanings Confucius expressed in *the Annals of Spring and Autumn (Chunqiu)*. As Kang explained in *A Study on Dong Zhongshu's Spring and Autumn*,

> The cardinal principle Confucius developed in *the Annals of Spring and Autumn* is the three stages of the historical progression. The first is the Age of Disorder characterized by political chaos and social anomie; the second is the Age of Approaching Peace marked by gradual restoration of political order and economic well-beings; and the third is the Age of Unity (*datong*) when the world develops toward an utopia in which people enjoy harmony and equality . . . with fully-developed political order and peace . . . This is the first and foremost principle from *the Annals of Spring and Autumn*.
>
> (Kang, 1981)

This served as the foundation for Kang's painstakingly "refashioning of Confucius as a reformer." As Kang's most significant disciple and successor, Liang Qichao followed Kang's steps and expanded on the theory by borrowing insights from Western theories on political systems classifications:

> There are three types of governance. They are characterized by the rule of multiple rulers, of one single ruler, and of the people, respectively. There are two sub-categories of the rule of multiple rulers. One is under the rule of sachem; and the other is the rule of feudal and hereditary lords. There are also two sub-categories of the rule of one single ruler. One is monarchy; and the other is characterized by the shared ruling of the monarch and the people. There are still two sub-categories of the rule of the people. One is under the rule of the president; and the other is without the president. The rule of multiple rulers is the signature of the age of disorder. The rule of one single ruler is the signature of the age of approaching peace. The rule of the people is what the age of unity actually means.
>
> According to Yan Fu, the reforms in Europe take three different approaches, namely, Monarchy – people under the rule of kings, Aristocracy – noblemen-enabled republic, and Democracy – the rule of people.
>
> The global trend is evolving toward peace, which is not unique for Taixi (the Western world) nor evitable for Cina Sthana (China). I reckon that in less than a hundred years the entire world will adopt the rule of the people with no exception to China.
>
> (Liang, 1936c)

These passages strike remarkable resemblance to Aristotle's classification of constitutions. In *Politics*, Aristotle groups constitutions into six categories: royalty, aristocracy, constitutional government, tyranny, oligarchy, and democracy. Among these six constitutions, royalty, aristocracy, and constitutional government belong to the group of true, ideal constitution while tyranny, oligarchy, and democracy belong to the group of ominous, perverted, and actual constitution. Based on the number of people who participate in the magistracies, the six constitutions can be divided into three types: government of one, government of a few, and government of many (Wang, 1984, p.61). Liang adapted and contextualized this classification of constitutions to an evolutionary system. Liang's ideas of political evolution were inspired and influenced by Western thought via Yan Fu, who had obviously learned Western evolutionary theory that described the progress from tyranny to royalty and then to democracy through his translations of Montesquieu's *The Spirit of Laws* (*Espirs de Lois*). Yan noted in his translated version that

> in Mengzi's classification of government, there are the government of the public, the government of a single ruler, and absolutism. Given the absence of the concept of the citizens and of the limited power of the king, the government of a single ruler actually implies that the ruler is also abided by laws.
>
> (Yan, 1996, p.395)

Yan thus developed a relatively systematic social progression theory from a combination of Western evolutionary theory concerning political systems and the thought asserting that society was evolving successively from the age of disorder to the age of approaching peace and the age of great unity.

We would be astonished at the similarities between Kang's and Liang's theories about the three stages society and relevant Comte thoughts. Comte divides the development of human intelligence into three periods: theological (or imaginary) age, metaphysical (or abstract) age, and positive (or scientific) age. In the theological age, human beings tend to explain a variety of phenomena by referring to personified deities. The metaphysical age is characterized by explanation by impersonal abstract beings, such as nature. In the positivity age, human beings explain phenomena through observations and establishing cause-and-effect relationships. Scientific methods first make inroads into fields such as mathematics, astronomy, physics, chemistry, and biology and then expand into social science by facilitating the establishment of sociology. From his theory on three stages of knowledge development, Comte inferred that there are also three corresponding stages for social development – namely, militant, interim, and industrial ages. Comte (1907, pp. 2–3) maintained that the law of three stages was "his great discovery of fundamental laws which abide by unvarying necessity and which rest on a solid foundation. This solid foundation is based either on positivism from our perceptions of organization or on historical examinations through discreet analysis."

To our bafflement, Yan Fu seemed not to be interested in Comte's ideas, although Comte was more well known than Spencer, and Yan's translation of Comte's work predated that of Spencer's work. He was able to make (rather subtle) connections between threads in Spencer's work and the gist of *Daxue* and *Zhongyong*. However, he was rather blind to the (visibly) profound meanings behind subtle words in Comte's literature that resonated with *the Annals of Spring and Autumn.*

One of the reasons for Yan's preference for Spencer lies perhaps in the fundamental distinction between Spencer and Comte when it came to the origin of social progression laws. While Comte's theory of social progression was based on his laws of human intelligence development, Spencer's theory was an application of Darwinian theory to the social organism. Therefore, they were often grouped into the category of "positivists," but their theoretical groundwork could not be more different. When talking about this dissent, Spencer said,

> What is Comte's professed aim? To give a coherent account of the progress of *human conceptions.* What is my aim? To give a coherent account of the progress of the *external world.* Comte proposes to describe the necessary, and the actual, filiation of *ideas.* I propose to describe the necessary, and the actual, filiation of *things.* Comte professes to interpret the genesis of *our knowledge of nature.* My aim is to interpret . . . the genesis of the *phenomena which constitute nature.* The one end is *subjective.* The other is *objective.*
>
> (Spencer, 1904, p.570)

Spencer's stance was closer to the academic trend in the later part of Qing dynasty in China when intellectuals in their collective revolt against the Confucian school of idealist philosophy of the Song and Ming dynasties turned to positivism. It is also in line with reformers' tendency to propose reform motions out of the paradigm that emphasizes "the harmony between heaven and man" and "no separations of (Western) function from (Chinese) foundation." Particularly, Spencer's social Darwinism stressed "the survival of the fittest," which for reformers who were preoccupied with wealth and power of a nation was an overdue rain after a prolonged drought.

Yan Fu's prejudice in favor of Spencer might have caused certain misinterpretations of the latter's ideas. One of Spencer's significant ideas was concerned with structural transformation from militant society to industrial society. Differing from Comte's classification of the society based on the level of progression, Spencer defined the types of society based on social structure constitutions. While militant society is structured around "forced" relationships, industrial society is based on "voluntary and contractual" relationships, from which we can already get a glimpse of Émile Durkheim's division between "mechanical solidarity" and "organic solidarity." Those classical modernization theories that focus on the transformation from traditional society to modern society are all based on the same definition of structural constitution and the hypothesis on social transformation, whether it be the division between status society and contractual society (Henry Sumner Maine), or *Gemeinschaft* and *Gesellschaft* (Ferdinand Tönnies), or folk and urban societies (Robert Redfield), or premodern and modern societies (Max Weber), or religion and secular society (Ulrich Beck). Driven by his quest for wealth and power along with his attention to military and economic power, Yan not only failed to emphasis the distinction between the militant stage and the industrial stage in Spencer's theory but also considered them equivalent from time to time. That is because in Yan's mind, the pursuit of wealth fit the goal of military power. Another example of Yan's misinterpretation is that he found collectivism ideas that stressed state and socially collective power in Spencer's magnum opus, whereas Spencer was a classic supporter of laissez-faire from nineteenth-century Britain.

The extension of evolution theory to social changes serves as a theoretical foundation for reformers as well as the groundwork for Liang Qichao and Yan Fu's theorizing of "qun study." Before "Public Vehicle Petition" in the spring of 1895 in *From Changes to Reform and From Reform to a Long Reign*, Kang (1981, p.110) urged, "Heaven cannot be of Yang without Yin, the Earth cannot be firm without soft, humans cannot stay static without changes." In the introduction to *On Changing Institutions* published in 1896, Liang opens as follows:

> Why we must seek reform? Anything on the planet is constantly changing. Nighttime and daytime become a day; summer and winter build into a year. Earthquakes, volcano eruptions, and the flow of lavas and the drifting of glaciers all gradually transform the Earth. Generations after generations of sea grass, aquatic animals, enormous trees and large birds, fishes, and alligators experience shifts in birth and extinction, transforming what the world looks like. Humans have blood circulating within the body alternating the color from red to alizarin crimson; while inhaling oxygen and exhaling carbon dioxide unremittingly, humans experience dramatic changes within. If they remained unchanged, the Heaven, the Earth, and human beings are soon to vanish. Therefore, change is the axiom throughout the history.
>
> (Liang, 1936d)

In Yan Fu's publication of *On the Origin of Strength*, he also introduced Darwin's theory of evolution and then discussed Spencer's "qun study." He explained, "Although Spencer's work is published earlier than Darwin's *The Origin of Species*," it "extends evolutionary theories to human society with an emphasis on human relations, morality, and governance." Along this line, Yan argued that the transition from evolution to social change reflects a path that "sheds light on the thriving and governing of a nation":

> To understand why body grow, one must learn biology. To appreciate the magic of mentality, one must study the mind. One can start to learn qun study after completing these studies. As far as the substance and the function are concerned, qun, after its formation, is not different from a unified biological body. The size might be varied, but the way of governance has little difference. Just as one who knows the key to biological growth would understand the development of qun, one who knows the secret to longevity would know what leads to a nation to long-term prosperity . . .Consequently, the intellectual

practice shall return to qun study. Only qun study would shed light on the thriving and governing of a nation. Alas! It is an essential field of study.

(Yan, 1996d, p.20)

Reformists such as Liang Qichao and Yan Fu were deeply convinced that both nature and human society are guided by the same unified law, so they believed for a nation to become powerful and a people to prosper, they must conform to such a law and reform themselves. In addition, with a deep-seated notion of the harmony between heaven and man, Liang Qichao maintained, "Universal cause-effect laws" work behind all kinds of natural and social phenomena "not by chance." But natural laws cannot function on their own independent of humans or "evolve from unconscious movement to social change" (Ge & Jiang, 1984, p. 221). We can tell there is a contradiction here, which Liang also confessed in his later thinking. Namely, on one hand, he believed that history and nature alike abide by the universal cause-effect laws, but on the other hand, he acknowledged that cause-effect laws have limited applicability to history as the latter is created by human's joint effort.

In his later years (in 1922), Liang Qichao changed his view regarding universal cause-effect laws and raised questions as to "whether there are cause-effect laws to history" and "whether there is a progression in historical phenomena." He also thought of himself as "completely wrong." For the universe is divided into nature and culture, in which "the territory of nature is ruled by cause-effect laws, the cultural realm belongs to liberal spirit," and historical phenomena are at most "inter-related" rather than of "causality." While nature that is evolutionary and subject to cause-effect laws can be explored through induction, culture is the opposite (Liang, 1936e).

Qun study: "inner sage and outer ruler" and qun-oriented principle

As I mentioned earlier, Yan Fu repeatedly said that he discovered ideas from Spencer's work that "coincide with" traditional Confucian notions concerning knowledge acquisition through studying the natural phenomena, self-cultivation, family regulation, rightly state governing, and making the world at peace. From the present perspective, Spencer's theory on social organism evolution and Confucianism are two completely different ideologies, and they are contradictory at many places. So what in Spencer's work struck Yan Fu as "coincident?"

With the differences between Eastern and Western thinking in mind, Western philosophy is more like puzzle games (the study of human intelligence), while Chinese philosophy is more like wisdom about living (life philosophy). A majority of Yan Fu's translations of Western literature belong to the family of studies on statecraft with pragmatic utilities, including sociology, economics, laws, and politics with much less concern for humanities such as philosophy. Literature on statecraft caters to Chinese intellectual's taste in favor of pragmatism. Moreover, just as Spencer and Comte self-righteously claimed that sociology is the queen science, a comprehensive discipline of all social science, Yan held that the ideas of self-cultivation, family regulation, rightly state governing, and making the world at peace that are conveyed in *Daxue* represent Chinese Confucian scholars' fundamental point of view on the laws of life and social development. Furthermore, Spencer thought of human society and biological evolution are in accordance with the universal law of "the survival of the fittest," which has a plausible resemblance to Chinese traditional thinking of "the harmony between heaven and man." Finally, Spencer's ideas on social evolution were very appealing to reformists such as Yan who were yearning for China to regain power and wealth, even more so given the economic and social prosperity in Britain. Around 1873 when Spencer wrote *A Study of Sociology*, Britain emerged as the center of the world economy. Its foreign trade surpassed the combination of that of France, Germany, and Italy, and it was almost four times larger than that of the United States. Britain controlled the oceans, and that its navy was invincible is beyond question. When the European continent was caught in the swirls of wars and revolutions, Britain enjoyed its peace and well-being domestically and internationally. No wonder Yan, who studied at the British Naval College, connected British economic growth to its progressive thought. That translations of works such as *Evolution and Ethics* caused a sensation in China had as much to do with Chinese intellectuals' collective aspiration for the country's wealth and power.

Like Comte and Spencer, Chinese reformist scholars were ambitious about finding a comprehensive social science disciple and a unitary law to explain social development. Their intellectual pursuit, to a large extent, was a reaction to Western academic methodology, which meant discovering "texts" – laws and rules – behind codes (letters or social phenomena). For reformists, that meant finding "sublime words with profound meaning." In Liang Qichao's eyes, the "text" in Chinese learnings that revealed the rule of "survival of the fittest" was the teaching of "inner sage and outer ruler," which is also the highest goal for Chinese intellectuals. He said, "Confucian philosophies are broad, but the use of them can be summarized by what *the Analects of Confucius* has said about 'self-cultivation and reassuring others.'" The highest goal for intellectuals is summarized by the term "inner sage and outer ruler" from *Zhuangzi*. Perfection of self-cultivation would lead to an inner sage, and the end of reassuring others is an outer ruler. The progressive path leading to inner sage and outer ruler is made explicit and straightforward in *Daxue*. The so-called knowledge acquisition via investigation, sincere thoughts, rectified hearts, and self-cultivation from *Daxue* are what is needed for one to reach the stage of inner sage; the "family regulation, rightly state governing, and making the world at peace" from *Daxue* are what is needed for one to reach the stage of outer ruler (Liang, 1936f).[11] Liang also points out the consistence in Confucian learnings and modern social science when it comes to research questions. Liang (1936a) said,

> Modern social science is interested in many problems that also attract attentions from Confucianism. In line with the outer ruler aspect, family system concerns family regulation; government institutions concern rightly state governing; social customs relate to the making of a peaceful world. Therefore,

we must appreciate Confucian thought comprehensively instead of simply apply modern philosophy to it. Confucian conceptualization of outer ruler encompasses sociology, political science, and economics and so on; Confucian conceptualization of inner sage includes education, psychology, and anthropology and so on.

In short, from Liang's perspective, sociology was first and foremost learnings on the outer ruler – namely, learnings about family regulation, rightly state governing, and making the world at peace, which he maintained were more important than political science and economics.

Liang Qichao and Yan Fu expanded on the social evolution theory and developed a theory of "qun study" that consists of a series of concepts such as "qunben (groups as the center)," "baoqun (preservation of groups)," "hequn (be gregarious or getting well along with others)," "shanqun (skilled at organizing groups)," "qunde (social morality)," "qunshu (group tactics)," and "qunzhi (the governance of groups)." At its core is a qun orientation that "qun is the constitution and change is the function," and the theory is fleshed out by the principle of "hequn (be gregarious)."

In his explanation of qun orientation, Liang Qichao pointed out that the spirit of "qun" is common to all living things. There are people who are "good at it" and who are not. Gregariousness leads to procreations, but staying away from qun is subversive. Those who are good at qun survive, but the rest will extinguish. No species has only one type; no type stays unchanged. With the passage of time, one replaces another, which is the law of generational succession. While "the freshly-formed qun gets stronger and stronger," its "predecessor becomes weaker and weaker"; the civilized qun triumphs over the barbaric qun. This is almost identical to evolutionary ideas of natural selection and the survival of the fittest. Etymologically and linguistically speaking, the concept and the meaning of "qun" is rooted in Chinese culture and Confucian learnings, but hermeneutically and semantically speaking, the theory and texts of "qun study" are derived from Darwinian evolution theory and Spencer's social organism theory.

In his translation of *Evolution and Ethics*, Yan Fu pointed out that Huxley arguing that human forming groups of sympathy misplaces its focus on trifles, as compared to Spencer who argued that humans forming groups is driven by interests. Yan's ideas about "preserving groups" is almost identical to the "natural selection" theory:

Huxley's argument on preserving groups is appealing. But we must take a critical approach toward his reasoning that human form groups out of sympathy mistakenly treats the effect as the cause. Human form groups because of interests and the need for safety, the same as animals are in herds for survival and proliferation. Human forming group is not driven by sympathy. Given shared interests and the need for safety, human groups evolve over time. Those who are able to form groups survive, the rest extinguishes; those who are good at organizing groups survive, the rest extinguishes. Who are good at organizing groups? Those who have sympathy with others. Human sympathy, however, occurs after, not before, natural selections took place. Could it be that the human species does not have members who lack sympathy from the beginning? They were wiped out in the natural selection and are extinct now. Huxley treats the effect as the cause. Thus his theory of qun is not as rigorous as Spencer's.

(Yan, 1996, p.323)

Although Yan Fu put much emphasis on nationalism and racialism, as he translated Adam Smith's *An Inquiry into Nature and Causes of the Wealth of Nations*, he seemed to accept the liberal economic idea that explains how "self-interests" are guided by "an invisible hand" for "public good." He thought the reason for the political impasse in China lay in the separation of *yi* (righteousness) from *li* (profit), which often promotes junzi (man of honor) as a person who puts righteousness before profit. Yan thus believed the most significant contributions economics makes is to allow for the combination of righteousness and profit. He continued by mentioning that he had tears in his eyes while reading *The Wealth of Nations* because "I have never seen a free country where its people are deprived of the right to freedom; I have never seen a powerful country where its people are deprive of power" (Yan, 1996, pp. 341–2, 379).

When being compared to Yan, Liang Qichao syncretized more threads about how to get well along with people from Chinese wisdom in his theorizing of qun study. On one hand, he recognized the importance of social association (hequn, or forming groups), because humans forming groups is the outgrowth of natural selection needed for preservation. On the other hand, Liang distinguished formal communities from substantial communities in that the former lacks unity, whereas the latter is built on the qun-oriented, altruistic morality (qunde). The spirit that advocates collectivity triumphing over individuality, large group over small group, and being selfless and devoted to the public cause becomes the prime principle for the future reformers and revolutionaries when it comes to mobilizing and organizing the masses. Liang was obviously among the first to promote this spirit as the principal implication of qun study:

Private persons form groups. According to the axiom of natural selection, the more united the group is, the more powerful it is. This is self-explanatory even for the beginner of philosophy. Aren't there any groups in China? Our country has more than four hundred million people who have inhabited in this land for thousands of years. Moreover, local self-governance has well-developed, and there are numerous small associations in individual provinces. Industrial associations are so common that countless associations are seen among four occupations.[12] Groups lacking unity are bound to fade away, because they are not united by group-oriented morality. Group-oriented morality means when in a group private persons are able to always put the group before themselves and when in a larger group smaller groups are able to always put the larger group before their own smaller groups. When groups are cohesively united, they are able to defeat other groups from outside.

(Liang, 1936g)

Liang's theorizing of "group tactics" and "the governance of groups" further shows his premise that social integration is rooted in morality, especially collective morality:

> Tens of thousands of people unite to form a nation, and the entire world consists of hundreds of millions of people. Without group formations, how comes there are nations and the world! The making of groups rely upon tactics that regulate groups. Groups would fail to come into being if individualism prevails. One group thrives at the expense of other group's failure. Individualism means everyone refuses to see anything beyond self-interest and is blind to the external world. Gentlemen only mind their households; officials only mind their positions; peasants and farmers only mind their arable fields; merchants and traders only mind their business and the price of their products; individuals only mind their own interests; households only mind their fertility; kindred only minds the passage of the family name; villages only mind their land; associations only mind their villages; teachers only mind their schools; scholars only mind their teachings; therefore there are four hundred million countries among four hundred million people, which is actually without a nation. A great ruler of a nation understands that he and the people are members of the same group. The knowledge about the group and the group norms which tie group members together and prevent the group from falling apart are called group tactics. The world is divided by different countries and thus qun is divided as us versus them. The age of chaos is characterized by groups separating from each other; and the age of great peace is characterized by unification of various groups. A group that is dominated by individualism still has the chance to save itself if the group it fights with is dominated by the same doctrine. But it is a matter of time for its demise if it met a group that is governed by group tactics. Westerners have been skilled at group tactics in recent hundred years, in which lies the cause to their prosperity.

(Liang, 1936b)

Thanks to Yan Fu's introduction of Spencer's theories, Liang Qichao was exposed to Western sociological thought and later on developed his own theory of qun study. But his theoretical groundwork of collectivism aligned more with Comte, whom Liang knew less about then but it contradicted Spencer's endorsement of laissez-faire. Comte's sociological theory stresses collectivity and order. From his perspective, social order is based on the uniform morality. Organic social life can never build on the premise of individual contracts or natural rights, but on legitimate authorities, hierarchy, and uniform morality instead, or otherwise the society would be rendered as disconnected as loose sand. He also argued that the scientific spirit demand individual need or self-interest not be treated as the unit of society. The most elementary social unit is family instead of the individual, since the impulse for self-interest is almost already constrained within a family to comply with social interests. "The collective organism is essentially composed of families which are its true elements, of classes and castes which form cities and villages" (Coser, 1990, p.10). Comte was once the secretary to Henri de Saint-Simon, a French socialistic philosopher, who had a great impact on Comte's embrace of social progress, social order, and collective authority, and his rejection of anarchism. Liang Qichao adopted "collective morality (qunde)" as the foundation for his theory of social integration is owed to his mentor Kang Youwei.

Liang Qichao was the best among his contemporaries when it came to knowledge about and profound command of Western learnings, even though those contemporaries were already at the intellectual frontiers then. In *On the Left and Right Forces in the Academy* published in 1902, Liang listed "ten meritorious men" and their significant contributions to the construction of world knowledge. They were Copernicus and his theorizing that "the earth is round"; Francis Bacon and his advocacy for "knowledge production via empirical investigation"; René Descartes and his insistence on the role of "reason"; Baron de Montesquieu and "the separation of power among a legislature, an executive, and a judiciary"; Jean-Jacques Rousseau and "contractual relationship between human" on the basis of natural rights; Benjamin Franklin and "electrics"; James Watt and "mechanics"; Adam Smith and "the study of wealth"; Johann Kaspar Bluntschli and "the study of nations";[13] and Charles Darwin and the "evolution theory." Liang Qichao also listed Isaac Newton's "gravity"; Otto von Guericke and Robert Boyle and the invention of "vacuum"; Carl von Linné and botany, Immanuel Kant and "a pure and comprehensive philosophy"; Joseph Priestley and chemistry; Jeremy Bentham and utilitarianism; Johann Friedrich Herbart and education; Saint-Simon and Comte's "socialism" and qun study; John Stuart Mill's "ethics, political science, and feminism"; and Spencer's qun study, as well as litterateurs such as de plume Voltaire from France, Fukuzawa Yukichi from Japan, and Leo Tolstoi from Russia (Liang, 1936i). Reformists were selective about Western thought, as the aspiration for national wealth and power guides the selection of intellectual works. Johann Kaspar Bluntschli, in Liang's list of top ten, is not comparable to the rest of the nine scholars in terms of either social prestige or academic influence. Out of his obsession with "constitutional monarchy," Liang raved about Bluntschli's theory of "nation state" and criticized Rousseau's social contract theory relentlessly for its "liberalism" foundation. He even failed to capture the strong tendency toward collectivism in the latter's writings. Liang insisted on the inapplicability of Rousseau's theory to suit the purpose of China's state building, to which Bluntschli's theory of "nation state" would serve well. What China needs the most is a unified organism and effective order so that "civilians" can be transformed into "citizens" (Liang, 1936j; Chang, 1993, pp. 169–86). Liang overstressed the nation state and the collective community, while overlooking society and individuals, as the political theme in his theories of qun study and qunlun largely shaped his intellectual thinking and paved the way for his future turn to political conservatism.

Modernization: reform and institutional transformation

Sociological thought on reform and academic institutionalization

Sociological thought emerges out of the practical needs for social integration and an intellectual complex. When Comte wrote *The Course in Positive Philosophy* and established sociology discipline in 1848, France was on the eve of revolution, with social turmoil and disorder in the aftermath of economic recession and an intelligentsia and a middle class caught in the moral and faith crises. During his lifetime, Comte lived through seven different regimes with countless riots, uproars, and citizen revolts, and rare peaceful and stable times. Therefore, searching for social integration mechanism that would lead to stability and order, and the mission to realize social progress through reforms, became the main feature of Comte's sociological thinking, which also become one of the definitive characteristics for the future discipline of sociology. From 1862 when Spencer published *First Principles* to 1873 when he published *A Study of Sociology*, Britain was at the middle of the Victorian age (1815–1914). Different from the turbulent France that Comte lived in, Britain, free from revolutions and upheavals for a long time, had almost reached the end of its industrial supremacy over the world. Intellectuals commonly had a sense of danger and wanted new forms of social integration. Spencer's sociology reflects this public need since his social organism theory provides theoretical groundwork for new social integration and a balanced social order. In short, from its outset, sociology seemed to link to an essential social reform thinking – with respect to making social progress through gradual, nonviolent, nonrevolutionary evolution and to reform the social institutions and conceptions via structural transformations. When it comes to the relationship between the sociologist and the French revolution of 1848, French sociologist Raymond Aron commented that sociology, which was conceived and established by Comte and further practiced by Durkheim, centers on society instead of politics, or rather subordinating politics to the category of society. This rationale results in depreciating the role of the political system and meanwhile giving prominence to the changes in social reality. For instance, Durkheim was passionate about social and moral problems, as well as restructuring of occupational organizations, yet showed little interests in, but much contempt for, the parliamentary system (Aron, 2005, pp. 278–79).

Comte's sociological thinking cringed in regard to social reform and social order invited vehement attack from revolutionary theorist Karl Marx, of course. Marx's attack was completely different from his critical adoption of and praise for Adam Smith's economics and Georg Wilhelm Friedrich Hegel's dialectics. In 1866, Marx wrote to Friedrich Engels with disdain for Comte's positivism, in a typically German rigorous tone he said,

> I am studying Comte on the side just now, as the English and French are making such a fuss of the fellow. What seduces them about him is his encyclopedic quality, *la synthèse*. But that is pitiful when compared with Hegel (although Comte is superior to him as a mathematician and physicist by profession, i.e.,

superior in the detail, though even here Hegel is infinitely greater as a whole).
And this shitty positivism came out in 1832!

(Marx, 1963a, p.236)

By the time Marx was drafting *The Civil War in France* in 1871, he originally
devoted one section titled "Workmen and Comte" to excoriating Comte for
his defense of capitalist political and employment system. He wrote in a harsh
manner,

> Comte is known to the Parisian workman as the prophet in politics of Impe-
> rialism (of personal *Dictatorship*), of capitalist rule in political economy, of
> hierarchy in all spheres of human action, even in the sphere of science, and
> as the author of a new catechism with a new pope and new saints in place of
> the old ones.
>
> (Marx, 1963b, pp. 423–4)

The tendency toward social reformation and fierce conflicts between refor-
mational and revolutionary ways of thinking that marked the birth of Western
sociological thought repeated itself for its Chinese counterpart. At the end of the
nineteenth century when Liang Qichao and Yan Fu tried to theorize qun study,
freshly defeated in the First Sino-Japanese War in 1894, China was reminded of
the decline of its royal court and stricken by domestic poverty and humiliations
from outside. It is natural that qun study theory is pragmatic with obvious goals to
preserve qun and the entire Chinese race, and it is characterized by the tendency
toward social reformation that is driven by a desire for social order as well as the
evolution theory.

Yan Fu had a stronger tendency toward reformist ideas than Liang. Earlier,
Yan cried out for a social reformation and salvation movement, opposed dictatorship and advocating for constitutional monarchy, and promoted democracy as the
function and liberty as the foundation. But in his later years, Yan gradually turned
to political conservatism as he showed little sympathy toward the Revolution of
1911 (the Xinhai Revolution) and led public opinions to support the Yuan Shikai's
restoration of monarchy with himself as the Emperor (Zhang, 1995, pp. 23–4).
Nonetheless, a tread persists in Yan's thought in a modest and steady approach
toward social reforms, which is hardly a contingent political attitude but based on
his theorizing of qun study. When he first came across *A Study of Sociology* at the
age of 28, Yan Fu thought, "[he was] confined by one-sided arguments, but now
[saw] the flaws." Yan stressed that qun study purported to value construction and
oppose destruction.

> What is qun study for? Using scientific method to understand social changes
> and historical trends . . . I believe that our country's recent dramatic change is
> caused by what our people have done over the history. Superficial yet reactive
> folks, without a deep understanding of the breath and the magnitude of the
> historical problems, took to the streets, demanding overnight changes, with

the hope that by so doing our country would rise from the decay to confront enemies who once defeated us. When they failed, they once again urged for blind but radical destructions of everything. Even if destructions worked, construction does not necessarily fix the problem. We might as well take prudent steps toward reform and consult studies first for remedies!

(Yan, 1996, p.123)

This is also why Yan Fu insisted on "making incremental social reforms instead of leaping forward."

Liang Qichao was drastically different from Yan Fu in that he was not only a prominent scholar but also a leader of and a big card in social reformations. He articulated his nuanced ideas that fell between reform and revolution in "An Explanation of 'Ge' " published in 1902. First, he believed the Chinese term "ge" contained meanings of both reform and revolution. While reform is translated into Chinese "gaige," revolution is translated into Chinese "bian'ge." The differences are "'Ref'" indicates steadiness while "Revo" indicates suddenness; "Ref" means partial, while "Revo" means the whole; "Ref" points to the portion of progress, while "Revo" points to the portion of opposition. Second, "'ge' is the inevitable universal law in evolution." Everything in nature or in the human society abides by the rule of the survival of the fittest and the washout of the misfit. They are "natural selection" and "human-made elimination." Human-made elimination is "ge," which includes reform and revolution. Third, what people refer to as "revolution" is reform by its nature. Revolution occurs in not only the political realm but also in an array of fields such as religion, morality, academics, literature norms, and industries. Even when there is a political revolution, it does not necessarily mean the alternation of dynasties. Dynasty change does not necessarily mean there was a revolution. The term "revolution" was first used after the British "Glorious Revolution" of 1688, but the dynasty changes prior to that do not qualify as "revolutions." Fourth, the French Revolution of 1789 left people with the impression that revolution means violence and dynasty change, which also stirred fear among people toward revolution. But civil reforms can also be revolutionary such as the Meiji Restoration of 1868 in Japan. What China needs is a revolution like the Meiji Restoration, not restricted to reforms such as abolishing "the eight-legged essay," promoting political argumentation, abolishing the traditional system of civil service exams, and establishing new schools. China is at the crossroads where its existence is at stake and "at the risk of being eliminated by natural selection," so the so-called revolution is the same as reform, which is also "the single and only way to save our nation." "Other than that, any attempt making futile efforts to quench the desire for survival and power, no more than making mirror from stones and stir-frying sand for rice" (Liang, 1936h). Consequently, with respect to politics, Liang advocated for reforms under the centralized power of royal family (constitutional monarchy), with a strong mark of nationalism and racialism. Liang used to be a major fighter for reforms, running contradictory to revolutionaries led by Sun Yat-sen. He wrote an official denunciation against Zhang Xun's restoration of the monarchy, signaling an open break with his mentor Kang Youwei who wanted to preserve the monarchy, but the tendency toward social reforms while opposing violent revolutions is the lifetime brand of Liang's thought (Meng, 1980, pp. 106–18, 247).

The dominance of reformist ideas seemed to extend beyond a few sociologists' intellectual projects or attitudes and became the ideological feature for the entire sociology disciple. Precisely because of this, it was doomed to be reprimanded by Marxist revolutionaries who aspired to seize the power by armed forces as non-Marxism or anti-Marxism. Sociology was attacked as "bourgeois pseudo-science" in the Soviet Union in the 1920s and in China in the 1950s, respectively.[14] Sociology was eliminated from educational and research system in both countries, too.[15] It was not until 27 years after its disappearance in 1979 that the need for "reform and opening up" and the "construction" of modernization prompted Deng Xiaoping to reinstate sociology and political science in the higher education so that the disciplines finally shook off the stigma.[16]

Reformist ideas embedded in sociology failed to survive the political struggles in the first half of the twentieth century in China, which fell into disrepute. However, social reforms have had a subtle impact on the institutional transformation, during which sociology, as an academic field, has been institutionalized and thus modernized.

The ideal for modernization held by reformists was reflected in their longing for a wealthy and powerful nation. Their roadmap for a wealthy and powerful nation started from reforms in political, economic, and social systems, but eventually it boiled down to the problem of mass education. Thus reformists promote and participate in educational and academic reforms energetically. This perhaps is also driven by their intellectual natural instinct.

Yan Fu wrote in *On the Origin of Strength* in March 1895,

> After the lift of sea ban, our country has taken a few new looks: *Zongli Yamen*,[17] for one; the School of Combined Learning, for two; arsenals, for three; Chinese Educational Mission, for four; steamship and investment promotion, for five; manufacturing, for six; the establishment of navy, for seven; coast guard administration, for eight; Western style exercise and military drills, for nine; schools of new learnings, for ten; diplomatic envoy, for eleven; mining industry, for twelve; postal offices, for thirteen; railway, for fourteen, and the list may continue to twenties.

Yan Fu reckoned that transplanting those systems from Western countries to China would yield little fruit, so "today's mission" is "to teach the public their ABC, strengthen the country, and illustrate the public illustrious virtue."[18]

In May 1895, Kang Youwei, in the *Second Petition to Qing Emperor* (the renowned "public vehicle movement"),[19] listed pleas with regard to mobilizing the Chinese people, relocating the capital so that the country would resume its solid foundation, modernizing armies, and implementing reforms. Specifically, when it comes to the making of a wealthy nation, Kang had six suggestions. He wrote, "Six measures leading to a wealthy nation include the establishment of a monetary policy, the construction of railroads, the development of machinery and steamships, the exploitation of mines, mintage, and the postal service system." He also proposed educational reforms, affirming, "The key to Western richness and might lies in the emphasis they put on education instead of their cannons or armed force" (Zheng & Ren, 1994, pp. 14, 24).

In August 1896, Liang Qichao pointed out, "Nowadays whenever reformers open their mouth, they must bring up troop training, opening mines, and opening trade with foreign countries," in "On the Perils of Being Ignorant about the Core of Reforms," an article later collected into *On Changing Institutions*. However, railroads, steamships, banks, postal service, agriculture, and manufacturing would "by no means thrive despite their current boom" unless they were equipped with specialized schools where knowledge and skills were taught.

> To summarize, at the core of reforms is the talents. At the core of cultivating the talents is the educational system. To set up adequate education systems, we must reform civil service exams system. We must transform the bureaucratic establishments to make all these work.
>
> (Liang, 1936k)

In December 1898, a commentary titled "China's Reform Didn't Go Too Far" in the *Zhixin Newspaper* published a list of the kinds of "new reforms" adopted under the influence from the West and after the sea ban was lifted. The list was as follows: reforming civil service exams, bureaucratic establishment, and education; permitting petition and free press; retiring senior officials; sending princes on itinerate; organizing local militia; changing troop training into Western styles; letting go of Eight Banners soldiers; developing navy, opening inland postal offices and schools overseas; establishing department of agriculture, labor, and commerce; setting up modern medical school; building railroads; abolishing likin tax; raising salaries for government officials; abolishing torture and slavery; moving vagabond; reclaiming barren land; prohibiting drugs and gambling; promoting charity; protecting Chinese labor; establishing women's schools; banning foot binding; holding open competitions; relocating national capital; establishing parliament, constitution, and bureaus for policy making; getting rid of kneeling ritual; building police stations, bureaus of health and hygiene, and schools; and establishing agencies to protect self-governance at local level. Many of these systems have woven into the fabric of people's "everyday life" nowadays, but at the beginning of twentieth century, they all "symbolized" reforms and undertakings for a rich and powerful nation.

Just as these newly implemented systems have woven into everyday life, sociology as a discipline has been absorbed into the Chinese knowledge system and earned a place in the Chinese education system. This casual observation might have missed the "profound impact" of institutional transformation, but it is exactly what happened in the actual modernization process that took place in China during the dramatic years of political struggles.

Leaders of the Self-Strengthening Movement have built many new-style schools, mainly foreign language schools, schools of technology, and military academies, which include the School of Combined Learning in Beijing (1862), the School of Foreign Languages and Literature in Shanghai (1863), Imperial University in Guangzhou (1864), Hubei Self-Strengthening School (1893), Fujian Arsenal Academy (1866), Shanghai Machinery School (1865), Tianjing Naval Academy (1880), Jiangnan Naval Academy (1890), Tianjing Medical School (1893), and Tianjing Military School (1895). In addition to foreign languages, these schools also teach rudimentary knowledge about science and engineering.

Kang Youwei was among the first reformists to promote the spread of Western humanities and social science knowledge. In 1891, when Kang established the Changxing School, the enrollment slightly exceeded 20. However, it soon had to relocate twice because of expansion. In winter 1893, the school moved to the Yanggao Temple deep in the School of Guangzhou, with a new name: "Wan Mu Thatched Cottage." This is the first school where "qun study" was included in the curriculum. When Liang Qichao wrote *Biography of Kang Youwei*, he described the class and the education system in a vivid manner, based partially on his own experience with the school and partially on Kang's own account in *Note on Learnings at Changxing* (Liang, 1936l). Specifically, the education system groups disciplines into four categories – namely, the study of yi and li, textology, statecraft-ology, and letters. While the study of yi and li includes philosophy and ethics, textology includes history and natural science. While statecraft-ology includes political science and sociology, letters includes linguistics and literature. Contemporary disciplinary division among arts and humanities, social science, and science seem to take shape in the classification of this kind.

Kang Youwei taught at Changxing School (Wan Mu Thatched Cottage) in Guangzhou from the fall of 1890 to early 1894. Afterwards, he embarked on his trip to Beijing for the doctoral exams, alternating with lecturing back in Canton.[20] In 1895, Kang went to Beijing for the doctoral exams again and launched the "public vehicle petition." But in the first half of 1896, Kang still "taught at Changxing School located in the School Guangzhou," and "finished writing *Study of the Reforms of Confucius, A Study on Dong Zhongshu's Spring and Autumn*, and *A Study on the Annals of Spring and Autumn*." In June and July of 1897, Kang once again "returned to Canton to give lectures where a number of scholars gathered, discussing issues day and night" (Kang, 1981, pp. 19–23). There is no knowing when "qun study" was included in the curriculum at Changxing School. Kang did not put down any details about the content of the course in *Note on Learnings at Changxing, Oral History on Wan Mu Thatched Cottage*, or any other writings. That Kang is an old-fashion scholar with no knowledge of foreign languages and Western learnings casts doubt on the truthfulness of Kang having taught a course named "qun study" (see Kang, 1988).[21] Nonetheless, Kang purchased quite a number of translated Western learnings and guided his students in teaching themselves. Kang bought more than 3,000 translated books from a total sale of 12,000 by Shanghai Manufacturing Bureau. Liang Qixun, Liang Qichao's younger brother, who also studied at the Wan Mu Thatched Cottage, recollected that students:

> have to read plenty of Western learnings, including scores of scientific works on sound, light, chemistry, and electricity, and translations by earlier students studying abroad like Yung Wing and Yan Fu and by missionaries like John Fryer and Timothy Richard.
>
> (Lin, 1990, p.109)

Hereby, the "qun study" taught at Changxing School should be Spencer's sociology introduced by Yan Fu, because Kang did not record any of his thoughts about qun study in his work; he didn't even mention the term. However, Yan did not start to translate Western sociological thought until 1894. Yan's first translation of Spencer's work with regard to qun study was *On the Origin of Strength*, which was written in the spring of 1894 (halfway into spring of the year of jiawu) but published in March 1895.[22] There are two possible explanations for Liang's mentioning of the course "qun study" at the Wan Mu Thatched Cottage. The first one is that the course was set up after 1895, although the chance is very slim. The other possibility is that Liang's account of the education system only referred to the content students were exposed to or the knowledge they received from readings and discussions. Liang deliberately "recounted" the education system based on Kang's syllabus. That was not a course designed and taught by Kang, because it is unthinkable that he taught all these course by himself. After all, Kang was not an expert in mathematics, and as far as Western learnings are concerned, his only source was translations. Therefore, the alleged qun study course is no more than a localized illustration of what students at the Wan Mu Thatched Cottage have learned about Spencer's sociological thought after 1895.

Nevertheless, the classification of academic subjects in Liang Qichao's mind is fundamentally different from the classical Chinese knowledge system that hinged upon hundred schools of thoughts, Confucian classics, and history, yet closer to the modern knowledge system. In 1902, Liang Qichao held that theory is the mother of practice, which can be divided into the theory of theories and the theory of practice. While the former refers to philosophers and religions and so on, the latter refers to "political science, laws, qun study, economics, and so on." In the same year, when he raised the issue of new historiography, Liang pointed out that history is directly linked to disciplines such as geography, geology, ethnology, anthropology, linguistics, qun study, political science, religious studies, laws, and economics. And it is indirectly connected to philosophical fields of study such as ethics, psychology, argumentation, and literary studies, and natural science disciplines like astronomy, material science, chemistry, and physiology. After 20 years in 1922, Liang suggested expanding the definition of science, from chemistry, mathematics, physics, and geometry to include "political science, economics, and sociology and so on since science means a specialized knowledge about a field or a subject." He continued to define "science as seeking truth and seeking systematic true knowledge, as teachable knowledge." He went so far as to assert that without changing the bias against science, "Chinese can never declare their academic independence in the world" (see Li & Wu, 1984, pp. 345, 287, 794–7). It is thus clear that Liang's qun study, along with Chinese sociology, found its institutionalization in a constant struggle to define its place in the disciplinary subject system.

In China, qun study changed its name to sociology because Chinese scholars simply borrowed the term directly from Japanese translations of sociological work. Before the outbreak of Xinhai Revolution (known as Revolution of 1911), some scholars compiled and translated a few sociological studies from Japanese translations of the original version. For instance, in 1902, Zhang Taiyan (also known as Zhang Binglin) translated Kishimoto Nobuta's *Sociology*, in which the latter introduced the theories of Spencer and Franklin Henry Giddings. The book was published by Guangzhi Publishing House. In 1903, Wu Jianchang translated Ichikawa Minamotosan's *An Outline of Sociology*, which is the Japanese version of Giddens's work. In 1903, Ma Junwu translated the second volume of Spencer's *Principles of Sociology*. In 1911, the Commercial Press released Endo Ryukichi's *Sociology*, complied and translated by Ou'yang Jun. Endo's book was an introduction of the social psychological school of Giddings from the United States. Among other influential works were three books by American sociologist Charles Abram Ellwood, *Sociology and Modern Social Problems*, *An Introduction to Social Psychology*, and *The Social Problem: A Reconstructive Analysis.* Meanwhile, sociology started to enter universities. In 1908, St. John's University in Shanghai, founded by American missionaries, created a sociology course taught by American scholar Arthur Monn. In 1913, University of Shanghai also established a sociology course and in 1915, the department of sociology was founded by American professor Daniel Harrison Kulp. In addition to Professor Kulp, the faculty also included Harold S. Bucklin and J. Q. Dealey. In 1917, C. G. Dittmer started to teach sociology at the Tsinghua School in Beijing (later Tsinghua University). Yenching University (founded by American churches) established the department of sociology headed by G. S. Burgess, an American scholar, in 1919. Besides missionary schools, National University of Law and Political Science and Imperial University of Peking opened sociology courses in 1906 and in 1910, respectively. Kang Xinfu, Zhang Taiyan's pupil who returned to Peking University (Imperial University of Peking was renamed as Peking University in 1912) after studying in Japan, is perhaps the first Chinese who taught sociology on a university campus. He is also the teacher of Sun Wenben, China's first generation of sociologists.[23]

With the establishment of sociology discipline in China in mind, the only person comparable to the founder of sociology Comte was Liang Qichao. Yan Fu may have had deeper knowledge about Western sociology, but Liang's theorizing of qun study had a far more profound intellectual impact than Yan's. So who should be considered the Chinese Durkheim who facilitated the institutionalization of sociology in China? So far throughout the earlier development of sociology in China, no one is comparable to Durkheim. If we have to choose one scholar, Tao Menghe (original name as Fugong, 1887–1960) would be the first choice. Sun Wenben, a prolific scholar in comparison to other early sociologists, made the greatest contributions to the spread of sociology in China. However, his scholarship is more often than not second-hand studies. Tao Menghe, on the other hand, was one of the first to study sociology overseas and one of the first to write a sociological monograph based on sociological analysis of Chinese society. Tao co-authored with Liang Yugao in writing *Chinese Village and Urban Lives*, published in English by London School of Economics and Political Science in 1915. He was one of the earliest Chinese professors to teach sociology in China. As early as 1920s, he started to teach sociology and anthropology at the Peking University. He was also one of the first Chinese scholars who started social survey in China and was in charge of China's first agency of social survey. The investigative report he drafted concerning rickshaw pullers in Beijing was perhaps the earliest report written by a Chinese scholar. Indeed, from the a pure academic perspective, Comte was nowhere close to the scope of Liang's knowledge, but Durkheim was out of Tao's league when it came to the profoundness of the research.

The establishment of sociology in China reflects a more general institutional transformation process, which constitutes the path China takes to reach its modernity. The academic system set around sociology, along with the school system, the postal service system, and the railroad network, is part of a galaxy of "institutional symbols" for modernization through which scholars are able to decode and preserve the "texts" for modernization process. Conception, introduction, and establishment of these systems are progressive and subtle, or even inadvertent, processes. With the passage of time and the weaving of these systems into "everyday life," people perhaps forget their original intentions, but these systems take shape within conceptual ruptures, methodological innovations, and social transformations.

Academics to everyday life and some reflections

China's modernization is a long transformation process of its social structure, and institutional transformation is part of its component. Institutional transformation is not as polemic and dramatic as conceptual battles, but it has a significant impact on the base structural changes of everyday life because of its reference to ideological symbols and behavioral norms. In particular, stormy changes in the political system often become historical landmarks. In the modernization process, the base structural changes of everyday life are the longest, deepest, and most extensive, frequent, and fundamental changes that attract the least attention. Many scholars tend to treat conceptual transformations as something deeper than everyday life, but the adoption of modern sociological methodology has reversed this tendency.

Intellectuals in history seem to have only stressed the knowledge they learned from books, the relations with their mentors, and their ideological lineages. The intellectual depth depends on how well they polish the old concepts and whether they will find new sublime words with profound meaning on which they can build their own knowledge discourses and signs. Intellectuals consider everyday life as nothing more than oil, salt, sauce, vinegar, tea, food, clothing, house, transport, and leisure, and thus as not worthy of academic attention at all.[24] Modern sociological methods are an extension of scientific methods of observing, comparing, and analyzing "natural phenomena" into the social science field, which blazes the trail for knowledge production through observing social phenomena and reality. Doing research literally means raising questions. Before the mid-nineteenth century, few people believed that the social survey methods were appropriate research methods. Pierre Guillaume Frédéric le Play (1806–1882), a French sociologist, economist, and engineer, wrote *European Workers* on the basis of his fieldwork and case studies of worker families. His book made him one of the pioneers for using sociological methods. French sociologist Émile Durkheim (1858–1917), with his publication of in *Rules of Sociological Method* 1895 and *Suicide: A Study in Sociology* in 1897, succeeded in making sociological methods independent from their parent philosophical field.[25] Revolutionary theorists have long adopted a field research method for the sake of theoretical applicability. For instance, Friedrich Engels wrote *The Condition of Working Class in England* based on his field research when he was 24 in 1845. In 1880, at the age of 62, Karl Marx (1963b) designed *a Worker's Inquiry*, which listed more than 100 questions.

Sociology entering China also refreshes the approach Chinese intellectuals adopt toward research. Chinese scholars have suddenly come to a realization that observations of everyday life can lead to knowledge (which explains specific social phenomenon and deals with specific social problems). Field research methods also intensify the intellectual tendency toward pragmatism in China. One of the earliest social surveys in China was the one on rickshaw pullers from 1914 to 1915 conducted by the Beijing Social Progress Association (founded by college students in Beijing for social service in 1913). In addition, under the leadership of Chen Da, students from Tsinghua University examined 91 households in the nearby village of Chengfu and 56 households and 141 school employees in the village of Hubian in Xiuning, Anhui, province. From 1924 to 1925, Gan Bo, Meng Tianpei, and Li Jinghan examined 1,000 rickshaw pullers, 200 rickshaw rental places, and 100 rickshaw puller families. In 1926, Meng Tianpei and Gan Bo investigated the changes in price, wages, and costs of living over a 25-year period of time from 1900 to 1924 based on analysis of the accounting books from a couple of grain shops and bylaws of business associations and cross-referenced with the budget revealed by a few families. From 1926 to 1927, Tao Menghe used family bookkeeping practice to investigate the living expenses of 48 handicraftsmen's families and 12 elementary school teachers' families. His research report was published in *An Analysis of the Living Expense in Beiping* in 1930. Foreign professors who taught in China also supervised students completing in-depth research projects. For instance, Daniel Harrison Kulp at the University of Shanghai led students to study a village named Fenghuang with a population of 650 located in Chaozhou, Canton. Their research report was published in *Country Life in China* in 1925. China International Famine Relief Commission asked Carroll Brown Malone and J. B. Taylor to supervise 61 students from 9 different colleges in an investigation of 240 villages and 1097 households in Chihli, Jiangsu, Shandong, Zhejiang provinces. The commissioned investigation was published in "The Study of Chinese Rural Economy." In 1923, under the guidance of Professor

Harold S. Bucklin, the students in the sociological survey class at the University of Shanghai investigated 360 households in the village of Shengjiaxing in the neighborhood of Shanghai. They wrote *Living in Shengjiahang*, which was published by the Commercial Press in 1924, which is perhaps the earliest Chinese investigation report about Chinese countries (Yang, 1987, pp. 34, 55–7). Li Jinghan's *The Social Study of the Village of Ding*, which was published in 1933, is considered a groundbreaking sociological investigative report in China. I painstakingly listed all of these early sociological investigations in China only to illustrate that this research method was not born in China or the result of an outgrowth of traditional Chinese political culture. Just like the postal service, railroad, and modern schools, sociology coming to China is symbolic of the collision between Chinese and Western cultures and the departure of Chinese culture toward modernity.

Institutional changes only become prominent at particular historical moments. Ever since the beginning of the twentieth century, institutional changes in China (including regime revolutions and institutional reforms) became the definitive chapters in history, but a more frequent and lasting circumstance is when the institutions are stable in relative terms. Institutions per se represent a relatively stable repertoire of behavioral norms. People can never live under constant institutional changes, just as they cannot be on the road when traffic regulations are changing every day. Establishment of an institution reduces the cost of people's movement, so institutional changes occur at certain costs. Only when the benefit exceeds the cost can institutional changes be considered as rational. In contrast to institutional changes, changes to the base structure of everyday life are constant, which are constituted by numerous, taken-for-granted, and constantly shifting everyday phenomena. Continuous changes to social structures are the normal state for social development, although these changes sometimes seem inert and other times too dramatic to be accepted easily. The mission of sociology is to gain knowledge about the rules for base structural transformations of everyday life through social investigations. To gain this knowledge, there are no alternatives to synthetic analyses of everyday life experience.

The research method of this kind is not restricted to examining "practical problems." It is also applicable to historical studies. French renowned historian Fernand Braudel (1902–1985) focused on the changes to the most fundamental structure of people's everyday lives in his examination of the relationship between material life, economics, and capitalism from the fifteenth to eighteenth century. His work spares no pains in unearthing all kinds of details from everyday activities from clothing and food to shelter and transport that are often carelessly treated as a given by scholars. Braudel insists that such a method would reveal how market economy and capitalism take shape.[26] Indeed history written in the compliance of this historiography is not as concise as the history based on prominent historical figures and events, and sometimes it may elicit complaints that vigorous histories have been rendered mundane, tedious, and dull. However, history of this kind brings us closer to the core and truth of the history. China is a country that thinks highly of history. However, historians almost always only focus on official histories ("Twenty-Four Histories") and chronicles (*Zizhi Tongjian*, etc.) instead of all kinds of historical archives.[27] As for China's "Twenty-Four Histories," historians are more interested in basic annals, records of emperors, ranked biographies, and changes of regime, as well as other significant events. Recently, historians have paid attention to artifacts from archeology and history and relied on primary sources as references for history writing. They also became more attentive to a variety of aspects of everyday life revealed in the history, including annals about food and goods, criminal laws, geography, rituals, music, arts and literature, governmental officials rankings and responsibilities, rules on clothing and carriages, and elections.

Consequently, the development of China's modernization and social structural transformations in the past hundred years can be understood from different angles and at different levels. People are more familiar with events of the epoch, household names, and different schools of thoughts, but less attentive to "everyday life," which is equally significant. At the end of nineteenth century, imported commodities that "most Chinese were fond of" included machine-woven cloth, sateen, wool, camlet, velvet, carpet handkerchiefs, lace, buttons, needlework, umbrellas, paint, toothbrushes, toothpaste, soap, kerosene, coffee, cigars, cigarettes, wine, ham, jerky, cookies, candy, salt, nuts, fruits, liquid medicine, pills, tin plates, clocks and watches, sundials, thermometers, lightning rods, electric lamps, tap water, mirrors, photography, wires, microscopes, telephones, microphones, gramophones, and hydrogen balloons.[28] These goods are too common today to leave marks in people's memories in terms of the ways in which they have altered their way of life. However, their weaving into Chinese everyday routines reflects the slow process China went through for modernization, no less than the impact that manufacturing technologies of cannons and warships, institutions of education, postal service, and railroad, and the ideas of natural selection have made, if not more revealing in terms of fundamental changes of everyday life.

Introduction and establishment of sociology in China in the early twentieth century forced scholars to pay more attention to living conditions and to be more practical. Scholars acquired a strong sense of mission to search for a path leading to national wealth and strength. Thus sociology in China is characteristic of its involvement and intervention in daily lives, which has also prompted a large number of scholars to get out of their ivory towers and to turn to everyday life experiences. This also becomes an outstanding feature of Chinese academics – namely, to emphasize cultural "distinctiveness" in researches on Chinese issues.

As far as the issue of "distinctiveness" is concerned, earlier scholars brought this up because learning from the West yielded little progress. Taking an anxious perspective on China, scholars found the "reason" that Chinese culture was insufficient in following the West. At the beginning, they only found the insufficiency in the Chinese social structure and culture, but the "distinctiveness" soon extended to many academic fields, not the least of which were theories, regulations, and methodologies.

Liang Qichao was among the first (in 1906) to argue that there was a fundamental difference between the East and the West. He raised the issue of difference to prove his point that while the European countries were "caught in a situation when no alternative to revolution is possible," Chinese economy and society needed to "take a step-by-step approach toward development and evolution instead of taking the risk of revolution." He further explained,

> Current economic and social organizations in China is different from those in Europe prior to the revolution. There are several reasons to the difference. First is because of the absence of the aristocracy in China, a system that allows noble families in Europe to own large quantities of feudal land . . . Second reason is equal inheritance among all children whereas primogeniture in Europe reserves the right to the eldest son . . . Third reason is low tax rates. In many European countries, churches impose numerous exploitative taxes and means for contributions. While marquis and earls as well as monks are exempted from taxes, all the rest of the population have to shoulder the responsibilities . . . All these illustrate the contrast between Chinese economic and social organizations and their counterparts in Europe before the industrial revolution. There is no polarization between the richest and the poorest in China to begin with. This also can be explained by the aforementioned reasons.
>
> (Li & Wu, 1984, pp. 502–3)

Liang not only presented the distinctiveness of the Chinese social organization but also its superiority.

Before taking the faculty position at the philosophy department at the Peking University in 1915, Chen Duxiu published "On the Differences between Eastern and Western Thinking" in the *New Youth*, a Chinese magazine founded by Chen. For the differences, Chen maintained that first, "Westerners are belligerent but Easterners are peace-loving." Second, "Western society is centered upon individualism but Eastern society is centered upon family." Third, "Westerners are governed by law and practical interests but Easterners are regulated by kinship and emotional bonds and dead rules and regulations." Chen's Eastern society obviously means China. His comparison and contrast promotes Western characteristics while denouncing Chinese characteristics. He argues that the Chinese patriarchal clan system suppresses the development of individual personality, obstructs individual liberty, deprives the individual of equality before the law, and gives rise to dependence, which kills individual productivity. Therefore, he concludes that "in order to ameliorate the situation the society has to be reoriented toward individuals and away from family standard" (Chen, 1995, pp. 129–32).

Liang Shuming was perhaps most vocal about the differences between Eastern and Western cultures. Liang published *Eastern and Western Cultures and Their Philosophies* in 1920–1921. With the exception of his work on Indian philosophy and the "Treatise on Finding the Foundation and Resolving the Doubt," which secured him a position at the university despite him being a middle school graduate, the issue of differences is a thread running through all his work.[29] "Controversy over the Chinese Social History" that occurred in 1928–1929 certainly provoked Liang to think deeper about this issue. Liang asserted that, first, China is "a society dedicated to ethics." China is no longer a patriarchal society, out of which "a society dedicated to families" is born. Western modern society focuses on individuals – England and the United States in particular – or tends to stress society – with Soviet Union as an example. "Community and individual are two separate entities in West, while family has very weak connections to both. Chinese extend family relations onto the society, as ethics bond the two poles of individual and community together." Second, while the West is "dominated by religion in Middle Ages and by laws nowadays, [China] has replaced religion with morality and laws with social customs and etiquette." Third, Chinese has a society of "professional divisions," but the Western society revolves around "class antagonism," which is characterized by "the antagonism between the lord and the serf in the Middle Ages and the antagonism between the capitalist class and the working class recently." Lastly, China experiences periodic disorder and peace in history but no revolutions. However, there are both industrial and social revolutions in West. As Liang stressed the distinctiveness of Chinese culture, he tried to address the deep-rooted inadequacy of Chinese people. To remedy this inadequacy, China has to start from "self-governance in rural villages" rather than taking the path of Western capitalism (Liang, 1989b).[30]

After completing field studies, Fei Xiaotong used the comparative approach to examine the characteristics of rural China in 1947. He argued that the social structure of the Chinese village was formed by "social networks of personal relations" with the self at the center and "decreasing closeness" as one moves out, in contrast to the "Western structure of communities in which individuals are connected by mutual relations." Fei also believed that the modern West was a society ruled by law, whereas the Chinese village was a society ruled by morals; the Chinese village is a society based on bloodlines, which is also the foundation of social identity, but the modern West is a society based on geographical proximity on which a contractual society is based. He went on to point out that "the transition from bloodlines-oriented associations to geographical proximity associations is a character change for a society and a transformation in social history" (Fei, 1985, pp. 29, 48–9).[31] When Fei demonstrated the differences between the society of the Chinese village and modern Western society, he seemed to treat them as two separate cultural types. However, more often than not the influence of Western modernization theory on his discussion was remarkable (Ferdinand Tönnies' theory on structural distinction between community and society in particular) in that he tended to see the differences between traditional society and modern society as phase issues.

Cultural differences between the East and the West resurfaced among neo-Confucianism thanks to the economic takeoff in East Asian countries in the past dozen years. However, the proposition is different this time as Chinese no longer feel the need to belittle and make fun of their own culture. In 1983, Professor Ambrose King Yeo-chi from the Chinese University of Hong Kong presented his paper titled "The Confucian Ethos and Economic Development: A Reexamination of Weber's Theory" at the Chinese Culture and Modernization Symposium held in Hong Kong. Professor King casts doubts on Max Weber's assertion that Confucian ethos is the main hurdle for capitalism to flourish in ancient China. By doing so, he attempts to "reverse the verdict that has long been accepted as fixed by intellectuals." Professor King argues that the reality of economic booming in East Asia has posed "empirical challenges" to Weber's statement. But Weber's approach toward capitalism and the protestant ethic in *The Protestant Ethic and the Spirit of Capitalism* is applicable by providing "a cultural explanation" to the reality of economic development (King, 1993). In 1985 at the second Chinese Culture and Modernization Symposium, Chen Qinan deepened this line of inquiry in his paper titled "Family Ethics and Economic Rationalism – on Weber and Studies of Chinese Society." The article explores how Confucian family ethics contribute to the economic development and highlight how Confucian spirit emphasizes "bringing honor to one's ancestors" become the driving force for success and accomplishment (Chen, 1987a; 1987b). Through *Religious Intra-Mundane Ethics and the Spirits of Merchants in China* published in 1987, Yu Ying-shih sought to solve Weberian assertion by looking through China's long-term history. Yu (1987) argues that instrumental rationality elements such as diligence and frugality can also be found in traditional Chinese value system as in the protestant ethics. This is also why the second half of the Ming Dynasty witnessed business and trade thriving. Ever since Yu's publication, Chinese ethos and modernization soon became the main subject for neo-Confucianism, which was the de facto theme for the following Chinese Culture and Modernization Symposium in 1988.[32]

The academic endeavor that carries on the emphasis on the "distinctiveness" of Chinese social structure or culture is meaningful, but it is also not immune to academic pitfalls. Overemphasis on the distinctions gives rise to overgeneralization of what is otherwise temporary distinctiveness. The modernization process in the world shows that despite diversified value systems cultural, distinctiveness transforming into universality is also a widely acknowledged rule that remains true. Chinese academic undertakings would fall short if scholars extended the "distinctiveness" of Chinese culture to the realm of intellectual explorations. Science dissolves the boundaries between nation states, race and ethnicities, regions, and cultures. Sociology, as a scientific discipline, also belongs to the world. It may have many different schools, perspectives, standpoints, and thoughts. It may experience varied phases for theoretical development. It can be deployed to study different societies and cultures, but its fundamental logics and guidelines must stay the same.

Notes

This chapter was originally published as Chapter One, in Li, P., Sun, L., and Wang, M. (Eds.). (2001). *Chinese Academics and Society in the 20th Century (The Sociology Volume)*. Jinan: Shangdong People's Publishing House, pp. 1–58.

1 Raymond Aron (2005), the deceased well-known modern sociologist, vehemently denied Comte was the founder of sociology, arguing that Montesquieu not only predated Comte as a social theorist but also his theories were more original than Comte's, which is a simplistic version of deterministic philosophy. Therefore, Aron's course on social theories started from Montesquieu, differing from the common approach that begins with Comte.
2 This version is checked and annotated by Zhu Weizheng, which eliminates some errors commonly seen in the *Collected Works of Yinbingshi* (1936).

3 Liang's *Introduction to the Learning of the Qing Dynasty* was originally written as the preface to Jiang Fangzhen's *History of European Renaissance*. When putting it down, Liang confessed that "he can hardly stop himself" until he wrote tens of thousands of words, almost equivalent to the length of the book per se. Liang had to publish it as a separate book and in return invited Jiang Fangzheng to write the preface for the new publication.

4 The aforementioned Emmanuel Diaz Jeune, a Portuguese missionary, came to China in 1610 under the reign of Wanli Emperor in the Ming Dynasty. Franciscus Sambiaso, an Italian missionary, came to China in 1614 under the reign of Wanli Emperor in the Ming Dynasty. Ferdinandus Verbiest, a Belgian missionary, came to China in 1659 under the reign of Shunzhi Emperor in the Qing Dynasty, and Thomas Pereyra, a Spanish missionary, came to China in 1673 under the reign of Kangxi Emperor in the Qing Dynasty. They assisted Chinese courts to manufacture weaponry and improve firearms. See Liang (1929/1985, p.91).

5 In "Afterword to 'The Study of Sociology,'" Yan (1996b, p.127) wrote, "until the seventh and eighth year of Guangxu when I read this book I have been confined by one-sided arguments, but now I see the flaws. How unprecedented!"

6 Translator's note: the original title and the author's name are unknown, which is rare in Yan's translation works. The incomplete draft of Yan Fu's early translation appeared in Wang (1986).

7 The author adds the name in parentheses. Yan initially translated English sociologist H. Spencer's name into Xipengsai, later on into Sibinsai'er, and finally settled with Sibinsai.

8 The author adds the name in parentheses and bold is for emphasis.

9 Sun Benwen (1948) argues in "The Trend of Sociology in Recent China" that sociology was nominally introduced to China in 1896 when the term first appeared in the intellectual literature. However, the substance of the discipline was introduced to China six years later in 1902 when Yan Fu published the translation of Spencer's *A Study of Sociology* and Zhang Binglin published his translation of *Sociology* from Japanese scholar Kishimoto Nobuta. See Sun Benwen, "The Trend of Sociology in Recent China," in *Social Science in China* 1948: vol.6, p. 46. Sun did not mention who first used the term "sociology," but the year of 1896 is when Tan Sitong wrote *Renxue*.

10 In a letter to Yan Fu in 1897, Liang wrote, "Among contemporary outstanding intellectuals, Tan Fusheng from Xiangyang is no short of Xi Huiqing yet more forceful intellectually. What a weird genius! I found the first volume of *Renxue,* although he has published three volumes, already an unprecedented work in China" (Li & Wu, 1984, p.84). Translator's note: Tan Fusheng is the courtesy name of Tan Sitong. Xi Huiqing is one of the participants in reform during the reign of Guangxu emperor.

11 In addition, the well-known yet rather wordy passages on cultivation, regulation, governing, and world peace from *Daxue* read as follows:

> The ancients who wished to illustrate illustrious virtue throughout the kingdom, first ordered well their own States. Wishing to order well their States, they first regulated their families. Wishing to regulate their families, they first cultivated their persons. Wishing to cultivate their persons, they first rectified their hearts. Wishing to rectify their hearts, they first sought to be sincere in their thoughts. Wishing to be sincere in their thoughts, they first extended to the utmost their knowledge. Such extension of knowledge lay in the investigation of things. Things being investigated, knowledge became complete. Their knowledge being complete, their thoughts were sincere. Their thoughts being sincere, their hearts were then rectified. Their hearts being rectified, their persons were cultivated. Their persons being cultivated, their families were regulated. Their families being regulated, their States were rightly governed. Their States being rightly governed, the whole kingdom was made tranquil and happy.

12 Translator's note: the four occupations, also known as four categories of the people, was a hierarchical class stratification developed by Confucians and widely adopted by rulers in ancient China. They include the class of scholars, the class of peasant farmers, the class of artisans and craftsmen, and the class of merchants and traders.

13 Johann Kaspar Bluntschli (1808–1881) is a Swiss jurist and historian. He has published widely in the field of private laws and international public laws. Perhaps due to the fact that much of his writing were published in German, Liang has mistaken him as German and called him "a great political scientist." Bluntschli, however, is not among the world class in regard to academic reputation and influence. His being enlisted among the top ten is probably because of Liang's preference toward studies on nations and because the theory of this kind had greater impact on past Chinese reformists.

14 The attack at "bourgeois sociology" in China started in the early 1950s and later on continued in the anti-Rightist Movement beginning in 1957 (Hu, 1978).

15 Following the suit of Soviet Union, China crossed out sociology from the curriculum in a higher education institutions overhaul in 1952. This had a great impact on students of social science in general, such as finance, economics, politics, and law. Students majoring in politics and law constituted 24.33 percent of college student body in 1947, and the number dropped to 2 percent after the overhaul in 1952. In finance and economics, student enrollment plummeted to 2.9 percent in 1952 from 16.03 percent in 1950. See Mao and Shen (1989, pp. 78–9).

16 At the Meeting to Discuss Theoretical and Cognitive Problems in March, 1979, Deng Xiaoping suggested that

> it is a complex and hard mission to realize modernization . . . We are facing numerous economic theoretical problems . . . But I can by no means claim we have left no political problems untouched. We have long overlooked political science, laws, sociology, and researches on world politics. Now it is the time to catch up.
>
> (Deng, 1994, pp. 180–1)

In 1980, Nankai University reinstated the department of sociology, and then the Chinese Academy of Social Sciences established the Sociology Research Institute.

17 Translator's note: *Zongli Yamen*, meaning premier's office in Chinese, was established in 1861 by Prince Gong to function as a government body in charge of foreign affairs.

18 *On the Origin of Strength* was originally published in *Zhibao*, a newspaper based in Tianjin, from March 4 to 9, 1895. The quote is taken from a revised version. See Yan (1996d, pp. 17, 29).

19 Translator's note: "public vehicle" in the name of the movement is allusive in the sense that in ancient China candidates of civil service exams would be transported by the public vehicles to the national capital for the doctoral and final and imperial levels of the exams.

20 Translator's note: Chinese civil service exams take place at three hierarchical levels: provincial, doctoral, and final, imperial levels, respectively. Scholars have to pass the provincial exams before taking doctoral exams, which normally requires a reference.

21 Liang's description of the education system at the school mainly follows Kang's account in the *Note on Learnings at Changxing*, with some discrepancies. For instance, items like "dedication to Tao," "moral guidance," "ren as the foundation," and "extensive exposure to arts," along with their sub-items, were the same as listed by Kang. However, Kang listed "the study of yi and li," "textology," "statecraft-ology," and "poetry and prose" as four "general education" courses for traditional Chinese learnings. Specific disciplines contained in these four divisions as well as particular content on Western learnings (including qun study) were added by Liang based on his own interpretation. He also changed the name of "poetry and prose" to "letters." The most significant change is that Liang glossed over what Kang described as "the study of civil service examination" that originally included courses like "Confucian classic argumentation," "policy questions," "poetry and

rhyme prose," and "regular script," among others. Liang's move perhaps is because he believed that these courses did not correspond to Kang's orientation toward reforms.

22 In a letter to Liang Qichao in October 1896, Yan (1996, p.521) wrote,

> halfway into spring of the year of jiawu (1894) when situation was escalating [in the Yellow Sea], something simmered inside me. I let them out by writing *On the Origin of Strength, On Our Salvation* and other pieces that were published in *Zhibao*.

From this we can tell that *On the Origin of Strength* was written before the outbreak of the First Sino-Japan War. The publication date in *Zhibao* says March 4 to 9, 1895.

23 There are many records on the early history of sociology in China, but they all come from "The Mission, Process, and Scope of Chinese Movement of Sociology" published in the second issue of the second volume in *Sociology* (1929–1948) edited by Sun Ben-wen. See Yang (1987, pp. 243–60).

24 Translator's note: firewood, rice, oil, salt, sauce, vinegar, and tea are often used together as a Chinese idiom meaning "daily necessities." Food, clothing, house, and transport are often used together as a Chinese idiom referring to "basic necessities of life."

25 At the end of 19th century and the early 20th century, as the western empire expanded, the need for maintaining their colonies propelled the development of anthropology. Many anthropologists went to Africa, Australia, and Latin America to do fieldwork with indigenous people, which indirectly facilitated the spread of participatory observation methods used in sociology.

26 Braudel is the representative of the second-generation scholars of the Annales School in France. The school was cofounded by Lucien Febvre (1878–1956) and Marc Bloch (1886–1944). The Annalists uphold a style of historiography, influenced by anthropology, sociology, geography, psychology, economics, and linguistics, that stresses a "scientific" and "objective" research approach and values vetting the primary materials, especially archives, to reveal the historical causal relations among individual and particular social phenomena. The embrace of this new historiography makes Braudel's research on everyday life groundbreaking. See Braudel (1992).

27 Translator's note: *Zizhi Tongjian,* literally meaning "Comprehensive Mirror in Aid of Governance," is a chronicle published in 1084 AD that recorded Chinese history from 403 BC to 959 AD.

28 In 1895, Kang Youwei, in the *Second Petition to Qing Emperor* (the renowned "public vehicle petition") proposed four "means to support the ordinary people" – namely, strengthening agriculture, encouraging labor to participate in industries, nurturing business, and assisting the poor. The list of goods appeared in his discussions on labor participation in industries and nurturing business. He referred to these goods as imported industrial commodities associated with "national economy and the people's livelihood" that caused trade deficit. See Zheng and Ren (1994, pp. 19–20).

29 After graduating from the middle school, without any official trainings, Liang Shuming taught himself many subjects. In 1916, when he was 26, Liang (1989c) published his study on Indian Buddhism in "Treatise on Finding the Foundation and Resolving the Doubt" in *Oriental Magazine*, which caught Cai Yuanpei's attention. The latter invited Liang to teach Indian philosophy in the Department of Philosophy at the Peking University. At that time, almost all professors in the Department of Philosophy had studied overseas. This antidote soon became a story on everybody's lips that praised Cai's recruiting of talented people without overstressing qualifications. See Liang (1989a; 1989b).

30 Liang Shuming touched upon these differences between Chinese and Western society in his *Theory of Rural Reconstruction: The Future of Chinese Nation* published in 1937. According to him, these ideas and viewpoints were conceived in 1922, more or less thought through in the winter of 1926, and became mature in 1928. The quote here is taken from Liang's *The Substance of Chinese Culture*. Liang gave a lecture at Guangxi University in 1941, from which the book developed. He started the book in 1942 and published in 1949. See Liang (1990).

31 *Century Review*, a progressive periodical founded in 1947, invited Fei to write this book, which was adapted from Fei's course on the "sociology of villages" taught at the National Southwestern Associated University and Yunnan University.
32 Look no further than Hamilton (1991), Wong (1991) and Zhang (1991).

References

Aron, R. (1967). *Les étapes de la pensée sociologique*. Paris: Gallimard. Translation by Ge, Z., Wang, H., & Hu, B. (2005). Shanghai: Shanghai Translation Publishing House.

Braudel, F. (1979/1992). *Capitalism and Material Life, 1400–1800*. Vol. 1 (L. Gu & K. Shi, Trans.). Beijing: SDX Joint Publishing Company.

Cassirer, E. (1932/1988). *Philosophy of the Enlightenment* (W. Gu, Trans.) Jinan: Shandong People's Publishing House.

Chen, D. (1915/1995). "On the Differences between Eastern and Western Thinking." In H. Tan & S. Jiang (Eds.), *Archives in a Century (1895–1995)* (pp. 129–132). Beijing: China Archives Publishing House.

Chen, G., Xin, G., & Ge, R. (Eds.). (1989). *History of Pragmatism in Ming and Qing Dynasty*. Vol. 1–3. Jinan: Qilu Press.

Chen, Q. (1987a). "Family Ethics and Economic Rationalism – On Weber and Studies of Chinese Society." *Contemporary Age* (10), 54–61.

Chen, Q. (1987b). "Family Ethics and Economic Rationalism – On Weber and Studies of Chinese Society." *Contemporary Age* (11), 72–85.

Comte, A. (1907). *Cours de Philosophie Positive*. Paris: Schleicher Freres Editeurs.

Coser, L. A. (1977/1990). *Masters of Sociological Thought* (R. Shi, Trans.). Beijing: China Social Sciences Press.

Deng, X. (1994). *Selected Works of Deng Xiaoping*. Vol. 2. Beijing: People's Publishing House.

Fei, X. (1985). *From the Soil: The Foundations of Chinese Society*. Beijing: SDX Joint Publishing Company.

Foucault, M. (1966). *Les Mots et les Choese*. Paris: Gallimard.

Ge, M., & Jiang, J. (Eds.). (1984). *Selected Essays of Liang Qichao's Philosophical Thought*. Beijing: Peking University Press.

Hamilton, G. G. (1991). "Patriarchy, Patrimonialism, and Filial Piety: A Comparison of China and Western Europe." In S. Wong (Ed.), *Chinese Religious Ethics and Modernization (Collected Papers from Symposium)* (pp. 203–240). Hong Kong: The Commercial Press (H.K.) Ltd.

Hu, S. (1978). *Collected Essays of Hu Sheng (Zaoxi Luncong)*. Revised and Enlarged Edition. Beijing: People's Publishing House.

Huang, M., & Wu, X. (Eds.). (1988). *A Commentary on Kang Youwei's Posthumous Manuscript*. Guangzhou: Sun Yat-sen University Press.

Jiang, F. (1921/1985). "Preface to Introduction to the Learning of the Qing Dynasty." In Q. Liang (Ed.), *Two Treatises on the Academic History of Qing Dynasty* (p. 154). Shanghai: Fudan University Press.

Kang, Y. (1981). *Collected Political Commentaries of Kang Youwei*. Vol. 1. Beijing: Zhonghua Book Company.

Kang, Y. (1988). *On 'Note on Learnings at Changxing,' 'Q&A at Guilin,' and 'Oral History on Wan Mu Thatched Cottage.'* Beijing: Zhonghua Book Company.

Kang, Y. (1992). *A Chronological Autobiography of Kang Nanhai (Two Extras)* (L. Yulie, Ed.). Beijing: Zhonghua Book Company.

Keynes, J. M. (1953). *Théorie générale de l'emploi, de l'intérêt et de la monnaie*. Paris: Payot.

King, A. Y. (1993). "The Confucian Ethos and Economic Development: A Reexamination of Weber's Theory." In A. Y. King (Ed.), *Chinese Society and Culture*. Hong Kong: Oxford University Press.

Li, H., & Wu, J. (Eds.). (1984). *Collected Works of Liang Qichao*. Shanghai: Shanghai People's Publishing House.

Lin, K. (1990). *Kang Youwei: A Reformist Giant*. Beijing: Renmin University Press.

Liang, Q. (1929/1985). "Chinese Academic History of the Recent 300 Years." In Q. Liang (Ed.), *Two Treatises on the Academic History of Qing Dynasty*. Shanghai: Fudan University Press.

Liang, Q. (1936a). "Introduction to Chinese Progress over the Last Fifty Years." In *Collected Works of Yinbingshi*. Vol. 14. Issue 39. Shanghai: Zhonghua Book Co.

Liang, Q. (1936b). "Preface to A Discussion on Qun." In *Collected Works of Yinbingshi*. Vol. 2. Issue 2. Shanghai: Zhonghua Book Co.

Liang, Q. (1936c). "On the Transformations of Rule of the King and Rule of the People." In *Collected Works of Yinbingshi*. Vol. 2. Issue 2. Shanghai: Zhonghua Book Co.

Liang, Q. (1936d). "Preface to On Changing Institutions." In *Collected Works of Yinbingshi*. Vol. 1. Issue 1. Shanghai: Zhonghua Book Co.

Liang, Q. (1936e). "A Few Important Questions in Studying Cultural History – A Revision to My Previous Publication 'Chinese Historiography.'" In *Collected Works of Yinbingshi*. Vol. 14. Issue 40. Shanghai: Zhonghua Book Co.

Liang, Q. (1936f). "What Is Confucian Philosophy." In *Collected Works of Yinbingshi: Special Volumes*. Vol. 103. Shanghai: Zhonghua Book Co.

Liang, Q. (1936g). "On Ten Contradictory and Complementary Moral Virtues." In *Collected Works of Yinbingshi*. Vol. 2. Issue 5. Shanghai: Zhonghua Book Co.

Liang, Q. (1936h). "An Explanation of 'Ge.'" In *Collected Works of Yinbingshi*. Vol. 4. Issue 9. Shanghai: Zhonghua Book Co.

Liang, Q. (1936i). "On the Left and Right Forces in the Academy." In *Collected Works of Yinbingshi*. Vol. 3. Issue 6. Shanghai: Zhonghua Book Co.

Liang, Q. (1936j). "Great Political Scientist Bluntschli and His Theory." In *Collected Works of Yinbingshi*. Vol. 5. Issue 14. Shanghai: Zhonghua Book Co.

Liang, Q. (1936k). "'On the Perils of Being Ignorant about the Core of Reforms,' from On Changing Institutions." In *Collected Works of Yinbingshi*. Vol. 1. Issue 1. Shanghai: Zhonghua Book Co.

Liang, Q. (1936l). "A Biography of Kang Youwei." In *Collected Works of Yinbingshi*. Vol. 9. Shanghai: Zhonghua Book Co.

Liang, S. (1989a). "Treatise on Finding the Foundation and Resolving the Doubt." In *Complete Works of Liang Shuming*. Vol. 1. Ji'nan: Shandong People's Publishing House.

Liang, S. (1989b). "My History of Self Study." In *Complete Works of Liang Shuming*. Vol. 2. Ji'nan: Shandong People's Publishing House.

Liang, S. (1989c). "Theory of Rural Reconstruction: The Future of Chinese Nation." In *Complete Works of Liang Shuming*. Vol. 2. Ji'nan: Shandong People's Publishing House.

Liang, S. (1990). "The Substance of Chinese Culture." In *Complete Works of Liang Shuming*. Vol. 3. Ji'nan: Shandong People's Publishing House.

Mao, L., & Shen, G. (Eds.). (1989). *An Introductory History of Education in China*. Vol. 6. Ji'nan: Shangdong Education Press.

Marx, K. (1866/1963a). "Marx to Engels." In Central Compilation and Translation Bureau (Eds.), *Marx and Engels Complete Works*. Vol. 31. Beijing: People's Publishing House.

Marx, K. (1872/1963b). "Drafts of The Civil War in France (1872)." In Central Compilation and Translation Bureau (Eds.), *Marx and Engels Complete Works*. Vol. 2. Beijing: People's Publishing House.

Meng, X. (1980). *An Biography of Liang Qichao*. Beijing: Beijing Publishing House.

Schwartz, B. I. (1964/1995). *In Search of Wealth and Power: Yan Fu and the West* (F. Ye, Trans.). Nanjing: Jiangsu People's Publishing House.

Spencer, H. (1904). *Autobiography*. Vol. 2. New York: Appleton.

Sun, B. (1948). "The Trend of Sociology in Recent China." *Social Science in China*, 6, 46–48.

Tan, S. (1994). *Renxue – Collected Works of Tan Sitong*. Annotated by Jia, R. Shenyang: Liaoning People's Publishing House.

Wang, S. (1982). "Yan Fu and Great Works of Yan's Translations." In Editorial Board of the Commercial Press (Eds.), *On Yan Fu and Great Works of Yan's Translations*. Beijing: The Commercial Press.

Wang, Z. (1984). "Aristotle." In *Critical Biographies of Western Prominent Philosophers*. Ji'nan: Shandong People's Publishing House.

Wong, S. (1991). *Chinese Religious Ethics and Modernization (Collected Papers from Symposium)*. Hong Kong: The Commercial Press (H.K.) Ltd.

Xunzi. (1979). "Xunzi: On the Regulations of the King." In Peking University's Annotation Board of Xunzi's Work (Eds.), *A New Annotated Xunzi*. Beijing: Zhonghua Book Company.

Yan, F. (1986). *Collected Works of Yan Fu* (S. Wang, Ed.). Vol. 4 and 5. Beijing: Zhonghua Book Company.

Yan, F. (1996). *Social Upheavals and the Reconstruction of Norms: Selected Works of Yan Fu* (Y. Lu, Ed.). Shanghai: Shanghai Far East Publishers.

Yan, F. (1996a). "A Letter to Liang Qichao." In Y. Lu (Ed.), *Selected Works of Yan Fu* (p. 525). Shanghai: Shanghai Far East Publishers.

Yan, F. (1996b). "Afterword to 'The Study of Sociology.'" In Y. Lu (Ed.), *Selected Works of Yan Fu* (p. 127). Shanghai: Shanghai Far East Publishers.

Yan, F. (1996c). "Preface to and Notes on *Evolution and Ethics*." In Y. Lu (Ed.), *Selected Works of Yan Fu* (pp. 321–323). Shanghai: Shanghai Far East Publishers.

Yan, F. (1996d). "Notes on *On the Origin of Strength*." In Y. Lu (Ed.), *Selected Works of Yan Fu*. Shanghai: Shanghai Far East Publishers.

Yan, F. (1996e). "Notes on *the Wealth of Nations*." In Y. Lu (Ed.), *Selected Works of Yan Fu* (pp. 341–342, 379). Shanghai: Shanghai Far East Publishers.

Yan, F. (1996f). "Preface to the Translation of *A Study of Sociology*." In Y. Lu (Ed.), *Selected Works of Yan Fu* (p. 123). Shanghai: Shanghai Far East Publishers.

Yang, Y. (1987). *History of Sociology in China*. Jinan: Shandong People's Publishing House.

Yu, Y. (1987). *Religious Intra-Mundane Ethics and the Spirits of Merchants in China*. Taipei: Lianjing.

Zhang, D. (1991). "Confucian Ethics and the Motivation for Accomplishment: Reality and Myths." In S. Wong (Ed.), *Chinese Religious Ethics and Modernization (Collected Papers from Symposium)* (pp. 62–76). Hong Kong: The Commercial Press (H.K.) Ltd.

Zhang, H. (1993). *Liang Ch'i-Ch'ao and Intellectual Transition in China (1890–1907)* (Z. Cui & F. Ge, Trans.). Nanjing: Jiangsu People's Publishing House.

Zhang, Z. (1995). *A Study on Yan Fu's Intellectual Thought*. Beijing: The Commercial Press.

Zheng, D., & Ren, J. (Eds.). (1994). *On Strength – Political Commentaries from Hundred Day's Reform*. Shengyang: Liaoning People's Publishing House.

4 "Chinese School" of sociology in the first half of the twentieth century

The first half of the twentieth century for China was a time of dynasty collapsing, scrimmages between warlords, foreign invasions, and boiling domestic resentment. With respect to cultural and academic realms, it was also a time of intellectual surges, seething outcries, and people of talents coming forward in multitudes. Chinese sociology, for that matter, also developed at a rapid pace. Some of the studies reached the peak of the time, which has barely been topped today.

At the turn of the twentieth century, there was an intellectual exuberance comparable to what happened during the time of the Spring and Autumn and Warring States Period.[1] What causes such an exuberance in troubled times? There are perhaps three reasons. The first cause is the dissemination of Western learnings and the reflection and introspection springing from the impact of Chinese culture meeting with the West. Second, anti-tradition goes to the mainstream because of the spread of an array of new thoughts and because waves of reforms, modernization, and revolutions have intensified the inclination of critical thinking. Third, as intellectuals turn to real life, practice, and pragmatism, how to reform the society becomes a key subject matter in academia.

Liang Qichao, in his speech of 1923 titled *Chinese Academic History of the Recent 300 Years*, traced the origin of pragmatic thinking in the Chinese academe way back in the history. He considered Chinese academic mentality during the recent 300-year period a revolt against the Confucianism of the prior 600 years. "Our age is characterized by the tendency toward objective examinations and the sickness of subjective reflections" (Liang, 1985, p.91). Liang was not alone. As Jiang Fangzheng wrote in the preface to Liang's *Introduction to the Learning of the Qing Dynasty*, "The academic spirit in the Qing Dynasty when the subjective deduction gave way to objective induction is synchronous with European Renaissance spirit" (Liang, 1985). Many scholars have summarized the trend of Chinese thoughts from the sixteenth century to the1840s as "humanistic pragmatism" or "pragmatism of Ming and Qing Dynasty" (Chen, Xin, & Ge, 1989).

Sociology setting its foot on China's soil fits the general development process of natural science and intellectual thinking in the society, but the tendency toward reality, practice, and utility is particularly outstanding in sociology. This tendency is manifest in the emphasis on social investigation, which evolves into a cult and a movement of social survey.

The spectrum of Chinese sociological thought in the first half of the twentieth century can be roughly grouped into six fields: historical materialistic sociology, studies of social principles, rural reconstruction theory and practice, anthropological investigation and community studies, social history studies, and studies on laws, politics, economics, culture, and ethics. The division of this kind is by no means encompassing all sociological branches, but for the sake of description, it is not completely appropriate either in that one field is united by one school but another is filled with many schools and still another is void of any school.

Two threads would help us better understand these six fields – namely, the thread of theory and practice and the thread of Chinese learnings and Western learnings. The two threads are intertwined with each other. For instance, with respect to theoretical sociology, there are the Marxist historical material school (such as Li Da), the school of Western sociological academism (such as Sun Benwen), and the school of Chinese culture with a sinology tradition (such as Liang Shuming). With respect to empirical sociology, there are also the Marxist historical material school (such as Chen Hansheng), the school of Western functional sociology (such as Wu Wenzao and Fei Xiaotong), and the school of Western sociological culture with an emphasis on Chinese cultural elements (such as Lin Yueh-Hwa and Francis L. K. Hsu). After all, it is a rough categorization. Indeed, historical materialism, Western sociology, and sinology are the main forces that catalyze the emergence of sociology thought in China. Constrained by limited space, this chapter only focuses on the "Chinese School" that takes place in the development of anthropological investigations and communities studies.

The making of the "Chinese School"

The making of the "Chinese School" of sociology is inseparable from one name: Wu Wenzao. Or rather, Wu is the founding father of the Chinese school of sociology. He earned his PhD from Columbia University in 1927 with a dissertation titled *The Chinese Opium Question in British Opinion and Action*. He returned to Yenching University in 1929, taking a position as professor of sociology. In 1933, he became the director of the sociology department. Wu is one of the pioneering thinkers with regard to localizing anthropological investigations and studies of communities.

At the beginning of the twentieth century, there were two approaches when it came to sociological research and pedagogy. One was to fill Western social science and humanities theories with existing Chinese literature and other one was to describe contemporary Chinese society using social survey methods that were widely used by British and American sociologists. Sociology and anthropology started to expand after Wu Wenzao returned to China; he strongly advocated and pushed for the localization of sociology in China. Wu believed that the most important task for the localization of sociology in China was to study Chinese characteristics.

In 1929, the creator of human ecology, Robert E. Park, came to China and helped spread the knowledge of the human ecology theory. From 1932 to 1933, during his second trip to China, Park took students from Yenching University to visit slums, overpasses, prisons, and the neighborhood of Eight Hutongs in Beijing to experience various living conditions.[2] In 1935, Alfred Radcliffe-Brown visited China and elaborated the theory of structural functionalism of anthropology and the methodology of "ethnography." Having drawn insights about functionalism from Polish English anthropologist Bronisław Malinowski and human ecology theory from American sociologist Park, combined with anthropology and sociology, Wu Wenzao suggested that "community studies" should be at the core of localizing sociology and reforming Chinese social structure.

Wu Wenzao argued that when it comes to modern community studies, sociological investigation differs from social investigation in that the latter is a collection of social life observations but the former is to test of a sociological hypothesis through examining the social reality. The purpose of social investigation is to solve real social problems. The goal of sociological investigation is to discover, learn, and interpret the society.

Wu's suggestion of putting "community study" at the core, which combines anthropology and sociology, was the cornerstone for early Chinese sociological researches. Anthropologists such as Bronisław Malinowski called the academic team under Wu's leadership "Chinese school of sociology." He trained a number of scholars who hold PhDs from overseas institutions but took part in exploring Chinese characteristics, including Lin Yueh-Hwa, Fei Xiaotong, Li Anzhai, and Qu Tongzhu.

Wu pointed out that "community study" means "to apply the ideas and methodology of ecology and culture to study varied communities in different regions." For instance, ethnologists should examine tribal communities or colonial communities at the borders. Rural sociologists should study rural communities in the hinterlands or communities of migrants. Urban sociologists should focus on urban communities along the river or in the coastal regions. By doing so, research on static communities analyzes social structures, while studies about dynamic communities reveal knowledge about the social process. Attention to both respects would help us understand social organization and transformation as a whole. Thanks to Wu's efforts and extensive repercussions of numerous scholarship under his influence, the "Chinese School" became the academic mainstream for the future development of sociology in China, which also led the research direction for the field for a long time thereafter (Wu, 2002).

Within this academic mainstream, there are two different branches, with one being social anthropology represented by Fei Xiaotong and the other being cultural anthropology represented by Lin Yueh-Hwa. While the former pays more attention to analysis of social organization as associated with economy, the latter is more interested in examining the informal institutions that associate with culture, such as clans, religions, and customs. Early anthropological work in the West concentrated on the study of indigenous people in the preliterate colonies to meet the need of expanding colonialism. Fei's and Lin's contributions, for that matter, apply anthropological methodology to the study of China – a country with a long history and established civilization.

Cultural anthropological investigations

Representative figures of early Chinese cultural anthropology include Lin Yueh-Hwa, Ch'ing-k'un Yang, Francis L. K. Hsu, and Tien Ju-Kang. They combine the anthropology theory with the practice of fieldwork in China, breaking the ground for a field that studies Chinese cultural characteristics. Their studies focused on Chinese clans and religions match the studies on Chinese grassroots culture in a nice manner.

When studying at the Yenching University, Lin Yueh-Hwa worked under the mentorship of Wu Wenzao. Per the request of a community study project, Lin conducted fieldwork on the clan of Huang in his hometown, Yixu, Fujian, and completed his master's degree with a thesis titled *A Study on the Clan in Yixu.* His thesis involved a systematic analysis of the mechanism deployed to keep the clan in order, which includes the rituals concerning births, weddings, deaths, and funerals. In this way, Lin examined the clan as a unique Chinese cultural and functional institution. Influenced by newly emerging functionalism, Lin provided some original analysis in regard to the clan's functions. Since he considered the kindred extended family as the basic unit in the clan system, his examination spanned from individual's status in a single family to the extended kindred family structure and then to the functional structure of the clan. His research approach presented a clear line of reasoning, which expanded the horizon for understanding Chinese clans. In *Chinese Clan Village from An Anthropological Point of View*, Lin Yueh-Hwa (1937) elaborated on his new approach toward lineage. "Clan village is a type of village. Extended families that share the same ancestor are a clan. A country is a clustering of people in the geographical proximity, and a village is a political clustering of countries. I use the term *clan village* as a group with both consanguinity and geographical proximity – namely, *community*."

Prior to Lin, there were many studies on Chinese clans, but they tended to be historical studies. For instance, Lü Simian (1929) studied the Chinese clan system and wrote *A Brief History of Chinese Clan System*, the first of its kind on the Chinese clan system. His book engaged with the concepts of ancestor and clan, addressing many issues concerning the hereditary family and the offshoot families in a clan, sacrifice, anthrophony, genealogical tree, collective living of an entire clan, the patriarch, and the property of the clan, which was groundbreaking work. Tao Xisheng (1934), in his *Marriage and the Clan*, put forth a chronology of the family system: the Western Zhou Dynasty to the Spring and Autumn period was the dominated lineage system; the Warring States period to Five Dynasties was dominated by the organizational system of family relatives living together as a clan; the patriarch system started to gain ascendancy during the Song dynasty, and the twentieth century was dominated by monogamy. Gao Daguan (1944) took a sociological perspective in his *A History of Family Clans in China* to examine and compare the family clans in the Zhou, Song, and Qin dynasties, respectively.

As for the researchers on clan history, in *The Transplant History of Chinese Clans*, Liu Jie (1948) dwelled on the origin and meaning of clan, epoch and generation, and totem. Liu's work had a great impact on later rigorous historical research methods on the question of clan. Liu graduated from the Tsinghua

Academy of Chinese Learning. He was deeply influenced by figures such as Wang Guowei, Liang Qichao, and Chen Yinque. When he was at the Tsinghua Academy of Chinese Learning in 1929, Chen Yinque, as requested by Liu and others, wrote the epigraph for the Wang Guowei monument. There was one passage from the epigraph that expressed the literati character that became the motto for future generations of mentors. It said,

> Mr. [Wang]'s scholarship at times is not outstanding and open to debate. Only his spirit of independence and freedom of thought would last long as the universe exists and shed light on the earth like the sunlight, moonlight, and starlight.

Monographic studies on the social history of clans exert great influence over the emergence of sociology, among other historical studies on clans, which includes Liu Xingtang's (1935a, 1935b, 1936) articles on bloodlines: "The Public Properties of Kinship in Song Dynasty," "Kinship Organization in Fujian Province," "Kinship Organization in Henan Province." Lang Qingxiao's (1933, 1936) articles on the clan focused on armed fighting: "Causes and Organization of Armed Fighting in South China" and "Folk Fights in South China in the Recent Three Hundred Years."

Pan Guangdan is a genius in interdisciplinary studies who has many exquisite conceptions in the fields of sociology, psychology, eugenics, and social history. He combined eugenics and policy on the talents into the study of clans and wrote up *Distinguished Families in Jiaxing during Ming and Qing Dynasties*. According to his calculation, which is based on mapping out the bloodline, kinship networks, and generation networks, each distinguished family in Jiaxing has a bloodline to pass on to the next 8.3 generations on average that will last more than 200 years. Pan (1937) argued that the key to the rise and fall of the distinguished families lies in ancestral powers such as genetics and education, as well as the status of migration, marriage, and early death.

Lin Yueh-Hwa's approach to clan studies based on fieldwork extends clan studies from history to reality. His *the Study of Yixu Lineage* paved the way for the publication of *Golden Wing*, which took shape during Lin's years studying at Harvard University. The initial subtitle was "A Family Chronology," but it was changed to "A Sociological Study on Chinese Family Institution" in the revised edition published in 1947. All materials in *The Golden Wing* were from real life, which described stories that happened in the Huang village in the lower reach of the Minjiang River in the Fujian Province during the early twentieth century to the 1930s. The stories touched on traditional agriculture in south China, business, politics, local folk associations, feng shui, the vivid life moments from worshiping the kitchen god and ancestors, wedding and funeral ceremonies, and other festival and entertainment activities. The book documented the kinship, etiquette, and disputes in the namesake village among an extended family of four generations in China. *The Golden Wing* also broke a new path in writing style in that it presents a scholarly work in the form of a novel – a complete anthropological story that is constituted by segmented, scattered, and miscellaneous materials from the investigation. Although Raymond Firth, an internationally respectable economic anthropologist, thought highly of the scholarly value of *The Golden Wing* in his preface to the book, the writing style has invited constant doubts in the decades since its publication. Is the book a fictional story, or scientific research? Lin has repeatedly stressed that the stories in the book are true; they are the epitome of the oriental village society and family structure, and the research outcome based on socio-anthropological investigation. Lin's ingenious "literary summarization" method was always considered an "outlier" in the academic world. The only comparable writing style is from American sociologist William Foote Whyte of the Chicago School. Whyte also tried to examine investigation materials from a unique perspective that renders his *Street Corner Society* as something between scholarly work and fiction. However, the department of sociology at the Chicago University, which is known for its rigorous academic tradition, accepted *Street Corner Society* as a dissertation that later became one of the representative works of the Chicago School and even a standard "storytelling method for the outside world." New scholars of case studies and interview-based investigations have imitated the exemplary text.

All stories in *The Golden Wing* revolved around clans and lineage systems, but these stories are not merely the footnotes to the clans and lineage systems. Instead, as an intricately knit web, the book connects every part of the network no matter which clue one follows. *The Golden Wing* pays attention to not only the life circumstances and experiences of individuals but also the complicated relationship between individuals and their living community from the perspective of cultural functions of clans and lineage.

Ch'ing-k'un Yang (also known as C. K. Yang) is another important figure in the field of Chinese anthropology. He wrote *A North China Local Market Economy: A Summary of a Study of Periodic Markets in Chowping Hsien, Shantung* while studying at Yenching University. Based on his investigation into 14 bazaars in the village of Zouping, Yang examined various factors of bazaars including goods, transaction, sellers, and organizations. His work marked a starting point for many researchers. William Skinner was inspired to construct the analytical framework for China's market network as a result of the text.

Early anthropological studies in China value long-term fieldwork in the targeted villages. Ch'ing-k'un Yang conducted his fieldwork in the "Lujiang village" close to Guangzhou, and based on three years of fieldwork spanning from 1947 to 1950, he wrote *A Chinese Village in Early Communist Transition*, which has been translated into many languages and made "Lujiang village" well-known as an academic village. Among early anthropological studies done by Chinese, Fei Xiaotong's *The Economy of Jiang Village*, Martin C. Yang's *A Chinese Village – Taitou, Shantung Province*, Lin Yueh-Hwa's *The Golden Wing*, Francis L. K. Hsu's *Under the Ancestors' Shadow*, and Ch'ing-k'un Yang's *A Chinese Village in Early Communist Transition* are all milestones for the development of anthropology in China.

Nonetheless, the most influential work of Ch'ing-k'un Yang is *Religion in Chinese Society* published in 1961, in which Yang dwelled on various types of beliefs in Chinese society and the relationship between those beliefs *and* political, economic, and Confucian doctrines. The book is known as the "bible" in the field of Chinese religion studies, where the place of religion in China and whether Confucianism is a religion are always controversial subjects. Hu Shih, for instance, once said that China is irreligious country and Chinese are a people without superstition and religion. Liang Shuming also pointed out that religion has its weakest base in China across the world. Chinese are the least enthusiastic about religion, and the occasional rise of religion in China's history is motivated by inferior causes. Max Weber, in *the Religion of China: Confucianism and Taoism*, also argued that popular beliefs in China are the "instrumental hodgepodge of deities." Indeed, contrary to Europe, in most of China's history, there was no powerful and highly organized religion, and there were no long-term and never-ending struggles between the church and the state.

Yang's contribution is twofold. On one hand, he successfully proved the existence of religion in China since

> [there] was not one corner in the vast land of China where one did not find temples, shrines, altars, and other places of worship. . . [which is] a visible indication of the strong and pervasive influence of religion in Chinese society, for they stood as symbols of a social reality.
>
> (Yang, 1961/2007)

On the other hand, Yang also disclosed the distinctions between Chinese religion and the Western religions, and demonstrated that the religious perception from the West is not applicable for shedding light on Chinese religion since the latter lacks "salient structure" – that is, the absence of a stand-alone organizational system that cannot exist independent of the secular institution. As a result, as opposed to the nation's political authority, religion may only absorb secular morality for its own survival and meanwhile provide supernatural basis for political governance. The cultural order between religion and Confucian ethics of this kind determines the persistence of religion in Chinese society.

Yang borrowed from Joachim Wach's categorization of two religious organizations of "natural groups" and "specifically religious" in the *Sociology of Religion*, and divided Chinese religions from the perspective of structure function into two groups: one being "institutional religion" and the other "diffused religion." The "institutional religion" is featured in its independent existence beyond secular social institutions and to a certain extent separable from the latter. The "diffused religion" also has its functional system of theology, sacrifice, and technically trained personnel, but it is part of a social institution because of the integration with the secular system and the social order of either its inner spiritual cores or symbolized organization of ceremonies. Religion in diffusion loses meaning and the significance of its independent existence. To elaborate on these two key concepts, Yang borrowed analytical the framework and methods from Western sociology and anthropology (Durkheim has already examined the characteristics of "diffused religion") and built his argument on local experience and empirical investigations. Yang argued that the place of Chinese religion is ambiguous not only because of "polytheism" but also because of the economic mode and geographical conditions. For instance, facing the constant threat of sea waves, people in the Baoshan region worship the god of the sea, while residents in Foshan in Guangdong Province tend to worship the god of fire because they are affected by the threat from firecracker factories, and so on. The religious utilitarianism and secularism were common until this date. For example, businessmen who wish to make a fortune worship the god of wealth; people who want a child worship the goddess of mercy or Sung-Tzu-Niang-Niang; when they wish to be free of hunger, they worship the kitchen god; and when they wish for rainfall, they worship Dragon King, and so on so forth.

In the Western scholarship on religion history, the development from pantheism to polytheism to monotheism is considered a kind of "social evolution" in religious beliefs. For pantheism is a primitive religion, and Christianity makes people explore the uniform law of the nature by overthrowing the "heresy theory of all souls," which gives rise to the emergence of modern science. This argument suggests, by extension of its conclusion, that polytheism is the cultural reason for the underdevelopment of science in the oriental countries. Ch'ing-k'un Yang, however, argues that it is untrue to claim that there is no religion in China. Instead, religion took a cultural shape as a decentralized organization, wherein religion in diffusion served for secular social institutions, which in turn reinforced its organization. Pervasively diffused religion relied upon the institutional structure of the traditional society for support and exerted systematic influence on the public life via its specific theology, gods, beliefs, and ritual ceremonies. Why Chinese religion has such characteristics, Yang explained, is above all because religion in China has thoroughly subsumed by the monarchical power so that the subordinate religion, when at its incipient stage, tended to be diffused and integrated with social institutions and failed to develop into an organization with independent function and structure. The second reason is that social inclusiveness of polytheism precluded the possibility that a single religious belief and organization stood out and improved itself. C.K. Yang's last point on the underdevelopment of Chinese religion contradicted to his assumption that the religion in China is a cultural existence, which is indicative of his unavailing struggle against the established conclusion of the Western study of religion.

Tien Ju-Kang also conducted unique research on Chinese folk religion on the basis of fieldwork. Tien was a research member in the Yunnan Kui Ge sociology research laboratory supervised by Fei Xiaotong. Around 1940, Tien conducted a ten-month long fieldwork in the Namu village in the city of Mang in Yunnan Province where he investigated in the religious ceremony around *Pai-i* conducted by Dai people. His research was published in *Religious Cults of the Pai-i along the Burman-Yunnan Border* (also known as *The Pai in Pai-i*) in 1946. "Pai" (originally known as Pai-i) was a folk religious activity among local Dai people. While examining the economic life in the village along the border, Tien discovered the significance of "Pai," for it "connected to the entire living activities of Pai-I," although the ceremony was simple. Influenced by *Magic, Science and Religion and Other Essays* by Bronisław Malinowski and *The Elementary Forms of Religious Life* by Émile Durkheim, Tien elaborated and analyzed the difference at length between religion and witchcraft, Pai and non-Pai, and the religious ceremony and the supernatural worship ceremony. In Tien's eyes, "Pai-i" as a religious ceremony was non-utilitarianism since people collectively consumed properties in the ceremony and the purpose of the ceremony was "consumption" per se. However, "non-Pai" was utilitarian in the sense that non-Pai ceremony, like performing witchcraft, attempted to solve real-life problems by utilizing supernatural power. Tien (1946) argued that "Pai-i" was a religious means to overcome social stratification for the Dai people, and the accumulation of wealth was not to differentiate individuals but for the sake of "consumption" at the religious ceremony to balance out the social discrepancies.[3] Tien's study to a certain extent challenges the simplistic judgment call that Chinese religions are based on utilitarianism and reveals the dual character of both utilitarianism and non-utilitarianism of the religion in China.

Francis L. K. Hsu is another important figure in Chinese anthropology, whose representative work was *Under the Ancestors' Shadow: Chinese Culture and Personality* published in 1948 (it changed into *Under the Ancestors' Shadow: Kinship, Personality & Social Mobility in China* in its 1967 revised edition, hereafter as *Under the Ancestors' Shadow*). The book was based on the fieldwork conducted by Hsu in the West village, the Xizhou village in Dali, Yunnan Province, from 1941 to 1943 when Hsu worked for the sociological fieldwork lab in Yunnan. Having set the argument in *Under the Ancestors' Shadow* on the cultural worship of ancestors in the Chinese personality with the axis of parental relationships, Hsu revealed the completely different cultural characteristics and psychological structure of Chinese than the Western culture, which made Hsu the pioneer in Chinese psychology. In Hsu's eyes, ancestor worship and the clan family organization played crucial roles in building individual Chinese personality in that every individual, living and growing under the ancestor's shadow, spent his/her life making the ancestor's legacy last longer, which in turn eternalized the short and corporeal lives of individuals. Since Chinese ethical system gave priorities to and subsumed individual interest under the interest of family, nation, and other forms of collective beings, the independent and self-reliant individual is almost nonexistent in the traditional Chinese society (Hsu, 2001). *Under the Ancestors' Shadow* presented vivid ethnographic description and systematically anthropological analysis, and it explained why Chinese cultural is collectivism oriented. Hsu's argument, however, did not ring as original for Chinese readers. Instead, the mainstream opinion since the late Qing dynasty was that the revolution in the Chinese personality and culture must smash the ancient tradition by breaking through the curse of the ancestor's shadow and thoroughly transforming the individual self. Hsu made his major contribution in resting this kind of judgment and explanation on concrete fieldwork and in successful utilizing psychological methods in anthropology.

Under the Ancestors' Shadow raised the question about the causes for the rise and fall of the clan family – that is, the so-called question of why "wealth won't be able to pass down three generations or further" – and he attempted to answer those questions through fieldwork investigations. However, Hsu's academic aspiration was beyond shedding light on individual families' situations. In his view, the rise and fall of an ordinary family in a small community had causes in common with that of dignitary families and the imperials, so he linked the rise and fall of families to that of nation state and society, although the latter is much more complicated than the former as he would admit. Hsu argued that there are two schools of thought in the established Western literature to explain the rise and fall of a society. The first school is the Malthusian theory of overpopulation. This theory maintained that population growth during peacetime engenders conflicts between the population and the resources of land and technology. When overpopulation reaches its peak, unrest ensues that may kill a large number of people, and then the nation once again evolve into a new dynasty. The other school is represented by Karl August Wittfogel's strata loop circle theory. The theory maintained that Chinese society is divided into the ruling class, bureaucrat stratum, and civilians. Land accumulation by bureaucrats and upstart (dignitary, locally evil tyrants and gentry, and merchants) gives rise to land crisis leading to economic and social crisis. The vicious cycle of this kind may be periodically alleviated by the rise and fall of dynasties, but it can never be completely eradicated. Nonetheless, Francis L. K. Hsu argued that personality is a crucial factor in the rise and fall of the family; while cowardice often relates to family decline, a powerful persona is emblematic of the prosperous family. In his investigation in West village, he discovered that under the ancestor's shadow, authority and competition are the two most important factors in shaping individual personality. While poor people compete against each other for survival, rich people compete for power and reputation. Although paternity is the same formal relationship, the economic disparity distinguished the two classes from each other in terms of personality development. Sons born into the rich family tend to be completely at the mercy of the paternity, but sons born into the poor family are relatively more independent and reluctant to being manipulated by the traditional paternity. Along this line, one's economic condition determines one's character, which in turn determines the development prospect for oneself. The psychological anthropology completed by Hsu was under great influence of the Western behavioral school of psychology on one hand, but on the other hand, it was a significant endeavor initiated by a Chinese scholar to localize the discipline of anthropology. To a certain extent, Francis L. K. Hsu's work breaks the ground for the localized Chinese psychological studies on themes such as "the art of dealing with people" and "face."

Community studies from the field of social anthropology

Sociology and anthropology has always been unfathomably intertwined in China, and many anthropologists hope to establish anthropology as a stand-alone tradition and system, separate from the discipline of sociology. As a result, when it comes to early anthropological fieldwork studies in China, scholars often make reference to Martin C. Yang's investigation in Taitou, Shangdong Province; Daniel Harrison

Kulp's investigation in Phoenix village in Guangdong Province; Lin Yueh-Hwa's studies on Yixu in Fujian Province and Huang village in his *The Golden Wing*; Francis L. K. Hsu's work on West village in Yunnan; and C. K. Yang's Nanjing village in Guangzhou. Scholars tend not to count Fei Xiaotong in this team of anthropologists. Early social scientific studies in China actually do show clear-cut disciplinary distinctions between sociology and anthropology. Fei's work leaned toward an economic perspective, and back then valuing economy not only meant the study was swayed by functionalism but also indicated its turn to the left.

Investigation into villages is a typical research method used in early sociological studies in China. Professor Daniel Harrison Kulp at the University of Shanghai led one of the first village studies. He led students to conduct fieldwork in the Phoenix in Guangdong Province in 1918, 1919, and 1923, respectively. Their research report was published in China in 1925 under the title *Country Life in South China: The Sociology of Familism.*

Martin C. Yang's *A Chinese Village: Taitou, Shantung Province* was praised for beginning the era of localized anthropological community studies, as Ralph Linton wrote in the preface to the book. Yang was born and raised in the village of Taitou. Following the suite of Fei Xiaotong and Lin Yueh-Hwa, Yang conducted his fieldwork in his familiar hometown, which invited suspicion concerning the methodology, for one may find it difficult to step out of the perspective of "one of the insiders" as far as the investigation on one's hometown is concerned and thus the analysis was partially based on "affective" perception. It is almost always a controversial question as to whether the investigation on the "hometown" would be swayed by the observer's angle and what the difference is between an insider hometown study and an outsider's investigation. However, an insider "hometown" study has the advantage over the outsider's in terms of avoiding cultural misunderstanding and misinterpretation. Martin Yang used real names in his description of the village life in Taitou and his analysis centered on his own family. Relying on his familiarity with the village life, Yang described and examined at great length the family life, internal conflict, crop planting, children's games, and many other aspects.

Marin Yang argued that the key to the Chinese village study is to put village life against the context of a series of social relations, especially family relations and village relations – two layers of analysis that scholars cannot afford to ignore. Because villages did not exist in isolation, the analysis also needed to count in intervillage relations and the impact of urban centers on the village.

When it comes to social relations in the village, Yang takes a completely different approach from George William Skinner. Skinner, taking the rural "market" as an analytic unit, in fact put more emphasis on the influence of urban commercial civilization on the village social life and render peasants at the periphery of the "market circle." Martin Yang, however, also stressed the link between the village and the outside world, including the connections to the market, but he put peasants at the center of the "village circle." Focusing on life in the village and family life, Yang took a close examination into village agricultural civilization. Yang found that many villagers left for Qindao for jobs, but their wives and children were still in the village. The population reproduction took place in the village, which set in motion a benign and orderly interaction between the rural and urban regions, so Yang further argued that this situation was much better that in ghettos in American cities.

Martin C. Yang's study on the village of Taitou has made an extraordinary contribution to the research on village organization. He believed that some interim organizations between family and village, such as the family, the neighborhood, the religious organization, and the organizations were built on family unions. He divided these organizations into three categories based on the organization size: the village organization, neighborhood organization, and the organizations built on family unions. In Martin C. Yang's view, the management of the village depended on the traditional local organizations to mediate disputes; the delivery of legal knowledge alone to the rural places would cause the collapse of the community. Yang (2001) also applied multiple social stratification theory to the analysis of the hierarchy in the village. He argued that the hierarchy was not only manifested in the economic disparity but also in gender, age, family name of the clan, social status, reputation, and religions.

In his later book, *The Evolution of Rural Society in China*, Yang sorted out and summarized his research on the Chinese village. In particular, he extended his argument on village organization, which first took shape in the *A Chinese Village: Taitou, Shantung Province*. He defined social development as the transition from a disorderly situation to an orderly situation. Whether it is a tribe of fishing and hunting developing agriculture that later on inhabits in an area and builds a village, or it is migrants that reclaim a wild area and build a village, the social organization is initially triggered by specific problems or special needs, such as the clan. Once the scope of "mutual help, protection, and support for the sick" spreads onto the entire village and the relationship built around this rationale is widely accepted by all or a majority of the villagers, community activities emerge out from the needs but rise and fall because needs and functions may vary over the time. The community activities include village self-defense, youth league, employment system for trade and industry, paying celebratory or condolence calls to each other, festival gathering to welcome gods, fairs, building schools, and disaster prevention and emergency relief, and so on.

Yang also divided social relations in the Chinese village into two categories: primary social relation and secondary social relation. In addition to family, the "neighborhood" is the basic unit in the primary social relation. The social meaning of the "neighborhood" in the village refers to the social connections established among the families within the said neighborhood. The social connections afterward would transcend geography and develop into social relations network, on which social connection is the link and affective cohesion of "our group," and the common behaviors and actions form the nodes. Next to the neighborhood is the "clan group" in the village. There is the clan group or the family group with the nature of clan in all the large- and medium-sized rural villages in China. The "clan group" is also a social relation unit in the village and many social organizations with the clan nature derive from this unit, including private school, clan barn, senior nursing homes, organizations to look after the poor and the orphans. In addition, the primary social relations include informal social communities such as those that help out during funerals and festivals.

Yang pointed out that the secondary social relations are reflected in educational groups, religious groups, and family groups, as well as tenancy relationships that lack obvious organizational structure. Education provides an upward mobility path, and with no exception to the village. Educational groups in village refer to private school or school operated by the clan and regular school. The religious groups and organizations in the village include both official religious organization and social community relations reflected in folk beliefs activities like temple fairs, praying for rain, and worship. "Family groups" are a social class of families that connect to each other in an unfixed and loose manner because of similar economic situation and social status, such as family groups bound by the master-apprentice relation, job exchange families, and pure family popularity. Tenancy relations are the relations between residential landlords and their tenant peasants. People are prone to speculate and believe that the landlords have an upper hand in this relation, and their power exerts downward pressure on the tenant peasants who lack the privilege and channels to petition, and who have to be humble and at the mercy of the landlords. The reality, however, is that this assumption may not be true and is subject to changes from factors such as family relations, cooperative relations, and dependent and confrontational relations.

Fei Xiaotong is undoubtedly the leader in community studies of the village. He inherited the academic tradition initiated by Wu Wenzao. In the interval from 1950s to 1980s, sociology in China went through destruction to restoration and reconstruction. Given the unique role played by Fei Xiaotong in the restoration and reconstruction of the discipline, his village community studies become the only pathway for Chinese sociology to continue along the academic tradition.

The work that establishes Fei's name is *The Economy of Jiang Village*. In 1936, Fei Xiaotong went to rural villages in Guangxi Province to conduct fieldwork but lost his beloved wife 108 days into the marriage. While he stayed in his hometown for recovery, he conducted fieldwork in Kaixuanggong village of Miaogang town in Wujiang, Jiangsu Province. Later on, he took the fieldwork data with him and went to study in England. Having built on these materials and received advices from Bronisław Malinowski and other mentors, Fei wrote *Peasant Life in China: A Field Study of Country Life in the Yangtze Valley*, which was translated into Chinese with the title *The Economy of Jiang Village*. What is unique about Fei's approach is that he was the first person to apply the "community" research method of participatory observation from social anthropology to the rural economy in the developed areas of south of the Yangtze River in China. His study on Kaixuanggong village (formal name as "Jiang village") in Wujiang, Jiangsu, breaks the new ground in terms of examining industrial development problem from the perspective of rural social organization. In the 1930s, the academic world overwhelmingly neglected the problem of rural industrialization. Given the prior position of land in rural studies and even for Chinese revolution, a great majority of rural researchers and revolutionary theorists had to focus on the problem of land. They paid preponderant attention to the questions about the survival of peasants and how to organize them, and the question of industrialization seemed to be on the margin.

In Fei Xiaotong's opinion, if the family sericulture in the Jiang village was an inward development because of the pressure caused by population outnumbering the land, then the entry of factory industry to the village reflected a response from the village to save rural industry from the external challenges. For Fei, these "external forces" sometimes meant the introduction of modern technology and sometimes the imperial invasion and the industrial expansion led by the Western imperialist powers, or something accompanying the combination of both. Fei argued that land is the fundamental problem of the rural village, and the ultimate solution to the problem of land was not tightening peasants' expenditures but increasing peasants' income. Therefore, restoring rural enterprises is a fundamental measure. He further illustrated that foreign invasion threw the land problem into stark and making it a matter of life-and-death. Only through rational and effective land reform and resolving peasants' anguish can a brand-new China rise from the ruins of suffering (Fei, 1939/2006).

Many of the contemporary scholars always criticized Fei Xiaotong and Li Jinghan for the lack of hypothesis in their community investigations. However, the community studies of this kind are not without hypothesis. Fei's hypothesis that foreign power led to the collapse of rural industry has constantly elicited "criticism" and "disproving" from Western scholars.[4] Prior to studying in England, Fei did nothing more than purposefully refuse the theoretical hypothesis, rather than putting forward a hypothesis and verifying it. When he edited and wrote the social organization of Hualanyao, he also talked about how he tried to avoid theoretical stretch and insisted that there is no place for theory in fieldwork. For theory is no more than "a reasonable order arrangement for the narration of the facts." When he conducted the fieldwork in Jiang village, he also advocated Fei (1990, pp. 11–12), "investigators were supposed not to bring theories with them to the rural villages. It would be best if they thought of themselves as a roll of photographic film open for automatic projection of the facts from outside;" and after studying in England, Fei had the feeling that this methodology "threw many of the significant observations into oblivion." While he was writing *The Economy of Jiang Village*, Fei (1990, pp. 11–12) felt that "without a coherent theory, [he] cannot organize all facts under a single theme, which is an undeniable shortcoming." Consequently, *The Economy of Jiang Village* is "a transitional work from social investigation to sociological investigation or community study." What differentiates sociological investigation from social investigation is whether it is a collection of observations on a group's social life or it aims to test sociological theory by examining certain part of social reality, or if it is a "trial hypothesis."

Fei's aspiration is to look through Jiang village and examine the broader and more complicated "Chinese society" instead of making the Jiang village investigation into a community research model for functional analysis method. Fei believes that it is practically impossible to survey every single village in China to grasp the panorama of the rural China, but scholars must conduct qualitative analysis for different types of village before embarking on applying random sampling method for quantitative analysis. The academic model he created out of "Jiang village," along with other models such as "Lv village," "Yi village," and "Yu village" he participated in organizing and establishing, have formed a typology of models to understand rural China societies that have organic connections but divided by economic organization modes.

Fei's complete conception of China's rural society is manifested in his *From the Soil: The Foundations of Chinese Society.* In the case of *The Institutions for Reproduction, From the Soil: The Foundations of Chinese Society*, the book was based on lecture notes on family and rural problems. However, the style of *From the Soil* is more vivid and readable, because the content was supposed to be published in journals. These two books have shown two academic characteristics of Fei – namely, the pursuit of typology and Chinese academic discourse. For instance in *From the Soil*, Fei created a series of academic typologies and Chinese academic concepts, such as a nonlitigation society and a nomological society, letter-less society and lettered society, differentiated social order and group society, consanguinity society and geographical proximity society, identity society and contractual society, and so on. In *The Institutions for Reproduction*, he also coined the topologic terms that have academic tensions and Chinese characteristics, such as "the basic triangle of social structure," "sociological weaning," "the continuity and replacement of society," "intergenerational irregularity," and "the pecking order."

Chang Chih-yi created a new type of rural industry through his studies on handicraft industry in "Yi village," a workshop-based industry that was different from cottage industry in "Jiang village." Chang's fieldwork was carried out in 1939 in Yi village – a village with relatively developed handcraft business in the county of Yimen, Yunnan Province. In the eyes of Chang, although workshop-based industry represented by the paper mill and family industry represented by weaving bamboo articles coexisted in Yi village, their natures were quite different as the former reflected another rural industry mode different from cottage industry. While weaving bamboo ware that did not require massive amounts of capital was a rural industrial activity that usually took place during the slack farming season for the purpose of making ends meet, the paper mill was to increase the value of capital. People whose livelihood was under threat found themselves having no spare money for paper mill construction. Through his studies on the differences between the cottage industry and the workshop-based industry in the handicraft business in Yi village, Chang raised an important academic question regarding significances of different industrial organizations in the rural areas. As he mentioned toward the end of *Handicraft Industry in Yi Village*,

> if this book reveals anything, it ought to be that we should not consider rural industry as a singular subject. The term entails many different types with each type having its own characteristics. The significance and impact of rural industry on rural economy may vary from type to type.
>
> (Chang, 2006)

In 1930s and 1940s, many rural regions witnessed the development of side-line occupations and workshop-based rural handicraft industry. Meanwhile, rural labor force started to enter small towns and cities for employment and business. This phenomenon aroused scholar's interests shortly, to which Kuo-Heng Shih paid special attention in *China Enters the Machine Age: A Study of Labor in Chinese War Industry* (the literary translation from Chinese is *Workers for Factories in Kun*, hereafter *China Enters the Machine Age*).

Kuo-Heng Shih considered his study an extension from rural community studies by Kuixingge, except that this extension was from village to city and from agriculture and rural handicraft industry to machined industry in factories. It was one of the rare sociological case study on enterprise. The factories in Kun referred to a state-owned military supplies factory with about 500 employees in Kunming where Shih conducted his fieldwork from August to November in 1940. The theme of *China Enters the Machine Age* was to explore the process of peasants transforming into workers, and Shih raised a few meaningful questions for China's industrialization: (1) The mode of transformation from peasant to work. When he examined the source of the workforce, he discovered that in the state-owned military supplies factory there were a large part of workers from rural families. Workers born into rural families were 31 percent less than those from nonrural families to work in the factory. At the same time, he also found that 68 percent of peasant-turned workers had prior interim jobs before working at the factory. Those without any interim jobs consisted of only 13.5 percent of the peasant-turned workers. The interim jobs included soldiers, businessmen, handicraftsmen, chore men, and layabouts. That meant that before entering the factory, they have more or less changed the unsophisticated personality of peasants and the consciousness bound to soil, and become a subsidiary of the urban life. This mode is different from the typical transformation mode of bankrupted peasants turning into industrial workers in the Western industrialization. (2) The relationship between individual change and social transformation. Shih believed that the transition from peasant to worker is individual change, which is far more complicated than the production change from agriculture to industry. For the process involved not only the changes in the mode of labor and labor relation but also lifestyle changes, including adjusting to two cultures (rural culture and urban culture), redesigning social values, balancing the psychological state in the turbulent times, and adapting management to the needs of new industries. "[This] indeed is an important social transformation." (3) The nature of state-owned factory. When Fei Xiaotong touched upon the new forms of rural industry in *Rural Recovery*, he pointed out that China's traditional industries could be divided into three types – namely, imperial monopoly, popular workshop-based industry, and cottage industry. Everything from salt, iron, military supplies and all supplies for the royal court were under the imperial monopoly. After the collapse of the royal dynasty, imperial monopolistic industry became "state-owned." Shih's investigation indicated, however, in the eyes of many workers the state-owned factory was yet one of the governmental agencies. Workers did not relate themselves to the waste and low efficiency seen in the factory, and they thought only the supervisors and managers are the main subject of the factory (Shih, 1946).

In *China Enters the Machine Age*, Shih emphasizes the analysis of individual factors. He explored the solutions for a variety of problems in the industrialization process by analyzing the social environment, family background, social situation, and human relations of the workers. This strong mark of human relations is obviously affected by the school of human relations from early American industrial sociology. In the postscript to *China Enters the Machine Age*, Fei Xiaotong introduced the "Hawthorne experiment" carried out by American sociology professor Elton Mayo (1880–1949). In 1943, Fei went to study at Harvard University. He translated *China Enters the Machine Age* into English precisely because of the Mayo's encouragement. Shih's investigation has shown that peasants-turned-workers in China then, regardless of whether they had a prior interim job or not, were not isolated phenomena. They might as well be generalized as another type of farmer worker who left the soil land and the village behind – a different type from the rural cottage industry and handicraft industry.

Kuo-Heng Shih's (1946) study on "workers for factories in Kun" and Tien Ju-Kang's study on "inland female workers" are perhaps the earliest studies on migrant workers in China. Tien Ju-Kang's *Female Labor in a Cotton Mill* was published as the appendix to *China Enters the Machine Age*. However, the research on female labor is especially important in China because women sustained a majority of the Chinese industries then. In Shanghai in the 1930s, about 55 percent of the workers were female, and the number would be 60 percent or more if female child labor were counted. It is not a coincident that China's industries largely build on female labor. This phenomenon shows that in China with lagging industries, the scope of industry is limited to light industry, which still needs cheap labor to develop. As Tien Ju-Kang put it, "Only pre-pubertal industry needs female care and nursing."

The main theme and pursuit of "Chinese School" of sociology is to understand the national conditions and to transform the society. As of today, sociology has seen rapid development in the 30 years into the reform and opening up. However, understanding the national conditions and transforming the society remains the main mission for Chinese sociology.

Notes

This chapter was originally published in *Social Science Front*, 2008, issue 12, but is adapted accordingly for this collection.

1 Translator's note: the Spring and Autumn Period and the Warring States Period refer to the time period approximately from 771 to 221 BC in Chinese history when China was torn apart by many small warring states. The Emperor of the Qin state ended it by unifying all of them. This period of time in Chinese history is also known for the flourish of philosophical doctrines, commonly known as Hundred Schools of Thought, including Confucianism, Taoism, Legalism, etc.

2 Translator's note: the neighborhood of Eight Hutongs refers to the red-light district spanning over about eight blocks near Dazhalan in what is now the Xicheng District in Beijing. "Eight Hutongs" even becomes a Chinese idiom for an area where brothels, prostitutions, and sex shops concentrate.

3 Tien Ju-Kang. Religious Cults of the Pai-i along the Burman-Yunnan Border. The Commercial Press, 1946.
4 Upon returning from visiting American sociologist circle in 1979, Fei wrote,

> during the time period when the diplomatic relation between China and the United States was interrupted, scholars who were interested in Chinese society can only go to Taiwan and Hong Kong for investigation. Many investigation reports were published in the past ten years. The authors more or less followed my method, but the arguments were set to criticize me, some of which tried to refute my ideas that "the decline of Chinese rural economy was caused by the invasion of imperial economic forces." The visiting scholar Potter is a case in point. He stresses that the Western industries brought prosperity and development to Chinese rural areas.

(Fei, 1985, p.149)

References

Chang, C. (2006). "Handicraft industry in Yi village." In X. Fei & C. Chang (Eds.), *Earthbound China: A Study of Rural Economy in Yunnan*. Beijing: Social Sciences Academic Press.

Chen, G., Xin, G., & Ge, R. (Eds.). (1989). *History of Pragmatism in Ming and Qing Dynasty*. Jinan: Qilu Press.

Fei, X. (1939/2006). *Peasant Life in China: A Field Study of Country Life in the Yangtze Valley (The Economy of Jiang Village)* (K. Dai, Trans.). Shanghai: Shanghai People's Publishing House.

Fei, X. (1947/1999). *The Institutions for Reproduction*. Shanghai: The Commercial Press.

Fei, X. (1948/1999). "From the Soil: The Foundations of Chinese Society." In *The Collected works of Fei Xiaotong*. Vol. 5. Beijing: Qun Yan Publishing House.

Fei, X. (1985). "Notes on Scholarly Visiting the United States." In *The Collected Sociological Works of Fei Xiaotong: Nationality and Society*. Tianjing: People's Publishing House.

Fei, X. (1990). "Cultivated Land in Lv Village." In X. Fei & C. Chang (Eds.), *Earthbound China: A Study of Rural Economy in Yunnan*. Tianjin: People's Publishing House.

Gao, D. (1944). *A History of Family Clans in China*. Hong Kong: Cheng Chung Bookstore.

Hsu, F. (1948/2001). *Under the Ancestors' Shadow: Kinship, Personality & Social Mobility in China* (P. Wang & R. Xu, Trans.). Taipei: Nantian Bookstore.

Lang, Q. (1933). "Causes and Organization of Armed Fighting in South China." *Eastern Miscellanies*, *30*(19).

Lang, Q. (1936). "Folk Fights in South China in the Recent Three Hundred Years." *The Monthly*, *14*(3–5).

Liang, Q. (1985). "Chinese Academic History of the Recent 300 Years." In *Two treatises on the Academic History of Qing Dynasty*. Shanghai: Fudan University Press.

Lin, Y. (1937). "Chinese Clan Village from an Anthropological Point of View." *Journal of Social Studies*, *9*.

Lin, Y. (1944/1989). *Golden Wing: A Family Chronicle* (K. Zhuang & Z. Lin, Trans.). Hong Kong: SDX Joint Publishing Company.

Liu, J. (1948). *The Transplant History of Chinese Clans*. Hong Kong: Cheng Chung Bookstore.

Liu, X. (1935a). "The Public Properties of Kinship in Song Dynasty." *Cultural Critique*, *3*(1).

Liu, X. (1935b). "Kinship Organization in Henan Province." *Cultural Critique*, *3*(3).

Liu, X. (1936). "Kinship Organization in Fujian Province." *Food and Goods*, *4*(8).

Lü, S. (1929). *A Brief History of Chinese Clan System*. Zhongshan: Zhongshan Book Company.

Pan, G. (1929). *Chinese Family Problems*. Shanghai: Crescent Bookstore.

Pan, G. (1937). *Distinguished Families in Jiaxing during Ming and Qing Dynasties*. Shanghai: The Commercial Press.

Pan, G. (1941). *Study on Consanguinity among Chinese Actors*. Shanghai: The Commercial Press.

Shih, K. (1946). *China Enters the Machine Age: A Study of Labor in Chinese War Industry*. Shanghai: The Commercial Press.

Tao, X. (1934). *Marriage and the Clan*. Shanghai: The Commercial Press.

Tien, J. (1946a). *Religious Cults of the Pai-i Along the Burman-Yunnan Border*. Shanghai: The Commercial Press.

Tien, J. (1946b). "Female Labor in a Cotton Mill." In K. Shih (Ed.), *China Enters the Machine Age: A Study of Labor in Chinese War Industry*. Shanghai: The Commercial Press.

Wu, W. (1934/2002). *Social Survey and Community Studies*. In Institute of Sociology and Anthropology at the Peking University (Eds.), *Community and Function – A Collection and Critical Study of Park's and Brown's Sociological Work*. Beijing: Peking University Press.

Yang, M. C. (1945/2001). *A Chinese Village: Taitou, Shantung Province* (X. Zhang, Trans.). Jiangsu: People's Publishing House.

Yang, M. C. (1970/1984). *The Evolution of Rural Society in China*. Taiwan: River Books Inc.

Yang, C. (1961/2007). *Religion in Chinese Society* (L. Fan, Trans.). Shanghai: Shanghai People's Publishing House.

Zhao, C. (1934/2002). *Social Survey and Community Studies*. In Institute of Sociology and Anthropology at the Peking University (Eds.), *Community and Function – A Collection and Critical Study of Park's and Brown's Sociological Work*. Beijing: Peking University Press.

5 "Chinese experience" of reform and development

The anchor of the world economic growth is gradually moving from the Atlantic Ocean to the Asia-Pacific region, which is even more so after the international financial crisis. As a country in the Asia-Pacific region with a population of 1.3 billion, China has developed its own "Chinese path" and "Chinese experience" in the rapid growth during the past 30 years, which is distinct from the rest of world when it comes to modernization process. "Chinese experience" is a valuable component of the world modernization experience. "Chinese experience" has several folds of meanings. First, different from "China model" or "China's miracle," "Chinese experience" conveys not only the "accomplishment" China has achieved but also the "lessons" it has learned, which cover all development experience. Second, "Chinese experience" refers to a family of new development rules that have to do with China's particularly large population, social structure, and cultural characteristics, which is of great value to deepen the understanding of modernization process. Third, "Chinese experience" is the experience of opening, tolerance, and exploration. It is not static nor fixed, but evolves in the practice. With due respect to other experience and options, Chinese experience is not framed as "oriental experience" as opposed to "Western experience." China never stresses the universality of its experience. On the contrary, Chinese experience proves the diversity of historical development and unlocks the new prospects for the historical development. There are many ways to describe the "Chinese experience," but what follows are the main characteristics from the perspective of social development.

The economic system reform synchronous with the social structural transformation

Besides the differences in political institutions, that the economic system reform coincides with the social structural transformation sets China's development apart from the new economic entities in East Asia and the transformed post-Soviet states in East Europe. Given that economic system reform is the de facto theme of the times in the past 30 years, people often consider the social structural transformation as the outgrowth or the side phenomenon. In fact, social structural transformation is a driving force for economic growth and social development on its own. China poses drastic differences from the post-Soviet states with the respect to the goal and the steps of reform, but people often overlook the differences in their social structures. Before post-Soviet states in East Europe take steps for reform, they have more or less accomplished industrialization and technologies have taken the place of labor in agriculture. Social structural changes entered a bottleneck and encountered the institutional rigidity. As far as the reform and the development in China is concerned, social structure is elastic, with much room for changes and flexibility for local operations. Therefore, when the reform stimulates the public's initiative and creativity, the society beams with vitality. Technology taking the place of agricultural labor, rural labor migrating to nonagricultural industry, and rural population concentrating in urban areas would all bring significant benefits to the society.

Progressive reform as the general rule for China's reforms

Progressive reform is characterized by taking the easy steps first and the difficult ones later, step by step, and replying on pilot programs, a "dual track," and incremental improvement and transition that lead to institutional reform. The merits of this type of reform include that it is easy for the government to control the reform pace. Government take into account both the overall reform strategy from top-down and the bottom-up creativity, sum up experience and lessons via trial and error in a timely manner, recalibrate the measures, and ensure social stability when reforms deepen. Grassroots reform experience ranges from household responsibility system, township and village enterprises (TVEs), construction of small urban villages, and state-owned business reform, to dismantling the urban-rural dualism and establishing social security system that covers urban and rural areas. Chinese progressive reform is also characterized by the expansion of reforms from the realm of economy to politics, society, and culture. Reforms are constantly taking place for employment, social security system, income and wealth redistribution, household registration, unit system, legislation, grassroots democracy, democracy with the party, and the cultural industry development.

Progressive reform has its own flaws. Friction cost of reforms is too high. It takes a long time for the new system to take over the old, during which institutional vacuum and disorder emerge frequently. Because China is such a vast nation and local circumstances vary, the request of "coordinating all the activities of the nation like moves in a chess game" demands that the local government comply with the national strategy for development on the one hand, while the central government finds it extremely difficult to make specific policies for the local governments due to the lack of sufficient knowledge. Unfortunately, more often than not, when policies implemented by the central government result in interest conflicts among established interests groups, policies would be distorted and morphed, which becomes a regular pattern known as "countermeasure from the bottom in response to top-down policy implementation." Relatively high "friction cost" is emblematic in the incipient market that is awash by the flood of counterfeits, in the corruption and the power-for-money deal commonly seen in the reforms, in the monopolistic hold on the established benefits and the hodgepodge of the good and the evil in the social organization development.

From the beginning until today, China's progressive reform has elicited many criticisms from institutions and scholars, domestically and internationally, who assert that it's time for China to get rid of this approach. However, China's reform is still marked by "progressiveness" as seen in the changes in the dual-track schemes for pricing and investment, in the transformation from the "structural layoff" system to unemployment governed by the market, and the floating exchange rates. With the passage of time, people increasingly realize that progressive reform is an effective means for a vast nation to avoid reform risks given the premise of "stability trumping all." Nonetheless, China's experience of progressive reform also indicates that in order to accomplish reforms it is far more difficult, and more significant, to establish new institution than dismantling the old ones.

Priority principle of social stability and proactive exploration for democratization

The high stakes given to social stability and the proactive yet cautious explorations for democratization characterize China's reform. This characteristic also attracts a good part of criticism from the Western mainstream, which is partially driven by theoretical thinking but more by ideological cause and national interests. According to the traditional theory of modernization, democratization accompanies industrialization, if it doesn't spearhead it, but the definition of democratization has never reached a consensus. The West also blames some nations in Eastern Asia (such as Singapore and Malaysia) for being "undemocratic" or even "authoritarian," despite their rapid development. According to Western standards, the stunning economic success in Singapore under the decades-long leadership of Lee Kuan Yew and in Malaysia under the regime of Mahathir Mohamad does not lead the countries to "authoritarian" regimes rather than democratic political regimes. In the days prior to its return to the motherland, Hong Kong, ruled by the appointed governors, did not fall into the "authoritarian" category, since Hong Kong was part of the "English democracy" under the royal family. Meanwhile, Philippines, a nation with all political and legal systems transplanted from the United States, is suffering from a sluggish economy and social unrest under a "democratic institution."

Western modernization theoretical assertions that economic growth and social progress are associated with a particular "democratic political system" that needs to be revisited in the face of national experience in the Eastern Asia and the changes in the Soviet Union and Eastern Europe, which is of more significance for the reality because of the "Chinese experience." From the perspective of Chinese pragmatism, whether a "political system" is superior or not depends on the fact and practice instead of theoretical principle. The yardstick is whether it benefits of the economic growth and social progress, and whether it raises the welfare standard of people's lives. Democracy unleashes people's creativity, keeps power in check, and safeguards the public's rights and interests. These are the merits of democracy, but the cost for coordinating interest groups is very high and is at the cost of effectiveness. There is also the pitfall of "the tyranny of the majority."

China stresses the internal association between democracy and the rule of law in the development. On one hand, China insists on the principle of "stability trumping all" in the political reform; on the other hand, it pushes for democratic elections at the grassroots and democratic explorations within the party, with the hope of building a socialist democratic system of laws in practice that is geared to the needs of Chinese development and to establishing a "consociational democracy" other than electoral democracy or representative democracy. In the midst of high-speed development, Chinese government, entrepreneurs, academia, and the public gradually have reached a consensus on the issue of social stability, which has transformed into political wealth for China's rapid structural transformation.

Unbalanced development in the rapid growth

Despite dramatic economic growth, China has seen serious unbalanced development. The gap between the urban and the rural widens. There are many modern cities in China, such as Beijing, Shanghai, Shenzhen, and Hangzhou, which are comparable to the big cities in the developed countries. On the other hand, vast rural regions in China remain in the premodern era. Tens of millions of people live below the absolute poverty line. A large number of the rural population lacks access to clean drinking water. Unbalanced development also exists among different regions. Against the backdrop of globalization, the economic hierarchy of the center-semi-periphery-periphery across the globe also affects the regional development in inland China. All three phases of development can be seen in regional China – namely, the capital accumulation phase in early industrialization, industrial upgrade phase in mid-industrialization, and the structural transformation phase in later industrialization. This reality poses daunting challenges, as China must simultaneously deal with problems that differ from each other by the nature of the development. Predicament thus emerges quite often. For instance, China has to develop labor-intensive industry with an enlarged appetite to absorb newly added labor as well as labor migrating from the rural areas. Meanwhile, it has to speed up the process of technological innovation and product renewals so that the ever-increasing labor cost can be offset by product added values, and the trade friction can be reduced. Still, China must enhance its measures for environmental protection and energy conservation for the sake of sustainable development. The third aspect of unbalanced development has to do with the gap between the rich and the poor. Last 30 years of rapid development have transformed China from a country of excessively even income distribution to a country of a relatively wide gap between the rich and the poor. Many Chinese have made into the global rich list, but a great majority of people earn only a low wage.

Make the most of labor comparative advantage

As a developing country, China enjoys the labor comparative advantage out of capital, technology, and labor, the three production elements. China has earned certain comparative advantage in manufacture, or been called "world's factory," can be largely attributed to the comparative advantage that is built on cheap labor. However, the golden age of cheap labor will see its end when the supply-demand relation shifts, which should not last more than ten years at most. Some of Chinese regions have seen "labor shortage" which is symptomatic of gradual increase of labor cost in the future. China needs to think of how to maintain its comparative advantage and competitiveness after cheap manufacturing. Future economic development for China has to shift from "made in China" to "designed in China" so that the labor comparative advantage can come from the quality of labor. Therefore, China has to take steps to improve the quality of labor on a massive scale and stimulate a sharp increase in social productivity. By doing so, China can keep its comparative advantage in the international competition and meet the needs of the new pattern of Chinese industrial structure and world economy.

Long-term policy of low fertility rate

China has implemented family planning policy since the early 1970s, imposing a strict control over the population and even taking the measure of "one couple and one child" in urban area. As the implementation of family planning policy in the rural areas goes violent and excessive occasionally, it attracts international public criticism. However, low fertility rates that last more than 30 years enables China to evade the possible crisis of overpopulation. If not because of this policy, China would have had 300 million more people and spent 30 trillion RMB more in providing for the elderly. Every year, "there would be a Canada born and a Portugal die in China, so China grows at a rate of an Australia." This description of population growth in China is no longer the case. China has passed the most difficult time for population control. Thanks to population control, China has earned the opportunity for development and for raising the standard of living. For example, China and India are both developing rapidly. In the 1950s, China's GDP per capita was lower than India's, but in the early 1990s, China's GDP per capita is almost equivalent to India's and now it is three times more than India's.

For a vast country like China, which has billions of people, changes in total population, demographic structure, and population quality would lead to many shifts in development outcomes and imperatives. Population increase in China has rigorous demands for development. Until today, the total Chinese population had a net increase of 600 million every year – a majority of which were concentrated in the rural areas. Under this circumstance, China must maintain a relatively high rate for economic growth and social development so that it can raise the overall living standards and materialize the social structural transformation. Differing from nations with zero or negative population growth, China faces an entirely different challenge for economic growth.

Reduce poverty-stricken population extensively

With a strict control over the population increase, the rural poor population has reduced significantly. Since reform and opening up, economic growth and anti-poverty policies have lifted hundreds of millions of people out of poverty, which is a major contribution to the global anti-poverty undertaking. From 1978 to 2007, rural absolute poor population that lives below the breadline has reduced from 250 million to 14.87 million, from 30.75 percent of total rural population to 1.6 percent. According to statistics released by the World Bank, two-thirds of the global anti-poverty achievement for over 20 years can be attributed to China. Without the Chinese contribution, the global poverty-stricken population would increase. China is the only country that has reached the UN millennium development goal of reducing the poverty-stricken population by half ahead of schedule. Based on the new poverty line of 1,196 yuan updated in March 2009 (equivalent of $1 at the current purchasing-power parity per day), the poverty-stricken population in China is 40.07 million, mainly concentrating in 600 townships in central and western regions.

The rate of rural poverty reduction slows down remarkably. The remaining poor population is increasingly difficult to lift out of poverty. The share of people who were already out of poverty who relapse into poverty is high. More and more peasants live in poverty because of debt caused by sickness and children's education. The income gap between the rural and the urban, among different regions is widening, and the widening tendency is difficult to reverse. A new poor population has emerged in the urban areas because of illness and unemployment. The mission to combat poverty remains daunting.

Focus on the investment in human capital including education

Valuing education used to be an important lesson from Japan and East Asian countries, which have accomplished leapfrog development. It means ever-greater potential for China because the quick drops in the Chinese birthrate brings the total burden coefficient down. With sufficient supply of labor nowadays, China has the opportunity for rapid development as long as it takes advantage of the vast room for improving the labor quality and competitiveness.

Chinese has a historical culture of valuing education, and even more so because of the one-child policy, which stimulates more family investment in education. Since 2000, education has become the second largest expenditure after food in the urban consumption structure. In the recent survey on urban residents' goals of saving, child education tops the list, followed by pension, housing, medical care, and employment. There were only 100 million college graduates in 1990s. The number climbs to more than 6 million in 2009. The average duration of education increases from 5.2 years in 1982 to 8.3 years in 2008. Indeed, the overall population quality lags far behind the developed countries. The gross entrance rate for college in China is approximately 25 percent, far below the rate of 60 percent in the developed countries.

The problem with the Chinese population has changed in nature because it stops being a problem of quantity but a problem of quality and demographic structure. Enormous elasticity of population quality and the transition from a populous country with huge human resource to a country with a large pool of talents indicate that there is great potential for China to improve productivity and knowledge output ability. In this way, China may make up for the relative deficiency in capital and technology and propel for robust economic growth.

Adhere to opening-up and international cooperation transcending ideologies

China's reform is closely connected to opening up, and the opening-up policy makes headway in a synchronous manner with the progressive reform. Opening up is also a progressive process fanning out from the coastal region over to the inland, from the economic realm to the cultural realm, and from general competitive field to monopoly field. While introducing advanced technologies and attracting foreign investment into the country, China also takes measure to "go global," participating in allocating world resource and reconstructing world order through overseas investment, acquisition, cooperation, and foreign aid. Opening up has generated tremendous profits for China, not only narrowing the gap to the developed countries in general technological field but also making China a popular destination for world investment. In particular, China launches international cooperation regardless of ideologies, which has earned China a broad spectrum for diplomacy. The international cooperation strategy of the kind, first, considers peace, development, and cooperation as the themes of the era and economic globalization as the trend, thus acts accordingly. Second, this strategy is pragmatic in that the mutually beneficial cooperation is never divided along the line of historical culture, social institution, or ideologies. Third, China upholds multilateralism and participates in building a new world economic and social order that is based on mutual trust, mutually beneficial, equality, and cooperation. China has reserved her own opinions on some of the assertions on universal values. Fourth, China tries to build an image of a responsible power that tackles emergencies with calmness, which has created a long-term peaceful environment for Chinese economic and social development.

Cope with the conflict between the rapid growth *and* the environment and resources

Given the huge population in China, intense conflicts erupt when the growing economy, rising living standard, and expanding consumption power encounter the environmental and resources conditions. At the stage of capitalistic primitive accumulation, Western countries were involved in a global plunder for natural resources. Politics becomes the extension of the economy, and the war ensues politics. Human beings have consumed more energy in the hundred years of the twentieth century than in all the years combined in thousands of years prior. Alternative energy resources made possible by the technological development are unlikely to meet the needs of high-speed production and consumption. There is still is the likelihood of economic crisis given rise by the shortage of energy and resource.

Rapid development forces China to seek resources and energy more broadly on one hand yet to rely on domestic resources and energy for the sake of economic security on the other hand. Either way, for such a large nation as China to modernize, it is impossible to replicate the high consumption lifestyle from the developed countries. As the awareness of environmental protection is enhanced, people have a refreshing knowledge about the high price paid for environmental governance.

The environmental change curve is the same as the income distribution change curve with regard to the unpredictability of the tipping point for overall improvement. However, as being rigidly restricted by the environmental and energy conditions, China has created new visions for development and life in spreading such concepts as "low carbon economy," "recycling economy," "environment-friendly society," and "resource-conserving society" and so on.

Note

This chapter was originally published in *Ganshu Social Sciences*, 2010, issue 4.

References

Bai, X. (2004). "Inequality in Education and Income: A Study of Chinese Experience." *Management World*, 6.

Bian, Y. (Ed.). (2002). *Market Transformation and Social Stratification: American Sociologists' Examination of China*. Shanghai: SDX Joint Publishing Company.

CCCPC Literature Research Office. (2004). *Deng Xiaoping: A Chronology*. Vol. 2. Beijing: Central Party Literature Press.

Chen, N. (2006). "A Literature Review of Fifteen Years of Overseas Debate on Chinese Market Transformation." *Social Science in China*, 5.

Chen, X., Chen, L., & Xia, C. (2003). "Rates of Return to Schooling in Urban China: Changes in the 1990s." *Peking University Education Review*, 2.

Chen, Z. (1991). *Income Distribution in the Economic Development*. Shanghai: SDX Joint Publishing Company.

Ding, R., Chen, Z., & Gu, W. (2003). "'Inverted U Curve' Hypothesis and Income Gaps during Chinese Transformation." *Economist*, 6.

Du, Y., & Gao, W. (2005). "How Far is China from a Unitary Social Security System." *China Labor Economics*, 2.

Fu, L., & Liu, J. (2008). "An Exploration into How to Solve Income Polarization." *Statistics and Decision*, 13.

Guan, X. (2006). "The Development of the Inverted-U Hypothesis and Its Testing in China." *Journal of Shanxi Finance and Economics University*, 5.

Han, L. (2009). "Ever Expanding Income Gap among Residents in Yangtze River Delta." *Pan-Yangtze River Delta Observation*, 3.

Hong, X., & Li, J. (2007). "A Review of Bi-polarization Measurement and Income Bi-polarization in China." *Economics Research Journal*, 11.

Jing, X. (1996). *A Study on Resident Income Distribution in Contemporary China*. Changchun: Northeastern Normal University Press.

Lai, D. (2001). *Education and Income Distribution*. Beijing: Normal University Press.

Li, C. (2004). *Rupture or Fragment: An Empirical Analysis of Contemporary Chinese Social Stratification*. Beijing: Social Science Academic Press.

Li, S., & Luo, C. (2007). "Re-estimating the Income Gap between Urban and Rural Households in China." *Journal of Peking University (Philosophy and Social Sciences)*, 2.

Li, P., Chen, G., Zhang, Y., & Li, W. (2008). *Social Harmony and Stability in China Today*. Beijing: Social Science Academic Press.

Li, Q. (2003). "An Analysis of Push and Pull Factors in the Migration of Rural Workers in China." *Social Sciences in China*, 1.

Lin, Y., Cai, F., & Li, Z. (1998). "Analysis of Regional Discrepancies in Chinese Economic Transformation." *Economic Research Journal, 6*.

Lin, Y., & Zhang, S. (2001). "A Review of the Studies on Chinese Income Distribution since 1990s." *Economic Review, 4*.

Liu, G. (2005, April 16). "More Attention to Social Equality." *Economic Observation Daily, 5*.

Liu, J. (2006). "The Change of Labor Market Structure and Returns on Human Capital." *Social Sciences in China, 6*.

Lu, X. (Ed.). (2010). *Contemporary Chinese Social Structure*. Beijing: Social Science Academic Press.

Ma, G. (2000). "Analysis and Measurement of Chinese Economic Marketization." *Qiu Shi, 10*.

Research Center of State Department. (2006). *Investigative Report on Chinese Rural Labor*. Beijing: China Yan Shi Press.

Shi, M. (2007). *Labor Relations in Informal Employment*. Beijing: China Labour & Social Security Publishing House.

Sun, L. (2008). "Social Transformation: New Issues in the Field of the Sociology of Development." *Open Times, 2*.

Wan, G. (2006). *Economic Development and Income Inequality: Methods and Evidence*. Shanghai: SDX Joint Publishing Company and Shanghai People's Publishing House.

Wan, G. (2008). "Inequality Measurement and Decomposition: A Survey." *China Economic Quarterly, 8*(1).

Wang, F. (2001). *Labor Mobility in Urban China: Employment Pattern, Professional Career, and New Migrants*. Beijing: Beijing Publishing House.

Wang, X., & Fan, G. (2005). "Income Inequality in China and Its Influential Factors." *Economic Research Journal, 10*.

Wu, Y., & Cai, F. (2006). "Informal Employment in Urban China: Size and Characteristics." *China Labor Economics, 3*.

Yang, Y. (2000). *Employment Theory and Governance of Unemployment*. Beijing: China Economic Press.

Yang, Z. (2009). "The Issue of Chinese Migrant Workers in the International Financial Crisis and its Solutions." *Chinese Cadres Tribune, 5*.

You, J. (Ed.). (2008). *China Employment report: 2006–2007*. Beijing: China Labour & Social Security Publishing House.

Zeng, X. (2006). "Employment and Unemployment in China: Scientific Measurement and Positive Analysis." *Economic Theory and Business Management, 6*.

Zhou, Y. (2004). "Commercialization, Change in Economic Structure and Transformation in Government Policies of Economic Structure – China's Experiences." *Management World, 5*.

6 Urbanization and a new phase for Chinese development

After taking off, China has entered a new phase of development with characteristics that have gone through fundamental changes. The problems and challenges China is facing have transformed as well. Problems and challenges that restrict economic and social sustainable development include rising cost of labor, declining return of investment, impeded trade, changes in labor relations, problem of accelerating aging, increasingly tightened constraints imposed by resources and environment, sluggish domestic consumption, to name a few. Meanwhile, international environment, development opportunities, and motivating forces have also changed dramatically. With all these new situations and changes in mind, many people keep asking whether China would fall into the "middle-income trap" as other takeoff countries.[1] If the answer is negative, where are breakthroughs and exits?

The greatest opportunity and driving force, among many others, is perhaps urbanization, which has become the new development engine after industrialization. China enters a new development era with dual engines of industrialization and urbanization.

Massive urbanization in China also attracts global attention. Nobel Prize recipient Joseph Stiglitz, for instance, asserts that China is facing three challenges in the new millennium. Urbanization is on the top of the list because it is significant new growth point to stimulate long-term domestic demand (Zhao & Zhou, 2002). In *World Development Report 2003*, World Bank (2003, p.9) pointed out that "urban areas can be the future engines of growth."

From take-off phase driven by industrialization to a new era of development driven by urbanization

After reform and opening up, the Chinese economy started to take off. The economic takeoff in China does not differ from other countries where economy takes off because of modernization, which is characterized by numerous labor flow from agriculture to industry, remarkable increase in foreign investment, polarized regional development, and a shift of competitive advantage from agriculture to labor-intensive industries. There are different viewpoints and debates concerning when China has accomplished economic takeoff and what it is like for China after takeoff. As far as urbanization is concerned, China has already entered a new phase of development that is driven by urbanization. This new phase has the following features.

Urbanization as the powerful engine for development after industrialization

Industrialization, urbanization, and marketization form the troika to drive the tremendous transformation of Chinese society. With ongoing urbanization, concentrated use of land and rapid increase in land values become main sources for economic growth and fiscal revenue. On one hand, people's fast-growing need for better housing conditions is in line with the need for changing economic development mode and expanding domestic demand. On the other hand, benefit game around the profits of land property affects the development of industrial enterprise, price stability, and fairness and justness of profit distribution. Therefore, how to find a satisfactory way out of the dilemma is the key for sustainably healthy development of the economy. The year of 2011 is a milestone for Chinese urbanization history as the urban population exceeds 50 percent and reaches 51.3 percent of the total population for the first time in the history. China has evolved from a peasant nation with thousands of years of agricultural civilization and history to an urban society, which marks a new era of development. It by no means is a quantitative change in population percentage, but implies fundamental transformations to production mode, professional structures, consumption behaviors, lifestyles, and value systems.[2]

Regionally phased development by urbanization

In recent years, a new phenomenon emerges is that economic growth in the central and western regions is leading the rest of the nation, which brings more balance to the regional development. In respect to industrial added value, while eastern region registered 12.2 percent year-on-year growth for the first three-quarters in 2011, central and western regions registered 18.3 percent and 17.1 percent, respectively. With regard to fixed assets investment, there is a year-on-year increase of 22.3 percent in the eastern region, but a 29.9 percent and a 29.5 percent increase in central and western regions, respectively.

Economic growth rate in central and western regions has exceeded the eastern region for seven consecutive years. Changes to regional development can be attributed to an outgrowth of industrial transfer and national policy for regional development. Rapid development in central and western regions is not a replica of the eastern region for urbanization has become the driving force after industrialization for central and western regional development.

Widening of the rural-urban divide slows down

Thanks to financial transfer payment with an increasingly support for rural areas and a series of measures to support and benefit farmers, especially rational increases in agricultural product prices, the farmers' standard of living has risen strikingly. The per capita net income for farmers increases at a faster rate than urban residents' disposable income in 2011, the same with in 2010.

This change is not an exception, but the beginning of a long-term trend. As the price of agricultural product and the cost of unskilled worker market rise, business revenue and wages are the two driving forces to increase farmers' cash income, which will constitute larger and larger proportion of farmers' net income.

However, the absolute disparity between the urban and the rural areas is wide. The chance is slim to have a landmark tipping point in near future, so China needs to enhance its policies that benefit farmers and improve their lives.

Dismantle dual urban-rural structure and the new theme of urban-rural integration

Balancing urban and rural development and integrating the urban and rural structure become the new theme for development across the nation. Further urbanization will precipitate comprehensive reforms in social institutions like household register system, employment, social security, income distribution, education, medical care, and social management. Thanks to the rapid spread of high-speed transportation networks, urbanization has entered its second phase of "one-hour" living circle of metropolitan areas from the era that is characterized by workers migrating to cities from the country. New urban-rural relation is taking shape. China puts an end to a thousand-year-long absence of social security for farmers, which brings about two hundred million farmers into the new rural social pension insurance system.

Stages of urbanization in China and its characteristics and effects

New phase of development featured mainly by urban population

China is a vast country with thousand years of agriculture civilization, but develops slowly in the modern industrial era. When the People's Republic of China was founded in 1949, China remained largely a peasant nation, with an urbanization rate of 10.65 percent and nearly 90 percent of the population peasants. Since the birth of the new nation in the early 1950s, China experienced an expanding urbanization and the urbanization level reached 17 percent in the early 1960s. However, the process of urbanization met with serious setbacks because of "Great Leap Forward," devastating natural calamity in the early 1960s, and the "Cultural Revolution" which sent massive number of youth to rural areas. For 16 years from 1962 to 1978, urbanization levels stopped at 17 percent, whereas the world average level of urbanization reached 42.2 percent in 1980 and in developed countries it reached 70.2 percent.

Since 1978, when China implemented reform and opening up, urbanization has expands rapidly. From 1978 to 2000, urbanization level rises to 36 percent from 17 percent, with an annual growth rate of 1.2 percentage point. It further accelerates in the new millennium. From 2000 to 2010, urbanization level jumps to 49.7

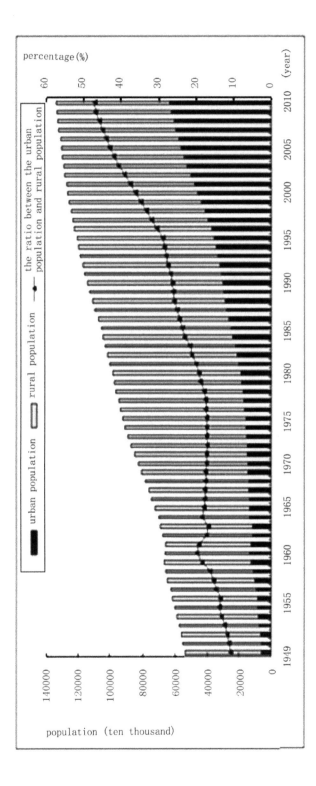

Figure 6.1 Urbanization process in China (1949–2010)

percent from 36 percent, with an annual growth rate of 1.37 percentage point. The urban population grows to 665 million from 459 million, adding 23 million urban population per year. This is the most massive urbanization undertaking in the world. The year of 2011 is a landmark point as the urban population account for more than 50 percent (51.3 percent) of the total population for the first time in the history. When industrial revolution erupted in the United States in 1870, the urban population constituted less than 20 percent of the total population. It takes the United States 50 years to raise the number to 51.4 percent in 1920. However, it takes China only 33 years to evolve from a vast rural country with thousand years of agriculture civilization to a new development era urban society.

The urbanization process has entered mid-term period

The process of urbanization in China after reform and opening up can be divided into three periods.

The first period is from 1978 to 1985, which is characterized by nonagriculturialization. As the household responsibility system is implemented universally, rural economy grows rapidly, small towns revive, and township and village enterprises (TVEs) rise unexpectedly, rural population begin to concentrate in small towns and to move to nonagricultural sectors. Mr. Fei Xiaotong published the well-known *Small Towns and Big Problems* in 1985, which attracted high attention from the central government and generated great social repercussion. Development strategy oriented to small towns was once called the urbanization path with Chinese characteristics.

The second period is from 1986 to 2000, which is characterized by "urbanization" of rural population pouring into the city. Since the late 1980s, rural laborers who "leave their land and homes" to work in the cities exceeds those working in TVEs who "leave the land but not their homes." This has become the main path for rural labor transfer. The reform of the state-owned enterprises has been intensified since the late 1990s, which has made the market more vigorous and brought all kinds of opportunities and hundreds of millions of migrant laborers to cities.

The third period is from 2000 until now, which is characterized by rapid expansion of city sizes and the emergency of urban agglomeration. The effect of urban housing system gradually shows up, car and house purchases becoming part of standard family consumption, a rapidly rising real estate market, ever-growing land values, and expanding cities into suburban areas. The construction of high-speed railroad and highways has significantly extended the scope of one-hour urban circle. Urban agglomeration has mushroomed, and it consists of cities one-hour from each other.

The process of urbanization across the world has experienced four stages – that is, population concentration into cities, suburbanization, counterurbanization,[3] and reurbanization.[4] China is currently at the stage of suburbanization when a majority of rural migrant population starts to concentrate in the suburban villages on one hand and on the other hand, some middle- and upper-class move to suburbia or outskirts to escape the deteriorating living conditions in the cities (traffic jam, air pollution, high cost of housing, and noises).

It is not necessary true that the higher urbanization level is the better. Urbanization rate in the developed countries stays in the range of 75 percent to 80 percent, but the agriculture population is less than 5 percent of the total population, about 1 percent to 4 percent. In other words, after "counterurbanization" is complete in the developed countries, roughly 20 percent of the nonagricultural population will stay in the rural areas. Urban-rural integration and improved transportation, utility, and information infrastructure in small towns, along with fresh air and the closeness to the nature, attract urban residents who are tired of turbid air and the city noise to move to rural region and countryside. The American urbanization rate is 80 percent, but its agricultural laborers only consist of 2 percent of the total population, meaning that 20 percent of the population lives in the countryside. Despite its high level of industrialization, 40 percent of German lives in the countryside. In contrast, the urbanization rate in some Latin American countries like Brazil, Argentina, and Mexico exceeds 80 percent, but a massive concentration of slums emerges in inner cities due to gigantic urban-rural divide and the extreme disparity between the rich and the poor. Therefore, narrowing the urban-rural divide and the urban-rural integration should be more important indicators for the urbanization stage and the development level.

Urban agglomeration economies that is constantly beyond the expectations

One basic feature of urbanization is population concentrating into the cities. However, it is not the case that the larger urban population is the better. Restricted by conditions like land, drinking water, housing, transportation, waste disposal, and environment, a city has to face the issue of an appropriate scale of its population. Many international research institutes and scholar have come up with a variety of models to analyze and evaluate appropriate population scale for cities. Economist Ernst Friedrich "Fritz" Schumacher (1973/1984) published *Small Is Beautiful*, in which he asserts that urban optimum population is 500,000. However, as international metropolitans spring out across the globe, the meaning of "appropriate population scale" has updated constantly. In practice, the effect of urban agglomeration economies is more and more salient, exceeding expectations and enhancing people's imagination that bigger is better.

From 1990 to 2010, the number of megacities that have more than 3 million people rose from 6 to 20 (Table 6.2). The agglomeration economy performance of all scales are improved significantly, with megacities having the highest growth rate (Table 6.3). By 2010, among 20 megacities with more than 3 million people, the average agglomeration economy effect (per capita GDP) is 62,775.6RMB, far more than that of big cities, medium cities, and small cities. The average agglomeration economy effect of the land output (10,000RMB/ km^2) is 13,341.1 RMB, also far more than that of big cities, medium cities, and small cities. Either urban agglomeration economy or the land agglomeration economy gradually declines from megacities to small cities.

Table 6.1 Agglomeration economy effect of population and the land output in Chinese cities of varied scales (2010)

	Number of Cities	Average Population (ten thousand)	Average Area (km²)	Average Agglomeration Economy Effect (per capita GDP) (RMB/Person)	Average Agglomeration Economy Effect of the Land Output (10,000RMB/ km²)
Megacities	20	608.3	5,153.0	62,775.6	13,341.1
Big Cities	110	159.4	2,233.5	45,242.4	6,113.1
Medium Cities	114	71.0	1,702.6	40,032.7	3,675.1
Small Cities	46	36.0	2,017.3	39,985.9	1,676.4

Table 6.2 Growth of urban areas of varied scales in China

Urban Scales	1990	2000	2010
Megacities	6	9	20
Big Cities	65	80	110
Medium Cities	79	103	114
Small Cities	90	69	46

Unit: Count

Table 6.3 Agglomeration economy effect of Chinese urban population (per capita GDP) (1990–2010)

	1990	2000	2010
Megacities	5,295.7	23,045.3	62,775.6
Big Cities	2,715.0	16,572.5	45,242.4
Medium Cities	2,977.2	12,390.5	40,032.7
Small Cities	2,898.7	13,253.3	39,985.9

Unit: RMB/Person

Source: Calculation based on *China Urban Statistical Yearbook 2011* released by National Bureau of Statistics.

Note: Cities in the Tables 6.1–6.3 refer to cities at the prefecture level and above, among which there are more than three million residents in megacities, one to three million residents in big cities, half a million to one million residents in medium cities, and less than half a million residents in small cities.

Cities becomes major consumer markets

One important result of urbanization is to change people's lifestyle and consumption behavior. Living in the cities from the countryside means a transition from material consumption to currency consumption and from consumption based on income and saving to credit consumption. Urbanization has also changed people's consumption structure and psychology. An array of new consumptions keep rising, including education, medical care, telecommunications, health and fitness, beauty produces, tourism, sports, culture and entertainment, and leisure activities and so on. Thousands of households pursue big-ticket items such as automobiles and houses, and urban consumption trend is often seen as the bellwether for popular consumption.

Since reform and opening up, the deep-rooted convention that "production comes first and consumption comes later" has changed, but the convention of "heavyweight on investment and lightweight on consumption" remains ingrained, which makes the consumption growth rate of urban residents long lag behind the economic growth. Income is the base for consumption. From 1991 to 2009, the disposable income of urban residents per capita increased 8.3 percent per year, but the net income of rural residents increased 5.5 percent, which was lower than the annual growth rate of GDP over the same period (10.4 percent) by 2.1 percentage points and 4.9 percentage points, respectively, and also lower than the annual growth rate of government revenue over the same period (18 percent) by 9.7 percentage points and 13.1 percentage points, respectively. Against the backdrop of changing the development mode in the past few years, urban areas have seen a rapid increase in residents' consumption, which contributes to a higher rate of growth concerning urban resident consumption than that of GDP. In 2010, per capita income of Chinese urban and rural residents has grown 7.8 percent and 10.9 percent, respectively. For the first time since 1998, per capita net income of Chinese rural residents grows faster than that of urban residents. In 2011, per capita net income of Chinese rural residents rose by 11.4 percent, the highest since 1985 and exceeding that of urban residents for two consecutive years.

Urbanization stimulates urban consumption. In 2010, household per capita consumption of urban residents is 13,471RMB and that of rural residents is 4,381RMB, meaning that one urban resident consume about three times of one rural resident. As far as income pattern is concerned, wage income is the main economic source for both urban-rural residents, but the household income structure is drastically different. In 2010, wage consists of 65.2 percent of urban household income, but 41.1 percent of rural household income. A great majority of the "business income" that constitutes about 50 percent of the household income of rural residents is non-monetary income converted from material objects. Material consumption outweighs market consumption in the distribution of farmers' consumption. The lower the income is, the higher the weight of material consumption is. Urbanization experience from other countries has proved that as rural population moves to the city, the "cumulative benefit" of consumption is enormous that would make consumption a powerful driving force for economic growth.

A nation's market size is not measured by population but rather by consumption capacity and total consumption. In this sense, China is a first-class nation of manufacturing but not a great consumption market. The pulling effect of consumption on economy is weak. From 2000 to 2010, Chinese final consumption rate has fallen to 47.4 percent from 62.3 percent, among which the consumption rate decreased from 46.6 percent to 36.8 percent. The final consumption rate in the United States and Japan is 70 percent and 65 percent, respectively. Three hundred million Americans spend $10 trillion, while 1.3 billion Chinese spend $2 trillion.

The increase in consumption in China will depend on the declining proportion of resident income in the national income, improving the living conditions for hundreds of millions of migrant workers in the cities, and narrowing the vast urban-rural gap in terms of consumption capacity.

Certainly, we must also advocate sustainable consumption, being cautious against the resurgence and the prevalence of "consumerism." If Chinese adopted American way of consumption, the natural resources on the planet would fall short to sustain Chinese modern life. Although GDP per capita in China is in the middle or even the lower end of the world's spectrum, China is the second largest luxury consumption market. Conspicuous consumption, excessive packages, and food waste are by no means an honor.

Elasticity of structural change and the significance of land appreciation for capital accumulation

What sets China apart from developed countries is the ongoing industrialization and urbanization, which still have tremendous elasticity and transformation bonus. The achievement of economic reform is impossible without the compensation of the benefits of economic reform to offset its cost. Therefore, China should take advantage of the transformation bonus and accelerate the transformation process.

In comparison to industrialization, one of the biggest benefit of urbanization is the appreciation of land. Land value increment, after the primary capital accumulation in industrialization, is a significant process for capital accumulation. Soaring housing price elicits discontentment from the public who thus see land appreciation as the root of all evils. As a matter of fact, land value increment is the outgrowth of urbanization and the path for farmers toward prosperity. Land appreciation per se is not the problem, because discontentment is caused by unequal distribution of land benefits. Some rural research specialists have argued that the fundamental route for rural areas and farmers lies in accelerating urbanization, integrating the urban and rural structures, reforming the dual system for household registration, along with all institutions associated with social welfare and public service (Guo, 1990).

Rapid economic growth and the national revenue growing at an annual rate of 20 percent to 30 percent are inseparable from the land value increment. According to relevant statistics, from 2001 to 2003, nationwide "land transfer fund" reached 910 billion RMB, about 35 percent of the local fiscal revenue over the same period. The number rose to 1.5 trillion RMB, roughly 46 percent of the local fiscal revenue over the same period (People's Daily, 2010). According to the statistics released by China Index Research Institute, the highest land transfer fund that is collected by a single city reached hundreds of billions of RMB in 2009. The profit from land-added value is the main financial source for expanding social welfare and improving public service. Land value is also the source of wealth for farmers, so land-added value is one of the driving forces for rural development. The key is to solve the distribution problem of the profit from land-added value.

Indeed, the lure of high profit from land-added value gives rise to many pitfalls. Some local governments are so obsessed with the short-term profit from the land that they would "overdraft" the land that should be made available for the future administrations, even a one-time charge for the land value for the next 50 to 70 years. "Rent-seeking behaviors" are rampant because of the enormous profits from land requisition and sales, which contributes to the economy bubble in the name of city management. The worst is unequal distribution of the land profits, which catalyzes frequent occurrence of mass disturbances led by farmers who have lost their land.

City provides space and muse for service industry

One feature of modern economic and social development is the growth of modern service industry. In general, the development level is associated with the proportion of service industry added value in the economic gross. The higher the proportion is, the higher the development level. Modern service industry and headquarters tend to concentrated in urban areas, including finance, insurance, consulting, education, and medical care. City is no long a space for manufacture, but a space for service industry. Service industry relies upon manufacturing. China is the world's factory, but its massive export products contribute to the urban development across the world except domestic cities.

Cities have not only the effect of the agglomeration economy but also the effect of agglomeration innovation. A nation's innovation competitiveness is also associated with urban development because the talents, information, capital, and all kinds of resources tent to flow toward and converge in the cities. For instance, there are 89 higher education institutions, more than 300 national mainstay research institutes, 86 state key laboratories, and 32 national engineering laboratories in Beijing. Among Chinese top-500 companies, 96 have their headquarters in Beijing. Among Global 500, 41 have their headquarters in Beijing and 187 have branch offices in Beijing. The intensity of intellectual resources in Zhongguancun, Beijing, is unmatched anywhere else in the world. To make the most of these resources for the sake of agglomeration innovation effects depends on adequate infrastructure and public service system. As the meaning of urban development keeps to be renewed, the definition of a city's competitiveness has expended from wealth concentration to economic and cultural prosperity, social harmony, environmental friendliness, open-mindedness and tolerance, and comfort and livability.

China is already a great manufacturing nation, but its future depends on whether we can leap from a "Made in China" nation to a "created in China" nation. Cities provide sources for innovations, which will become the center for China to construct an innovation-oriented nation.

Problems that stand out in Chinese urbanization process

Enormous urban-rural gap

While the urban development in China is getting closer than in the developed countries, the rural development is lagging behind. The urban-rural divide in China primarily manifests in the income gap, which was 2.5 to 1 in 1980, 2.2 to 1 in 1990, and 2.8 to 1 in 2000. By 2010, disposable household income of urban residents reached 19,109 RMB, while the rural family net income was only 5,919 RMB, with a widened gap of 3.2 to 1. Moreover, the disparity is even worse in social welfare. It is estimated that urban families spend dozens of times more than rural family on children's education, medical care, social security, and housing.

In addition to income and social welfare disparity, there is also a gap in the access to opportunities. Because cities are where all kinds of opportunities concentrate, entering cities is symbolic of a huge breakthrough for farmers' lives. If the urban-rural divide kept widening rather than narrowing, it would be an abnormal urbanization.

Urbanization lags behind nonagriculturalization and industrialization

Urbanization is marked as the population flow from the rural to the urban areas. Current urbanization levels are measured by permanent residents in urban areas, which count people who registered as rural residents who live in the cities for more than half a year.

In 2011, more than 51.3 percent of the total population in China lives in urban areas, 690 million out of 1,345 billion. But at the end of 2011, rural population is registered as 0.935 billion, which means among current 690 million urban residents there are only 410 million who hold urban household registers and another 280 million who hold rural household registers. The latter group consists mostly of migrant workers and their families who have stayed in cities for a long period of time. They are at most "peri-urbanized" because they are not entitled to institutional benefits such as employment opportunities, children's education, medical care, social security, and housing to the same degree as the urban residents. They are marginalized. According to 2010 national census data, there are 260 million in floating the population in China.

Regions where the floating population exceeds ten million include Canton (3.68 million), Zhejiang (1.99 million), Jiangsu (1.82 million), Shangdong (1.37 million), Shanghai (1.27 million), Sichuan (1.17 million), Fujian (1.11 million), and Beijing (1.05 million). A great majority of the floating population are "peri-urbanized" migrant workers and their families.[5]

Chinese urbanization rate (the proportion of urban population in the total population) lags far behind industrialization rate (the proportion of industrial added value in GDP). The ratio between urbanization rate and industrialization rate is too low—1.09 in 2010. The correspondent ratio in the United States is 4.1 – that is, the degree of urbanization is 4.1 higher than industrialization, 4.11 in France, 4.09 in England, 2.64 in Germany, and 2.48 in Japan. In the BRICS countries, the ratio of urbanization rate to industrialization rate in Brazil, Russia, South Africa, and India are 3.22, 1.97, 1.38, and 1.15, respectively, all higher than that in China (Zhou, 2011).

Consequently, a remarkable characteristic of Chinese structural transformation is that industrialization, nonagriculturalization, urbanization, and household

Table 6.4 National floating population distribution

Total Floating Population (0.26 billion)	Number of Provinces and Regions	Floating Population in Provinces and Regions
High Mobility (ten million and above)	8	Guangdong (36.81 million), Zhejiang (19.9 million), Jiangshu (18.23 million), Shandong (13.7 million), Shanghai (12.69 million), Sichuan (11.74 million), Fujian (11.07 million), Beijing (10.5 million)
Moderate Mobility (five to ten million)	14	Henan (9.76 million), Liaoning (9.31 million), Hubei (9.25 million), Hebei (8.3 million), Hunan (7.9 million), Inner Mongolia (7.17 million), Anhui (7.1 million), Shanxi (6.76 million), Guangxi (6.29 million), Yunnan (6.05 million), Heilongjiang (5.56 million), Chongqing (5.44 million), Shanxi (5.89 million), Jiangxi (5.30 million)
Low Mobility (below five million)	9	Tianjing (4.95 million), Jilin (4.46 million), Xinjiang (4.28 million), Gansu (3.11 million), Guizhou (4.63 million), Tibet (2.62 million), Hainan (1.84 million), Ningxia (1.53 million), Qinhai (1.14 million)

Note: The table is based on the sixth census data. The "floating population" refers to the population residing in the region for more than half a year whose household registration indicates they live elsewhere.

registration system lags behind one after another. On one hand, just like non-agriculturalization lags behind industrialization, transition in employment lags behind economic structural transformation. In 2011, the added value of agriculture declined to about 10 percent of GDP, but workers in agriculture constituted 38 percent of all employees. In other countries with similar industrialization rate, the proportion of workers in agriculture is below 25 percent. On the other hand, urbanization lags behind nonagriculturalization and urbanization rate (51 percent) grows slower than nonagriculturalization rate (38 percent). Lastly, household registration system lags behind urbanization in that 30 percent of the total population with urban household register is much lower than 50 percent of urbanization rate.

Population urbanization is behind the land urbanization

Chinese urbanization speeds up after the turn of twenty-first century, but a serious problem is that population urbanization is lagging behind the land urbanization. Enormous profits brought by land-added value allude people to enclose massive farmland and forced and violent demolitions occur frequently. According to statistics, despite the request of requisition-compensation balance, farmlands reduce by 124.8 million *mu*, from 2006 to 2008, with a decrease of 42 million *mu* per year.[6] These numbers are higher than the total decrease of 113 million *mu* and the annual decrease rate of 22.6 million *mu* by 12 million *mu* and 19 million *mu*, respectively (Ru, Lu, & Li, 2010). A new upsurge has come of rural residents "exchanging" their homesteads for urban expansion, which has triggered a wave of vicious conflicts and mass incidents that had negative impact on social harmony.

Weakened benefits of intensive use of urban land

The actual constraint on urbanization process in China is not the land. Many urban sprawl is like "making a pie" with low intensive usage. There is a significant gap in the output value per land unit between China and the developed countries. A study shows that current Chinese urban industrial land capacity rate is 0.23, much lower than the world average. For instance, despite the high level of urbanization and industrialization in Shenzhen, the output value per square kilometers (including construction land) is 0.4 billion RMB, but that of Hong Kong in the opposite of the river is 1.4 billion RMB and that of Singapore is 1.8 billion RMB. In another sense, even when the cities maintain their current size, Chinese economy has great potentials through a better way to use the urban space (Chen, 2012).

The upsurge of "land urbanization" reflects more about the stimulus of land finance than about the actual need for integrating the urban and the rural development and new rural construction. We must be cautious of making "the urban-rural integration" into "the urban-rural uniformity" which harms farmers' interests severely.

The emergency of "city disease" and "rural problem": air pollution, traffic congestion, and rural decay

A challenge facing China's urbanization is to deal with the urban-rural relation. The currently existing cities can never bear the enormous Chinese population if they were all living in the cities. Among 660 cities in China, there are more than 400 with a water shortage. To solve the urgent need for water, some municipal administrations mine irretrievable deep-water, disregarding the international ban on the procedure. Water resource becomes a major constraint condition for the urban development in China. Whenever people travel to foreign cities, they would feel that what sets foreign big cites from their Chinese counterparts is no longer urban infrastructure or the development level, but the air quality. The blue sky and white clouds are scare goods in Chinese big cities.

The so-called city diseases such as air pollution, traffic jam, and water shortage become salient. Consequently, while accelerating urbanization construction, China must improve rural construction and enable rural areas to absorb part of nonagricultural worker residents.

At present, there are also "rural problems" in the process of urbanization, which mainly refers to "rural hollowing." First, all industries are gone. With the upgrading of the national industrial structure and the rising of labor cost, the rural industry has lost its original competitiveness. Emerging industries gradually flow toward and concentrate in the large and medium cities, industrial parks, and New Technology Development Zone. The One Village One Product movement is on the wane. Second, younger generation is all gone. Youth moves to cities in search for job opportunities, finding themselves not willing to live in rural areas because of the wide gap between the urban and rural regions. Countryside becomes an elderly society and agriculture is the work for older people. Lastly, the house is vacant. In some developed areas, the renovation of housing is common and with a fast turnaround, but now very few people alter and renovate their houses. A majority of the rich rural residents have purchased and moved into the houses in the cities. In some places, one-third of the houses are left uninhabited. Long-term unoccupied houses, which also lack renovations, start to decay. The village becomes depressed and thinned out. As industries and youth are gone and houses are uninhabited, villages are in decline.

Strategic options to promote the development of urbanization

Give full play to the leading role of urbanization on economic and social development

We should be fully aware that industrialization and urbanization are the dual engines for economic growth and social development in China. Urbanization is the most powerful force for the development of China's economic and social development after industrialization. China must seize the opportunity to get rid of two urban-rural dualism, integrate the urban and rural development, narrow the urban-rural gap, and give full play to the role of urbanization in changing the lifestyle and the mode economy grows.

At present, the level of urbanization varies from province to province in China, which is consistent with the level of regional development. With the exception to Shanghai, Beijing, Tianjin, Guangdong whose urbanization level has reached that in developed countries, most provinces and regions stay at 41 percent to 60 percent, eight provinces and regions are below 40 percent, and the urbanization level in Guizhou and Tibet is below 30 percent. The difference of the level of urbanization is also the elasticity of urbanization structure, which provides a great opportunity for our country to promote economic and social development through urbanization.

Table 6.5 Different levels of urbanization in provinces, cities, and districts (2010)

Level of Urbanization	Number of Provinces, Cities, and Districts	Provinces, Cities, and Districts
High Level (61% and above)	4	Shanghai (88.6%), Beijing (85.0%), Tianjin (78.0%), Guangdong (63.4%)
Mid-level (41%–60%)	19	Liaoning (60.4%), Zhejiang (57.9%), Jiangsu (55.6%), Heilongjiang (55.5%), Inner Mongolia (53.4%), Jilin (53.3%), Chongqing (51.6%), Fujian (51.4%), Hainan (49.1%), Shandong (48.3%), Ningxia (46.1%), Hubei (46.0%), Shanxi (46.0%), Shaanxi (43.5%), Hunan (43.2%), Jiangxi (43.2%), Hebei (43.0%), Anhui (42.1%), Qinghai (41.9%)
Low Level (below 40%)	8	Xinjiang (39.9%), Guangxi (39.2%), Sichuan (38.7%), Henan (37.7%), Yunnan (34.0%), Gansu (32.7%), Guizhou (29.9%), Tibet (23.8%)

Source: Calculation based on data from *China City Statistical Yearbook 2011* released by National Bureau of Statistics, China Statistics Press, 2012.

Improve the intensive capacity of big cities

Population size and geographical scale of Chinese big cities have increased rapidly, but the urban aggregate economic capacity and scale are significantly lower than the world average, even lower than the developed countries. In most developed countries, the GDP output of megacity can reach more than 10 percent of GDP in the whole country. For instance, the GDP output of New York and Tokyo make about 18 percent of their respective national GDP. The GDP output of London make about 17 percent of English GDP, and that of Seoul about 26 percent of South Korean GDP. The country's largest Chinese cities like Beijing and Shanghai generate less than 5 percent of the China's GDP. The GDP of the Yangtze River Delta economic circle that is the region with a relatively higher economic intensive degree accounts for no more than one-sixth of GDP.

Urban development in China is still shaped by the idea of "making a big pie" as the size of the city expands rapidly with less favorable effect of agglomeration economics. Many well-designed skyscrapers encounter what is known as "rent evaporation" phenomenon. For the future development of the city, China must instill the management idea of the average output per square meters, and constantly improve the intensive ability of the city.

Development of urban agglomeration network

In recent years, thanks to the rapid development of expressway and high-speed railway in China, a number of one-hour distance urban networks have emerged, which drastically change the experience of time, urban space, and urban lifestyles, and accelerate the pace of life and improve the efficiency of social operations. Despite many problems emerging in the construction of high-speed railway, there is no denying the development path the high-speed railway has pointed to or the huge gains high-speed railways have brought. The high-speed rail and highway catalyze the formation of three metropolitan circles in the Yangtze River Delta, the Pearl River Delta, and around Bohai Sea.

The one-hour urban agglomeration network will continue to expand in the future, further accelerating the flow of people and logistics speed, generating a large number of satellite cities in the urban residential area, from where the formation of metropolis circles, urban agglomeration, and city strap take place.

Construct small towns

In 1980s to 1990s when small towns developed rapidly, Chinese academia found itself in fierce debate on China's "urbanization path." Many perspectives spring out, concerning the development of small towns, big cities, and medium cities, diversified development theory, and urban system theory and other views. After more than 20 years of practice, the academic community has reached a consensus. Namely, because China is a populous nation, it is impossible to rely on a few big cities to absorb the vast majority of the population like what happens in South Korean. Nor is it feasible to take the path of developing China into a nation dotted with small towns. Instead, China should balance and coordinate the development of large, medium, and small cities.

China should pay special attention to the development of small towns in its urbanization strategy. For the gap between urban and rural areas is huge; small towns connect urban and rural areas, and the main goal of urbanization is not only to develop cities but also to dissolve the development disparity between urban and rural areas. Small towns play a significant role to achieve this goal. For 20 years from 1990 to 2010, the number of cities in China increased from 467 to more than 660, while over the same period of time, the number of small towns in China increased from 12,000 to nearly 20,000. China has to focus on the construction of small towns, which are able to become an important channel to absorb rural population and relax the population pressure imposed on the large cities. This is an inevitable choice for China's urbanization direction.

Quicken the pace to urbanize migrant workers

Since the middle of 1980s, the urban economy has become the main channel to absorb rural the labor force. In the past 30 years, hundreds of millions of migrant workers flooded into cities for jobs and to do business. They constitute the world's largest floating population. A key criterion to assess the success of China's urbanization process is whether migrant workers can become urbanized. In fact, the decrease of agricultural population facilitated by industrialization in China is lesser than other countries. Japan's economic takeoff reduced agricultural population by 65 percent, and American economic takeoff reduced agricultural population by 72 percent. From 1980 to 2010, although the proportion of rural population fell from 80 percent to about 50 percent in China, the absolute rural population declined by only 15 percent. China should design specific and operable roadmap for urbanizing migrant workers and their families, in an attempt to solve urbanization problems facing 300 million migrant workers and their families including household registration, employment, children's education, medical care, and housing in the next 20 years from 2010 to 2030. That is to urbanize 150 million migrant workers per year.

A new way of urbanization to integrate the urban and rural development

By 2030, China's population will reach1.5 billion, and the urbanization rate will reach 70 percent, but the rural population still makes about 30 percent of the total population, which means 450 million people work and live in rural areas. The most challenging issues for China's urbanization are the rural regions. China must take the sustainable development approach toward urbanization by developing urban and rural areas as a whole, significantly raising farmers' income, improving farmers' living conditions and living standards, and protecting the ecological environment of rural areas. The future of urbanization is not about a lot of semi-urban migrant workers living in the cities, but a lot of nonagricultural workers and residents living in the countryside. China must adhere to the new way of urbanization, promote the coordinated development of large, medium, and small cities and small towns, focus on improving the city's comprehensive carrying capacity of aggregation effect, let cities to play a leading role to reignite the rural development, and gradually realize the integration of urban and rural development.

Notes

This chapter was originally published in *Jiangsu Social Sciences*, 2012, issue 5.

1 In 2006, World Bank used the term "Middle Income Trap" for the first time in the *Report on Economic Development in East Asia*. The term describes a dilemma faced by a country when it leaps from a low-income situation to a middle income level ($3,000 to $10,000 GDP per capita): on one hand, rising income brings down the competitive advantage of cheap labor and on the other hand, it lags behind in terms of technological upgrading so it is not competitive enough against developed countries. This has a "trap effect" because continuous economic growth will be hampered by the mode of current economic development with a per capita national income no more than $10,000 and an inclination of economic stagnation.
2 All statistics in this chapter are from State Statistical Bureau. Ed. *China Statistical Yearbook,* unless indicated otherwise.
3 "Counterurbanization" refers to a population movement since 1970s that runs counter to urbanization – people in the developed countries move from urban and suburban areas

further away from city to countries and small villages. Counterurbanization is often called "the hollowing out of cities," corresponding to "the hollowing out of countryside" of the early urbanization stage. "Suburbanization" and "counterurbanization" are deemed as "the middle stage of urbanization" and "the late stage of urbanization," respectively, with an urbanization rate ranging from 50 percent to 80 percent. "Counterurbanization" is in fact integrating of the urban and rural areas, whereby a majority people living in the countryside no longer work in agriculture and countryside revives in the sense that it is equipped with rich living facilities like shopping malls, bars, postal offices, schools, medical clinics, and saving banks.

4 The so-called reurbanization is part of the "post-urbanization" phase. In reurbanization, through industrial structure reforms and developing high technology and new tertiary industries, previously abandoned cities are able to provide more employment opportunities, improve urban environment and transportation infrastructure, and enrich cultural lives in the city. In particular, a large scale of young professionals return to and live in the cities because of the information gathering capacity of the city and great entrepreneurial opportunities. The process is called "reurbanization" which actually is a revitalization of urban industries, city functions, and urban lives.

5 It is estimated that migrant workers and their families account for about 70 percent of floating population, inferred from survey data released by the National Population and Family Planning Commission.

6 *Mu* is a Chinese measurement unit of area. One *mu* equals two thirds of 1,000 square meters or 0.165 acres.

References

Abe, K. (2001). *Urbanization: The Main Theme of China's Modernization*. Changsha: Hunan People's Publishing House.

Berry, B. J. L. (2008). *The Human Consequences of Urbanization: Divergent Paths in the Urban Experience of the Twentieth Century* (C. Gu, Trans.). Beijing: The Commercial Press.

Cai, F., & Du, Y. (2003). "Urban Expansion in Transitional China: Hierarchy of City, Financing Capacity and Migration Policy." *Economics Research Journal, 6.*

Chen, X. (2012). *Sum Up Experience, Improve Urbanization, and Achieve Sustainability.* Speech at China International Urbanization Forum. Available at http://www.ccud.org.cn/csph/201204/10/t20120410_537379.shtml

China Development Research Foundation. (Eds.). (2010). *A New Urbanization Strategy for China to Promote Human Development: Development Report on China 2010*. Beijing: People's Publishing House.

China Index Research Institute. (2009). *National Land Transfer Premium 1.5 trillion RMB.* Available at http://news.xinhuanet.com/fortune/2010–01/10/content_12784141.htm

Gao, P. (2004). *Comparative Studies on Urbanization in China and Foreign Countries.* Tianjin: Nankai University Press.

Gu, C. (2008). "China's Urbanization History, Status Quo, and Prospect." In China Society for Urban Studies (Eds.), *Report on the Development of Urban Science*. Beijing: China Science and Technology Press.

Gu, S. (1991). "Urban-Rural Dualism Strategy and Its Solutions." *Population Research, 5.*

Guo, S. (1990). *Unbalanced China – The History, Present, and Future of Urbanization.* Shijiazhuang: Hebei Press.

Li, P. (2001). *The End of Village*. Shanghai: The Commercial Press.

Li, Q. (Ed.). (2009). *Research on the Major Social Problems in Urbanization and the Solutions*. Beijing: Economic Science Press.

Lu, D. (2006). *China's Regional Development Report*. Shanghai: The Commercial Press.

Ma, C. (2008). *An Outline on Chinese Urbanization*. Beijing: Social Science Academic Press.

Mendras, H. (2005). *La Fin Des Paysans* (P. Li, Trans.). Beijing: Social Science Academic Press.

Pei, J., Niu, F., & Wei, H. (Eds.). (2009). *Development Report on Urban China*. Beijing: Social Science Academic Press.

People's Daily. (2010, December 27). Land Finance Is Unsustainable.

Ru, X., Lu, X., & Li, P. (Eds.). (2010). *Chinese Research Perspectives on Society for 2011*. Beijing: Social Science Academic Press.

Schumacher, E. F. F. (1984). *Small is Beautiful: A Study of Economics as if People Mattered* (H. Yu & G. Zheng, Trans.). Shanghai: The Commercial Press.

Takehiko, S. (2008). "A Study on Transportation Infrastructure Construction and the Income Gap between Cities in Japan in the Post-war Era." *Japan Studies*, *3*.

Tian, X. (2000). "Study on Influence of Population Urbanization on Promoting Consumption Demand." *Population Science of China*, *2*.

UN Commission on Human Settlements. (1998/1999). *A Urbanized World* (J. Sheng, Trans.). Beijing: China Architecture & Building Press.

Wang, M., Feng, B., & Xie, F. (Eds.). (2004). *Urbanization with Chinese Characteristics*. Beijing: China Development Press.

Wang, X., Lu, Q., & Wu, H. (2009). "A Cointegration Analysis on the Impact of Urbanization Level on the Urban-Rural Income Disparity." *Ecological Economy*, *2*.

The World Bank. (2003). *World Development Report 2003: Sustainable Development in a Dynamic World – Transforming Institutions, Growth, and Quality of Life*. The World Bank.

Yang, W. (2008). "Four Key Questions Regarding Urbanization with Chinese Characteristics." *Urban and Regional Planning Research*, *2*.

Zeng, G., & Wang, J. (2008). "International Comparisons in Urban-Rural Income Gaps." *Shangdong Social Sciences*, *10*.

Zhang, M., & Gu, C. (2002). "Rural Urbanization: A Comparative Study of 'Southern Jiangsu Model' and 'Pearl River Model.'" *Economic Geography*, *4*.

Zhao, Y., & Zhou, X. (2002). "Literature Review on China's Urbanization Path and Urbanization Theory since Reform and Opening Up." *China Social Sciences*, *2*.

Zhou, Q. (2011, November 5). *Agglomeration, Density, and Urbanization*. Speech at Media Transformation Forum, Sun Yat-sen University. Available at http://finance.qq.com/a/20121106/003433.htm

7 On the structure of class and stratum since China's reform

Chinese social structure is going through dramatic transformations, which manifest in demographic structure, urban and rural relation, employment, family and organizational structure, income distribution, lifestyle, and many other aspects. However, the change of the class structure is at the core content of social structural changes. After the reform and opening up, social structure changes in China are closely associated with policy alternations pertaining to the class and stratum.

Policy alternations pertaining to the class and stratum since the reform and opening-up

China's reform is in general seen as the market reform with the starting point of the reform of rural land contracting system. The story goes like this: in the winter of 1978, 18 farmers in Xiaogang Village, Fengyang, Anhui Province, took the risk in participating in the land contract responsibility by putting down their red handprints. This event is symbolic of the beginning of the rural reform. In fact, the prelude to reform, or the actual starting point, is to dismiss and repudiate the "class struggle as the central task." So the reform actually starts with a series of major adjustment surrounding class and stratum policies "to bring order out of chaos."

The analysis of interests of varied class and stratum has always been the basis for the Communist Party of China to formulate various lines, guidelines, and policies. In the early days of the Communist Party, Mao Zedong wrote *Analysis of the Classes in Chinese Society* based on his in-depth investigation into the rural areas. The article raised a primary question for the revolution by asking "who to rely upon, who to unite, and who to fight against." His article set the framework for the Communist Party of China during the democratic revolution period. The answers to "who to rely upon, who to unite, and who to fight against" also become then definitive line for Communist Party to distinguish class and stratum. After the foundation of the People's Republic of China in 1949, and upon the completion of the socialist transformation, the Communist Party of China held its Eighth National Congress in 1956, which stated that major domestic changes have proven that "the contradiction between the proletariat and the bourgeoisie in China has been resolved on the whole and the class exploitation system for thousands of years has basically ended."

China's major domestic contradiction is between people's demand for establishing an advanced industrial country and the reality of a backward agricultural country and between people's demand for rapid cultural and economic development and the reality that the current economy and culture cannot satisfy people's need.

Therefore, our country should enter a new stage of comprehensive construction of socialism. However, as the anti-rightist campaign escalated in 1957, China once again proposed that the proletariat vs. the bourgeoisie contradiction remains the principal contradiction in our society. This idea was soon absolutized, as it asserts that the bourgeoisie would exist throughout the historical period of socialism and try to stage a comeback, which would trigger the emergence of inner-party revisionism. As a result, class struggle needs to be repeated "year after year, month after month." These ideas served as the groundwork for "the theory of continuing the revolution under the dictatorship of the proletariat" and "route" in the "ten years of turmoil," which has engendered serious consequences in practice.

In the new period of reform and opening up since 1978, Deng Xiaoping put forward a series of important speeches, some of which had significant implications for the future conceptualization of the class and stratum structure. The first point is to switch the emphasis from "class struggle as the central task" to "economic construction as the core" (Deng, 1993, p.33). The second point is to eliminate equalitarianism and the practice of "common rice pot," and encourage some people and regions to get rich first through their labor (Deng, 1993, pp. 11, 155). The third point is that "the standard of judgment should be mainly to see whether it is conducive to the development of socialist productive forces, whether it is conducive to enhancing the comprehensive national strength of the socialist country, whether it is conducive to improving the living standards of the people" (Deng, 1993, p.110). Lastly, Deng urges China to take the path toward common prosperity (Deng, 1993, pp. 372–374). Although the reform practice of more than ten years has gradually perfected Deng's thoughts, they were put forward in the early stage of reform. Under the guidance of these ideas, the relationship between class and class has gone through a series of major adjustments in the initial reform stage.

The adjustments include as it follows (Hu, 1991, pp. 481–483). First, a large number of miscarriages of justice were vindicated. Millions of people have resumed their reputation from false accusations of being "counter-revolutionary," "capitalist roaders," "revisionists," and "gangster." Second, the label "stinking Number Nine" originated in "Cultural Revolution" was removed from the intellectuals who also restore their status as part of the working class, which corrected the wrongly cases that classify many intellectuals as "rightists."[1] Third, since January 1979 the labels "landlord," "rich peasant" and "capitalist" have also been removed from persons previously classified in those categories. They later regained the membership treatment of people's commune and their children were also classified as people's commune members. Fourth, since January 1979, China implemented policies concerning insurrectionary and surrendering personnel from the nationalist party and family members of Taiwan compatriots in the mainland. Meanwhile, it handled it with lenity and released former nationalist party cadres, military personnel, and special agents below the regiment level. Fifth, in the early 1980s, 700,000 out of 860,000 former industrialists and businessmen restored their laborer identities. Afterward, China specifically stipulated that former industrialists and businessmen were workers in the socialist society, and they fell into the membership of cadres or workers.

All these measures have brought major changes to the class and stratum relations so that the country can "unit as one in looking toward the future." They also motivate people from all walks of life to participate in the reform and opening up, and in constructing socialist society. These measures have expanded the mass foundation of the reform. These policy adjustments also imply a dismissal of the simplistic ideas from the "Cultural Revolution" that use "political thought" and "historical background" as the criteria for the class division.

The ensuing economic reform has engendered profound changes in the class and stratum structure, as well as the pattern of interests largely in three respects. First, the profound changes in ownership structure stimulate the non-public ownership economy to grow rapidly, which result in the formation of new social strata among private enterprise owners, individual industrial and commercial households, foreign investment and private enterprise senior management personnel and technical personnel. Second, industrialization and urbanization have turned more than 200 million farmers' professional identity into "new workers." Third, the scale of the middle stratum, which is connected to the modern economic society, has expanded rapidly, and social mobility has been greatly accelerated.

The rapid advancement of industrialization and urbanization push China to change from the traditional urban-rural dual structure to the modern social structure. The scale of population, the speed, and the degree of the social structural transformation is unprecedented in the world modernization history. Hundreds of millions of farmers leaving the land for nonagricultural industries and flooding into and concentrating in the cities form powerful driving forces for Chinese social structure transformation, which has greatly changed people's way of life and employment and the society as a whole.

Changes in social structure

As opposed to China's economic reform, changes in social structure have longer, deeper and wider implications.

Industrialization and urbanization process

Since the reform and opening up, as the economy grows rapidly, the industrial structure has also gone through swift changes. The proportion of the first, the second, and the tertiary industry in the total GDP rose from 31:45:24 in 1978 to 11.3: 48.6: 40.1 in 2008. During this period, China's service industry has increased rapidly, and the industry has also seen a smooth development, while the proportion of agriculture in the national economy has experienced a sharp decline. From the perspective of China's current industrial structure, China has reached the mid-industrialization stage.

Meanwhile, urbanization in China is booming. In 1949, when China was a freshly newborn nation, there was only 57 million in the urban population; the level of urbanization was at 10.6 percent, which was three percentage points lower than the 1900 world average. China was a typical agricultural country. From 1949 to 1978, the urbanization level increased gradually, which reached 19.7 percent in 1978, but the rate persistently stayed lower than 20 percent. After the reform and opening up, China's industrialization developed rapidly, which has accelerated the process of urbanization significantly. Within 29 years from 1940 to 1978, China's urbanization rate increased only by 7 percent, but in the 30 years from 1978 to 2008, it jumped by 26 percent from 19.7 percent to 45.7 percent. At present, there are 655 cities in China, 462 more than that in 1978. Among them, there are 118 metropolises and 39 megacities consisting of one million and above populations. China's urbanization lags behind the industrialization. For example, the current proportion of agricultural output accounted for only about 10 percent of GDP, but there are 45 percent of the total population employed in agriculture and 55 percent of the total population residing in rural areas. The lag of urbanization is closely associated with the household registration system in China, which causes huge gaps between the urban and the rural regions. Current urban household per capita income is about three times that of rural households, and the per capita income of nonagricultural workers is about five to six times that of farmers, which partially explains the emergence of China's 2.5 million migrant workers.

Changes in family and demographic structure

Historical changes have occurred to China's demographic structure – from the phase of a high birthrate, high mortality rate, and low growth rate, to the phase of a high birthrate, low mortality rate, and high growth rate, to current phase of a low birthrate, low mortality rate, and low growth rate. From 1952 to 2008, China's total population rose from 570 million to 1.328 billion, with the birthrate dropping from 37 percent to 12.14 percent, the mortality rate of 7.06 percent down from 17.00 percent, and the natural growth rate of 5.08 percent down from 20 percent. The main factors that lead to demographic transition include economic development, social transformation, and the family planning policy. Since the early 1970s, China implemented the family planning policy, and by the early 1980s, the policy of "one child for every couple" has been strictly carried out for urban residents. With a swift drop in the birthrate, China's demographic structure went through dramatic changes, as the total fertility rate of about 6 percent in the early 1970s dropped down to the current 1.8 percent, without which there would be 300 million more Chinese born to the land. Indices of social burden continue to decline, which has made great contributions to the Chinese economic and social development. However, at the same time, in less than 30 years, the Chinese age structure of population has moved from the expansive pyramid to stationary pyramid to constrictive pyramid. A 2005 survey of 1 percent of the Chinese population showed that 60-year-old and older people accounted for 12.9 percent of the total population and 65-year-old and above people accounted for 9.07 percent of the total population. The next few decades, China will see three peaks in the working age population, the total population, and the elderly population. According to estimates, the working age population from 15 to 64 years old will reach the peak of about 10.1 billion people in 2016. By 2030s, the total population will get to the spike of 1.5 billion, and by 2040s, the population 65 years of age and older will reach a peak of 3.2 billion.

Demographic transition results in significant changes to Chinese family structure and intergenerational structure. Nuclear family starts to dominate the population, with a gradual decline in the extended family and stem family. Household population dropped to 3.17 in 2006 from 4.41 in 1982. Changes in the intergenerational structure manifest in population size changes for each generation. In urban areas, the intergenerational structure 4–2–1 has gradually taken shape – namely, four grandparents, two parents, and one child, whereas in rural areas, the intergenerational structure is 4–2–2. The aging of population and the miniaturization of the family pose a daunting challenge to the traditional model that the family is obliged to support ever-aging parents.

Changes of regional development structure

A huge imbalance exists in Chinese regional development, which is not unprecedented, but it is intensified after the reform and opening up. China is geographically divided by a river (now the Heihe River) running from Aihui in northern Heilongjiang Province to Tengchong in southern Yunnan Province. It is also a population demarcation – about 94 percent of the population living in the region of southeast of the line which occupy 42.9 percent of the country's space while 6 percent of the population living on the northwestern side of the river which takes 57.1 percent of the country's space. The population distribution is related to natural conditions, because it is also a climate demarcation line which basically coincides with the 400 mm precipitation line, of which the northwestern region are areas of drought and little rain. Meanwhile, the river also indicates historical division, of which the southeastern territories are under long-term reign of Empires of in Central Plains throughout the history.

After the reform and opening up, the southeast coastal areas took the lead in opening up to the outside world. As the region develops rapidly, the regional development gap further widens. From 1978 to 2006, the ratio of the eastern, central, and western regional shares of GDP (with the western region as 1) changed from 2.36: 1.82: 1 to 3.17: 1.68: 1, and the ratio of per capital GDP (with westerner GDP per capita as 1) changed from 1.94: 1.20: 1 to 2. 63: 1. 23: 1. Overall, the gap between the western and the central regions is diminished but the gap between the eastern region and the rest of the country widens.

Change of ownership structure

Prior to the reform and opening up, China carried out a highly centralized planned economic system, pursuing a single public ownership system. There were basically only two forms of public ownership – namely, ownership by the whole people and collective ownership. Since the reform and opening up, the single public ownership economic system is challenged by the booming of individual economy and the appearance of private economy that have eight or more employees. As special economic zones are established and coastal areas open up to the world, foreign-funded enterprises emerge as the new economic sectors. The public-owned economy also diversifies, as many economic entities spring up across the urban and rural areas, across the boundaries of ownership, cross regions, and cross economic sectors. Now the new economic system is composed of a variety of economic sectors of state-owned economy, collective economy, individual economy, private economy, and other economic forms, which brings about a new ownership structure of keeping public ownership as the mainstay of the economy and allowing diverse forms of ownership to develop side by side.

The change of ownership structure and the fine division of social labor result in changes in and social strata, which not only is evident in employment categories but also manifests in social status, social prestige, lifestyle, income status, cultural level, consumption structure, and interpersonal communication and other aspects. Before the reform, the homogenous structure of professions and social strata prior to the reform has become more and more diversified. In current China, main professional groups include workers, cadres, agricultural workers, professional and technical personnel, staff, business managers, individual workers, private enterprise owners and so on. Social stratification and the diversification of enterprises generate multi-layers of benefit demand. The problems like the interest gap and the interest conflict and friction will become increasingly prominent. Over the past 30 years after reform and opening up, China has become a country with a large income gap from a country with a very evenly distributed income. According to statistical analysis of relevant departments and concerned scholars, the Gini coefficient, an indicator of the income distribution and concentration degree, after a brief dip in the early years of the reform and opening up, continues to climb since 1985, rising from 0.25 in 1984 to 0.49 in 2006.

Change of organizational structure

Before the reform and opening up, the government manages the society and individuals through basic institutions composed of pervasive "work units," which include state organs, non-profit sectors, enterprises and rural people's communes. "Work unit" is not only the workplace but also a community of living and social management. As "work unit" is in charge of nearly all aspects of personnel's life, from birth, illness, to aging and death, members of the "work unit" rely heavily on the work unit. In this case, protecting social life, managing social behavior, regulating social relations, and solving all the problems that occurred in social life are mediated and carried out mainly through the "work unit." Personnel and resources are locked within "work units," so the society lacks mobility and vitality. When the reform and opening up took off in 1978, China has more than 400 million "social workers." Among them, less than 0.04 percent worked outside the institution of the "work unit" (viz. 150,000 self-employed urban residents), and a vast majority of workers were affiliated with an array of "work units," including 74 million employees in the "units under the ownership by the whole people" and more than 20 million workers for "units urban collective-owned enterprises," as well as 300 million "social workers" in the villages who were all "members" of "people's communes." Since the reform and opening up, as ownership structure varies, a large number of "non-work-unit organizations" have emerged, which normally adopt a market appointment system. At present, more than 60 percent of urban employees work in the "non-work-unit organizations," while almost all rural laborers have broken away from the "work-unit institution" thanks to the disintegration of the people's commune and the implementation of the household contract responsibility system.

Moreover, with the reforms in government functions and social institutions, the original management scope of the "work unit institution" has shrank badly, especially after the privatization of housing, the socialization of social security, and the marketization of employment and logistics service. The basic unit of social management has also changed from "work unit" oriented to "community oriented," which greatly stimulated the demand for community service. Thus community construction that mainly serves the place of residence mushrooms everywhere. Thanks to changes in social management, a variety of grassroots organizations that link individuals to the government develop rapidly. According to the statistics released by the Ministry of Civil Affairs, at the beginning of the reform and opening up, there were only more than 2000 registered mass organizations in China. However, until the end of 2008, legal social organizations in China exceeded 413,700, which have 4.75 million full-time staff and about 5 million part-time employees, and more than 25 million registered volunteers. There are 200,000 social organizations in the records from the civil affairs departments at the levels of the urban, the rural, and the communities, and more than 1 million off-the-record organizations. Nowadays, the social organization grows by 10 percent to 15 percent every year, playing an increasingly important role in the society.

Changes to the class and stratum structure and the benefits distribution pattern

Marketization, ownership restructuring, and changes in the pattern of interests, all precipitate the social and economic stratification and cause profound changes to the structure of class and stratum.

Changes in social class and stratum

Before the reform and opening up, the social class structure of our country is mainly composed of two classes and on stratum – namely, the working class, the peasant class, and the intellectuals. After the reform and opening up, a differentiation occurred: migrant workers, individual business owners, the owners of private enterprises, and managerial personnel in a range of private companies and non-public enterprise all spring from the class or stratum they originally belonged. As professionals, personnel, or staff at the state organs, social groups and all kinds of enterprises and institutions, former intellectuals have obtained new, relatively independent social roles and status in the new labor relations (Lu, 2001).

From a perspective that combines the class analysis that is based on resource-possession and the stratum analysis that is based on professions, there are ten clear-cute categories of social class and strata in contemporary China. They are national and social administrators, managers, private owners, professional and technical personnel, service personnel, individual industrial and commercial households, commercial service workers, industrial workers, agricultural work-ers, and the unemployed or underemployed. According to the 1 percent national population sample survey from 2005, as well as statistics from State Industry & Commerce Administration and other departments, the social hierarchy in the urban and rural areas in 2005 is roughly as Figure 7.1 presents.

We may draw some preliminary conclusions from Figure 7.1 concerning the changes in social class and stratum in China. First, the urban social hierarchy dif-fers significantly from the rural one. Second, the rural social hierarchy is the shape of "pyramid," with a disproportionately huge base and an undersized middle rung. Third, the social hierarchy structure should proceed from the "pyramid-shaped" structure of the rural areas to the "olive-shaped" structure of the urban areas.

After the reform, the rapid development of industrialization and urbanization has accelerated industrial structural transformation. From 1978 to 2008, the share of China's first, second, and third industry in the GDP has changed from 31: 45: 24 to 11.3: 48.6: 40.1 in 2008. The outcome, however, is that a large number of farmers moved to the urban areas and changed the professional identity. While the employment rate of industries that focus on the material production slows down, the employment of finance, insurance, real estate, tourism, consulting, radio, television,

Distribution of Social Stratum in Rural and Urban Areas

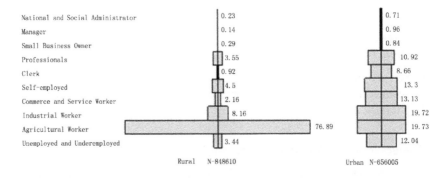

Figure 7.1 China's social stratum structure (2005)

Source: National Sample Survey Data 1% by National Bureau of Statistics in 2005.

as well as a variety of service and utilities and other nonmaterial production sectors, expands rapidly. From 1978 to 1993, the proportion of primary industry employment dropped from 70.5 percent to 39.6 percent, the number of employees in the secondary industry increased to 27.2 percent from 17.4 percent, and the number of employees in the tertiary industry rose to 33.2 percent from 12.1 percent.

The development of industrialization has greatly propelled urbanization. In 29 years, from 1949 to 1978, China's urbanization level increased by only seven percentage points. However, in 30 years, from 1978 to 2008, the urbanization level of China increased from 19.7 percent to 45.7 percent, 26 percent higher than that of 1978. This is a remarkably accelerating urbanization pace. At present, there are 655 cities in China, 462 more than that in 1978. Among them, there are 118 metropolises and 39 megacities of one million and above populations. Urban economic strength continues to grow, as cities at the prefecture level and above generate 63 percent of the GDP.

The group of "farmers" in the traditional sense has experienced the most dramatic changes since the reform. Until the end of 2008, according to the household registration system, agricultural population accounted for 60 percent of Chinese total population, based on the location of residence, the rural population made up 45.7 percent of the total population, and based on professional categories, agricultural workers was only about 39.6 percent of the total number of employees. In China, the concept of "farmer" used to include anyone who registered as "rural resident" in the household registration system and who did not have the access to the commodity grain consumption system – namely, undistinguishable "members of people's commune."[2] Since the reform, deep vocational differentiations have occurred to the traditional "farmer" category. While the "agricultural population" to a large extent has become the concept referred to the status in the household registration or the residential area, in reality, this category covers agricultural laborers, workers at township and village enterprises, migrant workers, rural workers, rural science and technology, culture and education of medical workers, rural individual industrial and commercial households, rural private entrepreneurs, managerial personnel at the TVEs, and rural administrative cadres and so on. Each group can be further divided into a number of subgroups based on the possession of income, wealth, and production means, or the status and occupational prestige. For instance, agricultural laborers can be divided into big business, by business, household and cooperative farmers, small farmers, and others. With ever more social mobility and the declining in the return of agricultural laboring, the trend of aging of farmers is increasingly noticeable. Rural youth normally migrate out working and agricultural laborers left behind are less and less. The living conditions as shown in the comprehensive survey of social conditions in 2008 are as follows in Table 7.1.

Changes in the class and stratum structure have the following three characteristics. First, thanks to industrial structure changes, both the proportion and the social influence of professionals associated with modern economy are reinforced. Moreover, there are more than 200 million farmers-turned-workers. Second, profound professionalization has led to a multiplication of social strata within a single class, which have varied economic status and interest. Income, status, and reputation that previously overlapped are split from each other. Lastly, after the reform of

Table 7.1 Social strata distribution of different birth cohorts based on current or final position (%)

Birth Cohort	Civil Servants and the Managers at the State-Owned Enterprises	Private Enterprise Owners and Managers	Professionals (Intellectuals)	Working Class	Self-employed	Peasants	Total
1938–1956 (Age of 52–70)	8.04	0.51	4.19	25.07	4.98	57.22	100
1957–1965 (Age of 43–51)	7.13	0.86	2.66	33.67	10.26	45.42	100
1966–1976 (Age of 32–42)	6.41	1.45	4.46	35.71	12.53	39.44	100
1977–1991 (Age of 17–31)	6.39	1.17	3.26	55.15	8.21	25.81	100

Source: 2008 CGSS, CASS.
Note: The age range of birth cohort refers to the age as of 2008.

ownership structure, a new stratum emerges composed of by private business own-ers and managers who possess certain amount of production materials.

Changes in interest pattern

Shifts in the structure of the class and stratum have brought profound changes to the established interest pattern. The reform is actually part of the process for interest pattern adjustment.

After the reform, family- and enterprise-based independent interest subjects appear thanks to the rural household contract and urban enterprise contract man-agement responsibility systems. Community- and region-oriented independent interest subjects emerge from "decentralizing" financial system and the imple-mentation of "serving meals to different diners from different pots" policy.[3] After the unitary public ownership system is broken down, and as multiple ownership systems coexist, individual and private-owned business, three types of foreign-funded enterprises and TVEs all become different interest subjects. State-owned enterprises become closer to relatively independent interest subjects because of "contracting system," "substitution of tax payment for profit delivery," "replac-ing direct financial allocation with loans," shareholding system reforms, and the abolition of mandatory plans and quota. A large number of public institutions join the free market and adopt means of enterprise management become keen aware of their interest subjectivity. In addition, the policy that "let some people get rich first through the labor" disrupts the deep-seated embrace of absolute equalitarianism," thus labor efficiency become more indicative labor income of than labor time. Lastly, validation and legal protection of the dividend, interest, and other capital gains acknowledge their legality, so the share of capital-based distribution in the income distribution grows. Among income influential factors, inherent factors like position, technical level, length of service, industry, and region still play their due roles, but work-unit distributions, enterprise economic benefits, and shareholding status become important new variables in determining income level.

A profound change in the interest pattern is a widening income gap between different classes and groups.

With regard to the urban-rural division, the ratio of urban and rural resident per capita income (urban household per capita disposable income / rural farmer per capita net income) expands from 1.72: 1 in 1985 to 3.33: 1 in 2008.

As far as regions are concerned, the average income of workers used to be higher in the western and remote regions prior to the reform, but now it is significantly lower than that in the eastern region. In 2008, the highest income among China's provinces (cities and districts) is in Shanghai and the lowest is in Jiangxi Province. The average income of a worker in Shanghai is 2.7 years higher than his/her counterpart in Jiangxi.

When it comes to different industries, heavy industry and material production sector do not show obvious advantage, and the average income is higher in the financial industry, real estate, IT industry, and lower in manufacturing and mining industry.

The phenomenon of "equal wages yet great disparity in income" is particularly noteworthy since all kinds of "hidden income," "extra-wage income," "income from a second job," "income in kind," and "business treatment" are influential factors to divide urban income level.

Income gap between different social class and strata continues to expand. The Gini coefficient, an indicator to measure the income distribution and concentration degree, after a brief dip in the initial years of the reform and opening up, has continued to climb since 1985, rising from 0.25 in 1984 to 0.47 in 2005, and reached 0.5 or so in 2008 (see Figure 7.2).

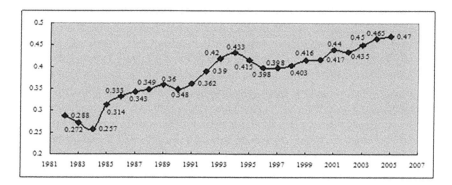

Figure 7.2 Trend of Gini coefficient of the income distribution in China (1982–2006)

Source: The Gini Coefficient from 1982 to 1999 is from Bi Xianping and Jian Xinhua (2002). The Gini Coefficient from 2000 to 2005 is from the data released by the National Bureau of Statistics. Gini coefficient of 2006 is based on the 2006 national sample survey conducted by this research project.

Questions for researches of Chinese class and stratum

An expanding income gap: periodical characteristic or part of a long trend

Regarding the relationship between income distribution and economic growth, American economist Simon Kuznets in mid-1950s proposed now the famous "inverted U-shaped hypothesis" based materials about limited number of countries from 1854 to 1950. The U-shaped hypothesis is almost regarded as a proven "law" in the development economics. According to the hypothesis, the long-term income distribution trend is presented as an inverted U-shaped curve. At the initial stage of economic development when the amount of wealth in the society is limited, the income distribution is in relatively fair fashion. When industrialization kicks in, inequality deteriorates in the rural areas and the income gap is getting wider because savings and wealth accumulation which are of particular import for economic growth are in the hands of a small number of wealthy class and urban workers have a higher income. A transient stable period ensues. As the country enters the later stage of economic growth reaching a higher level of development, the income gap gradually narrows down thanks to reforms in the property tax (particularly the progressive income tax and inheritance tax) and social welfare system as well as more heightened social mobility and an expanding middle-income class (Kuznets, 1955). The hypothesis, on one hand, is partially verified by cross-sectional and synchronic comparatives studies on in multiple nations. Statistics show that the turning point for the narrower income gap occurs when middle- and low-income countries develop into upper-middle-income countries. On the other hand, the hypothesis is also verified by longitudinal, diachronic comparative studies about a fraction of countries. Data analysis shows that the income gap in European developed countries narrowed down after the WWII, while the income distribution in some Latin American countries escalated rapidly in 1960 to 1970 when the economies developed at a high speed (Chen, 1994).

There are many different explanations to the causes of the U-shaped curve. Scholars who focus on class power believe that the deterioration of income distribution leads to intense social conflict which gives rise to the labor movement that exert significant political pressure on increasing labor wages and to a certain degree curbing the unlimited expansion of capital income. For scholars who stress the impact of the demand-supply relationship on the income distribution, the turning point of income distribution implies that prior to this point, the scarce capital and excessive labor in the elements supply lead to a higher capital income and lower labor income. Therefore, the income difference between the labor and capital continues to widen. However, after the turning point, capital becomes abundant and capital income starts to decline, and meanwhile labor force with improved quality become scarce and thus labor income starts to grow. Therefore, the average income gap also begins to reduce. Many scholars also believe that economic growth and income equality, like efficiency and equity, is substitute for each other. For countries that expect to have a rapid economic growth, an expanding income gap is the heavy yet inevitable price they have to pay. From a historical perspective, great economic development has always been associated with the prospect and the outcome of a big windfall gain. Along this line, the welfare distribution theory suggests that the solution to inequality is to make the welfare cake bigger through rapid economic development, so that there would be more surplus available for distribution and the state intervention into redistribution could be more effective.

The empirical challenge against Kuznets' inverted U-shaped hypothesis is from the development reality in the East Asia emerging industrial countries and regions. From 1960 to 1982, Singapore, South Korea, Hong Kong, and Taiwan have experienced rapid growth after economic takeoff. At the same time, the GNP per capita annual average growth rate is about 7 percent, but the income gap in the same period did not appear sharp deterioration, and in most cases, it was improved. With an exception to South Korea where the Gini coefficient grew slightly from 0.34 in 1964 to 0.38 in 1976, the Gini coefficient in Singapore, Hong Kong, and Taiwan, dropped from 0.49 in 1966 to 0.45 in 1980, 0.48 in 1966 to 0.47 in 1981, and 0.47 in 1961 to 0.3 in 1980, respectively (Fields, 1984). The situation in Taiwan is even more special as the income gap appears as a "U" shaped trend.

The per capita income of Taiwan was $186 in 1952, the gap between the top 20 percent and the bottom 20 percent is 20.47 times, which reduced to 11.56 times in 1961, 5.33 times in 1964 down, further down to 4.21 times in 1981, but when per capita income reached $2,500 in 1981, the income gap began to gradually expand, getting to 5.24 times in 1992 (Directorate-General of Budget, Accounting and Statistics, 1993). If such factors as family properties and rising property price in Taiwan are taken into consideration, the widening trend of the actual gap in wealth distribution is more salient.

China's development in the recent ten years have shown that against the backdrop of the long growth cycle, China is in transition period developing from a low-income country to a middle-income country, so it is characterized by the growing income gap which is also in line with the general economic rule. However, since the urban-rural income gap and regional income disparity are the main reasons for the overall income gap, the trend of an ever-growing disparity cannot be reversed in a short period. Consequently, the periodical characteristic of a widening income gap will persist for a long time. Furthermore, what sets China apart from other countries is the fact that income disparity in the rural areas is greater than that in the city. Therefore, urbanization in China, be it rural nonagriculturalization or the development of small towns or farmers migrating to cities for employment, is conducive to narrowing down the income gap, rather than the other way round. Finally, the income gap in China is so huge that it undermines social fairness and justice, triggers intense dissatisfaction among people. It is the deep-seated cause for many social problems, so China must adopt measures with regard to finance, taxation, social security and others to reverse the trend of an ever-increasing income gap.

Whether the introduction of the market mechanism caused worsening income disparity

Classical economists generally recognize that income inequality is an inevitable price paid for the market mechanism whose fundamental power refuses to yield to governmental intervention. Economics is a "dismal science that concerns the unchangeable distribution of income" because labor wages, land rent and capital profit are determined by the laws of the market, instead of political forces. If the state attempts to alter the rules by exerting its coercive power, the possible outcome is that the "pie" of the overall production gets smaller and the smaller "pie" might still be subject to the established way of distribution. Neo-classical economists are more inclined to believe that under the economic system of laissez-faire, the inequality and poverty circumstance in the Western industrialized countries in the nineteenth century may indeed be the same or even more terrible than the descriptions by Charles Dickens and other social criticism novelists. Later on, a series of reforms, such as antitrust legislations, a progressive income tax, unemployment insurance, social insurance, and monetary and fiscal policy that stabilize economy, and the establishment of all kinds of welfare systems, all contribute to facilitating the transition from a laissez-faire economic system to a mixed market economy system. These measures have leveled the ground, conducive to diminish extreme income disparity. Although the disparity in economic benefits may still be considerable, the era of "mass consumption" is finally here (Gillis & Perkins, 1989, pp. 93–96). The two aforementioned schools have notable disagreement on the role of the state intervention, but share their acknowledgment that the spontaneous role of the market mechanism will exacerbate the income inequality.

In recent years, Western scholars who are interested in Eastern Europe and China's reforms have different opinions based on a number of comparative studies. Among typical differing ideas is from some sociologists who suggest a "new institutionalism" theoretical framework. They argue that as socialist countries transform from a planned economy of "redistribution" to a market economy, the devolution of power effectively stimulate direct producers. A new pattern of opportunities emerge from the market, which has transferred the distribution from "redistribution" from the top to the market at the grassroots, so when the economy is transforming toward the market economy, the market mechanism is conducive to the weakening the income inequality (Stark & Nee, 1989, pp. 12–13). However, this point of view has not confirmed by statistical analysis of the long cycle of economic development.

Over the 30 years since China's reform and opening up, with the introduction and expansion of the market mechanism, the income gaps in urban areas, in rural areas, and between the urban and the rural areas have narrowed down initially before expanding. However, we can never jump to the conclusion that as economy in transition the impact of the market on the income gaps is positive in the early stage and turns to be negative later on, simply because associations do not mean causal relationship. For example, currently in China, the urban marketization level is higher than that in the rural areas, but the income gap between rural residents is greater than that of urban residents. In Zhejiang Province where the level of economic development and marketization is both higher than the national average, the income gap is lower than the national average.

What on earth is "social justice"

The understanding of "social justice" varies at different historical period and among different social classes who have different values. Generally, speaking, the connotation of social justice is determined by the shared values of the great majority of the people, but at the transitional period, people's values would go through profound changes and some basic social consensus would be shaken. So there are diverse understandings of what "social justice" means. For instance, how Chinese scholars understand "social justice" is as follows:

- The core of the social justice is economic equality, including equality in income and wealth, and any form of income disparity and difference in wealth possession is considered as the beginning of the "polarization."
- Social justice essentially is not the absolute economic equality, but the equality accommodating to people's needs, which means "equal treatment to the same people and different treatment to different people."
- Current social justice is measured by the standard of "distribution on the basis of labor" but it by no means is based on labor time, or rather is based on labor quality, efficiency and the actual output profits. Therefore, that remuneration differs even for the same amount of labor time is a natural outcome.
- Social justice conforms to the existing laws, which means everyone is equal before the law. Therefore, the legitimate distribution is reasonable distribution, legal income is reasonable income, and the income gap is reasonable as long as it is abided by the law.
- Social justice is different from fair market. While fair market is to foster production efficiency that is based on competition and improve the efficiency of resources allocation, social justice is to maintain social unity and promote social harmony and stabile development.

To grasp the meanings of social justice better, we must distinguish the concept of "social justice" from the concepts of "economic equality" and "equal opportunity."

"Economic equality" means that refers to the distribution of income, possession of wealth, and the distribution of welfare benefits as a whole. It indicates the distribution situation that is objective and measurable.

"Equal opportunities" suggest that what determines one's share in the current economic and social distributions are "achieved" factors, such as individual efforts and fair environment, instead of "ascribed" factors, such as family background and social status. As individuals differ in their talents and competences, even when equal opportunities are provided, the outcome of competition varies from person to person.

"Social justice" is based on common values that reflect certain social consensus on the basic rights of survival and development. It serves as a living principle that guides human beings to survive and protects them from social conflicts and collapse at times of scarcity. It is also the morality cornerstone for social order and institution.

The issue of "social justice" involves wealth possession, income distribution, the acquisition of power and rights, social status and prestige, the access to education opportunities, and professional options, and so on. In a word, it involves the allocation of all social resources and social welfare. Meanwhile, social justice does not only merely refer to the outcome of social welfare allocation. More importantly, it means equal opportunity of development – that is to say, people's access to development opportunities (e.g., education, employment) should never be restricted by family background, gender, race, status, and capital possession. Equality of opportunity for development is an important warrant for social justice. Moreover, social justice, in certain sense, makes up for market deficiency and restricts excessive competition. However, social justice is not the opposite of competition and efficiency since social justice and economic efficiency are not mutually exclusive. It is unimaginable that a society can operate properly based on values incompatible as fire and water. The social justice mechanism should be conducive to improving and maintaining the efficiency and effectiveness of resources allocation. If social justice were maintained at the cost of efficiency, then it is no more than encouraging laziness and back to the days of "common rice pot." Along this line, the "common rice pot" institution represents a type of "social injustice."

How to understand "middle class" and "xiaokang mass"

In sociological studies, "middle class" is always a concept of lasting glamor and of many disputes. Although scholars have conducted numerous research on almost every respect of middle class, including occupation, income, education and prestige, consumption, gender, race, tastes, identification, social and political attitudes, these findings seem keep raising new challenges, but fail to come to a consensus (Bulter & Savage, 1995). In spite of their different, or even opposite approaches toward the definition and operational measurement of middle class, scholar tend to agree on occupational classification as the most significant indicator for the middle class (Goldthorpe, 1990; Erikson & Goldthorpe, 1993; Wright, 1997). Empirical studies present different conclusions on the role of middle class in that while some show that the middle class is an important driving force for contemporary social change, some show that the middle class is the steadfast supporter of the traditional order (Goldthorpe, 1982). Some studies show that the middle class is a stable and progressive force for industrialization (Kerr, Dunlop, Harbison & Myers, 1973), while others show that middle class represents the radical force for democratization.

The important role played by the middle class in social changes in the new industrial countries and regions in East Asia has also attracted widespread attention from sociologists. However, empirical studies in South Korea, Singapore,

Taiwan, and Hong Kong also reveal that the middle class is both radical and conservative (Lv & Wang, 2003).

China is currently going through the world's largest social transformation in the history of modernization, which is featured by its intricacy in the context of globalization. Industrialization, urbanization, marketization, and internationalization all come together. Economic system transition and social structural transformation happen all at once. In the meantime, the capital accumulation required in the early stage of industrialization concurs with the demand for industrial upgrading in the midst of industrialization and the need for environmental governance in the latter stage of industrialization. These characteristics of complexity also pose some peculiar challenges for the middle-class studies.

First, the proportion of the middle class is small, and the definition of the group is not clear. On the one hand, China's urbanization level lags far behind the industrialization level, which reached about 90 percent (the share of industrial and service industry output in GDP) in 2009 when the former was only about 45 percent. This reality implies prematurely that the middle class is an "urban community" in China. On the other hand, the Chinese economy is predominantly driven by industries, whereas the share of the service industry in GDP and the share of employment lingered around 30 percent in the past few years. This also contradicts to the corresponding relationship between the middle class as "service population" and the level of economic development. It is estimated that the Chinese middle class makes up about 12 percent of the population and about 25 percent of the urban population.

Second, social transformation causes inconsistence between economic status and political standing. If defined by professions, Chinese middle class is on the low side of economic status, which also runs counter to the public perception and differs from the definition adopted by business institutions based on consumption level or habit.

Third, given the great urban-rural gap, the middle class defined by professions does not tally with social perceptions of people at "middle" rung, if not a complete divergent. For instance, nearly 42 percent of the migrant workers believe that they belong to "the middle stratum of the society."

There is a big difference between the social structure of China and that of the Western society, so the future of social direction and mass consumption may be subject to "xiaokang mass" (well-off mass) instead of the so-called middle class in China. For a long period, it was very difficult for the "middle class" to become the main social subject in China. "Xiaokang" is a description of a relatively well-off life in China. To achieve an overall well-off society is China's development goal by 2020. "Xiaokang mass" should include 80 percent of the population from the middle stratum. Sustained economic growth, accumulation of and increase in total welfare, expansion and radiation of the urban society, the improvement in rural surplus labor force transfer and labor productivity, and a rational income distribution system, undoubtedly, all pave the way for the rise of "xiaokang mass." At the current moment, more attention should be paid to enable the working class to obtain a certain amount of family-fixed assets and financial assets and agricultural workers to obtain a certain amount of production materials and development funds on their own. In short, it is to enable them to gain certain compensations beyond labor income, under the circumstance of an ever-growing added value from capital. In China, the historical cycle of order and disorder with a large time span has proven that "leave wealth with the people" can be an effective policy to foster social stability.

How to assess the role of "migrant workers" in the future of development

In China, "migrant works" refers to the labor force transferred from agriculture to non-agriculture whose identities in the household registration system say "farmers" but who work in nonagricultural sectors and rely on wages for a living. On January 18, 2006, when China's State Council promulgated the document titled "Opinions of State Council on Settling the Issue of Migrant Workers," the term migrant workers was written into central government's administrative regulations for the first time. There are two groups of migrant workers, those who work for nearby township and village enterprises (TVEs), known as "leaving the land without leaving the village" for one, and those who leave the hometown for jobs elsewhere, known as "migrant rural workers."

Over the past decade, the "migrant workers" in China has been a hot-button issue in academia and for policy makers and the press. In the initial stage of the reform before 1984, the main channel for the Chinese rural labor to nonagricultural industries is through TVEs. It is characterized by "leaving the land but not the villages and into the factory but not the city," which was once called "Chinese way of urbanization." In 1984, the government loosened the restrictions on farmers moving to cities, which ushered in an era of massive migrant workers working in the cities. From 1985 to 1990, there were 3.35 million farmers migrating out from the countryside whereas TVEs absorbed 22.86 million workers. Therefore, TVEs were the main means for nonagriculturalization. Things were drastically different from 1990 to 1995. According to a number of large-scale national sample surveys, migrant workers made up about 15 percent of the total rural labor force, which meant more than 66 million people in 1995, but over the same period of time, TVEs employed an additional 27.5 million people. TVEs' capacity to absorb rural labor began to shrink, while the number rural workers migrating to the cities kept growing rapidly. According to the statistics released in 2004 by China National Bureau of Statistics which was based on 68,000 the rural households and 7,100 administrative villages in 31 provinces (regions and municipalities), the number of migrant workers was about 120 million, 24 percent of the rural labor force. When rural employees at TVEs were included, the migrant workers in 2004 were about 200 million, with an average age of 28, the vast majority of whom were with a junior high school education or below, and who were mainly employed in manufacturing, construction, and service industry (Research Center of State Department, 2006, pp. 3–4). Because of its mobility, it is difficult to provide an accurate number of migrant workers. At present, a widely accepted estimate is 250 million, including 150 million of those working and doing businesses in the cities.

Migrant workers are facing daunting challenges in the future phase of development.

First, as China has entered the middle stage of industrialization, industrial structure will continue to upgrade, the contribution of technological progress to the economic growth will be increasingly prominent, the requirement of techno-logical quality from the labor force will become higher, to which migrant workers may not be able to adapt.

Second, with the development of urbanization in China, the impact of an aging population, and changes in the labor supply, the era of cheap labor in China will gradually come to an end. The future economic development must achieve the transformation from being "made in China" to "designed in China." The compar-ative advantage will come from the quality of China's labor force. Survey analysis has indicated that the educational level and technological competence of migrant workers are still generally lower than their counterparts in urban areas, which has a decisive impact on the former's income level.

Third, as massive migrant workers out from agriculture to industry and service industry, from the countryside to the city, they have been awash in the industri-alization and urbanization and their lives and social attitude have went through profound changes, and so has the entire social structure. The entire social manage-ment institution needs to accommodate for these changes, as do migrant workers.

Over the past 30 years, migrant workers' work, life, and social attitudes are significant influential factor for the overall China's economic and social develop-ment. It would be the same for the future 30 years.

Since the reform and opening up, changes in Chinese social structure are extremely far-reaching. The development trend built upon these changes will determine China's future.

Notes

This chapter was originally published in *Heilongjiang Social Sciences*, 2011, issue 1.

1 Translator's note: the term "stinking Number Nine" or "stinking ninth category" refers to class enemies next to landlords, reactionaries, and even spies, etc., a term of abuse by ultra-Leftists for teachers and other educated people in the 1966–1976 Chinese Cultural Revolution.
2 Translator's note: the system of commodity grain consumption and the agricultural grain consumption is a constructed binary between the urban and rural residents under the household registration system. Generally speaking, only those urban residents are entitled to the commodity grain consumption system.
3 Translator's note: "Serving meals to different diners from different pots" refers to the measures taken for the financial reform – namely, dividing revenue and expenditure between the central and local governments and holding each responsible for balancing their budgets.

References

Asian Development Bank. (2007). *The 2007 Key Indicators: The Uneven Distribution of Asia*. Beijing: People's Publishing House.

Atkinson, A. B., & Bourguignon, F. (1982). "The Comparison of Multidimensional Distributions of Economic Status." *Review Economic Studies, 49*, 183–201.

Bi, X., & Jian, X. (2002). "On the Relationship between Economic Structural Changes and the Income Distribution Gap." *Economic Review, 8.*

Bian, Y., & Logan, J. R. (1996). "Market Transition and the Persistence of Power: The Changing Stratification System in Urban China." *American Sociological Review, 61*, 739–758.

Bian, Y., & Zhang, Z. (2002). "Marketization and Income Distribution – An Examination into Urban Resident Incomes in 1988 and 1995." *Social Sciences in China, 5.*

Bulter, T., & Savage, M. (Eds.). (1995). *Social Change and the Middle Class.* London: UCL Press.

Cai, F., & Wang, D. (2003). "Migration as Marketization, What Can We Learn from China's 2000 Census Data?" *The China Review, 3*(2), 73–93.

Cai, F., & Wang, M. (2002). "How Fast Does Chinese Economy Grow?" *Expanding Horizons, 4.*

Campbell, K. E. (1986). "Social Resources and Socioeconomic Status." *Social Networks, 8*, 97–117.

Chen, G., & Yi, Y. (2004). *An Investigation into Chinese Middle Class.* Beijing: Tuanjie Press.

Chen, J., & Huang, Q. (2007). *The Report on Chinese Industrialization.* Beijing: Social Science Academic Press.

Chen, Z. (1994). *The Income Distribution in Economic Development.* Shanghai: SDX Joint Publishing Company and Shanghai People's Publishing House.

Chen, Z. (2002). *A Reconsideration on the Income Distribution in the Economic Development.* Beijing: Economic Science Press.

Deng, X. (1993). *Deng Xiaoping on the Construction of Socialism with Chinese Characteristics.* Beijing: The Central Committee of the Communist Party Press.

Directorate-General of Budget, Accounting and Statistics. (1993). *Taiwan Statistical Data Book.* Taiwan: Executive Yuan.

Erikson, R., & Goldthorpe, J. H. (1993). *The Constant Flux: A Study of Class Mobility in Industrial Societies.* Oxford: Clarendon Press.

Eyal, G., Szelenyi, I., & Townsky, E. (1998). *Making Capitalism without Capitalist: Class Formation and Elite Struggles in Post-Communist Central Europe.* London: Verso.

Fields, G. S. (1984). "Employment Income Distribution and Economic Growth in Seven Small Open Economics." *Economic Journal, 94*(373), 74–83.

Gillis, M., & Perkins, D. H. (1989). *Economics of Development.* Beijing: Economic Science Press.

Goldthorpe, J. H. (1982). "On the Service Class, Its Formation and Future." In A. Giddens & G. MacKenzie (Eds.), *Classes and the Division of Labour: Essays in Honor of Ilya Neustadt* (pp. 162–185). Cambridge: Cambridge University Press.

Goldthorpe, J. H. (1990). "A Response." In J. Clark, C. Modgil & S. Modgil (Eds.), *Consensus and Controversy* (pp. 399–440). London: Falmer Press.

Hao, D., & Li, L. (2006). "State Monopoly and Income Inequality in Regional Disparity Reform: Based on National Comprehensive Social Survey Data 2003." *Social Sciences in China, 2.*

Hu, B., Lai, J., & Hu, B. (2007). "Economic Growth, Income Distribution and Poverty Alleviation – Evidence from Rural China: 1985–2003." *The Journal of Quantitative & Technical Economics, 5.*

Hu, L., & Hu, A. (2007). "Middle Class: 'Stabilizing Engine' or the Opposite or Others – Review on Western Researches on the Social and Political Functions of the Middle Class." *Social Sciences in China (Internal Publication)*, 6.

Hu, S. (1991). *Seventy Years of Chinese Communist Party*. Beijing: Chinese Communist Party History Press.

Jones, D. C., Li, C., & Owen, A. L. (2003). "Growth and Regional Inequality in China during the Reform Era." *China Economic Reviews*, *14*, 186–200.

Kacapyr, E., Francese, P., & Crispell, D. (1996, October). "Are You Middle Class? – Definitions and Trends of U.S. Middle Class Households." *American Demographics*.

Kerr, C., Dunlop, J. T., Harbison, F., & Myers, C. A. (1973). *Industrialism and Industrial Man*. Harmondsworth: Penguin Books.

Khan, A. R., Griffin, K., & Riskin, C. (1999). "Income Distribution in Urban China during the Period of Economic Reform and Globalization." *American Economic Review*, *89*(2).

Kolm, S. (1977, February). "Multidimensional Egalitarianisms." *The Quarterly Journal of Economics*, *91*(1), 1–13.

Koo, H. (2001). *The Culture and Politics of Class Formation*. New York: Cornell University Press.

Krueger, A. (1992). *Economic Policy Reform in Developing Countries*. Oxford: Basil Blackwell.

Krugman, P. (1995). "The Myth of Asian Miracle." *Foreign Affairs*, *73*, 62–78.

Kuznets, S. (1955, March). "Economic Growth and Income Inequality." *American Economic Review*, *45*(1).

Lenski, G. (1996). *Power and Privilege: A Theory of Social Stratification*. New York: McGraw Hill.

Li, C. (2005). *Fracture and Fragmentation: Empirical Analysis of Social Stratification in Contemporary China*. Beijing: Social Science Academic Press.

Li, L. (2002). "Institutional Transformation and Changes in Stratification Structure: Dual Reproduction of the Pattern of Relative Inter-strata Relations." *Social Sciences in China*, 6.

Li, P. (Ed.). (1995). *Report on Chinese Class and Stratum in the New Era*. Shenyang: Liaoning People's Publishing House.

Li, P., Li, Q., & Sun, L. (2004). *China's Social Stratification*. Beijing: Social Science Academic Press.

Li, P., Zhang, Y., Zhao, Y., & Liang, D. (2005). *Social Conflict and Class Consciousness*. Beijing: Social Science Academic Press.

Li, Q. (2005). "T-shaped Social Structure and 'Structural Tension.'" *Sociological Research*, 2.

Li, Q. (2008). *Ten Lessons on Social Stratification*. Beijing: Social Science Academic Press.

Li, S. (2003). "Review and Prospect on Studies of Chinese Individual Income Distribution." *China Economic Quarterly*, *2*(2).

Li, S., Zhang, P., Wei, Z., & Zhong, J. (2000). *Empirical Analysis of Chinese Household Income Distribution*. Beijing: Social Science Academic Press.

Li, S., & Zhao, R. (2004). "Reconsidering Chinese Household Income Distribution." *Economic Research Journal*, 4.

Lin, J., Wang, G., & Zhao, Y. (2004). "Regional Inequality and Labor Transfers in China." *Economic Development and Cultural Change*, *52*(3).

Lin, Y. (1999). *China Miracle: Development Strategy and Economic Reform.* Shanghai: SDX Joint Publishing Company.

Lin, Y., Cai, F., & Li, Z. (1998). "Analysis of Regional Disparity in Chinese Economic Transition Period." *Economic Research Journal*, 6.

Lipton, M., & Ravallion, M. (1995). "Poverty and Policy." In J. Behrman & T. N. Srinivasan (Eds.), *Handbook of Development Economics vol. 3* (pp. 2551–2657). Amsterdam: North Holland.

Liu, Y. (2006). "The Definitive Methods and Empirical Measurement of the Middle Class in the Pearl River Delta." *Open Times, 4.*

Lu, X. (Ed.). (2001). *The Contemporary China Social Structure Research Report.* Beijing: Social Science Academic Press.

Lu, X. (2004). *Social Mobility in Contemporary China.* Beijing: Social Science Academic Press.

Lv, D., & Wang, Z. (2003). *Observations on the Situation of the Middle Class in Hong Kong.* Hong Kong: SDX Joint Publishing Company.

Maasoumi, E. (1986). "The Measurement and Decomposition of Multidimensional Inequality." *Econometrica, 54,* 771–779.

Mao, Z. (1973). *Mao's Selected Works.* Beijing: People's Publishing House.

Masao, W. (1998). *The Class Stratification in the Modern Japan and its Fixation* (Z. Lu, Trans.). Beijing: Central Compilation & Translation Press.

Nee, V. (1989, October). "A Theory of Market Transition: From Redistribution to Market in State Socialism." *American Sociological Review, 154,* 663–681.

Nee, V. (1991). "Social Inequalities in Reforming State Socialism: Between Redistribution and Market in China." *American Sociological Review, 56,* 267–282.

Poulantzas, N. (1973). "On Social Classes." *New Left Review, 78,* 27–54.

Przeworski, A. (1977). "Proletariat into A Class: The Process of Class Formation from Karl Kautsky's the Class Struggle to Recent Controversies." *Politics and Society, 7*(4), 343–401.

Ram, R. (1995, January). "Economic Development and Income Inequality: An Overlooked Regression Constraint." *Economic Development and Cultural Change, 43*(2), 425–434.

Research Center of State Department. (2006). *Investigative Report on Chinese Rural Labor.* Beijing: China Yan Shi Press.

So., A. Y. (2003). "The Changing Pattern of Classes and Conflicts in China." *Journal of Contemporary China, 33*(3), 363–376.

Stark, D., & Nee, V. (1989). "Toward an Institutional Analysis of State Socialism." In D. Stark & V. Nee (Eds.), *Remaking the Economic Institutions of Socialism: China and Eastern Europe.* Palo Alto, CA: Stanford University Press.

Sun, L. (1994). "Transformation of Chinese Structure since the Reform." *Social Sciences in China, 2.*

Todaro, M. P. (1969). "A Model of Labor Migration and Urban Unemployment in Less Developed Countries." *American Economic Review, 59*(1), 105–133.

Wade, R. (1990). *Governing the Market: Economic Theory and the Role of Government in East Asian Industrialization.* Princeton: Princeton University Press.

Walder, A. G. (1996, January). "Markets and Inequality in Transitional Economies: Toward Testable Theories." *American Journal of Sociology, 101*(4), 1060–1073.

Wang, T., & Wang, F. (2005). "Group Factors in Income Distribution in Chinese Urban Areas: 1986–1995." *Sociological Research, 3.*

Wang, X. (2007). "The Gray Income and Income Distribution Gap in China." *China Reform, 7.*

The World Bank. (1993). *The East Asian Miracle: Economic Growth and Public Policy.* New York: Oxford University Press.

The World Bank. (2004). *China: Promoting Equitable Economic Growth.* Beijing: Tsinghua University Press.

Wright, E. O. (1997). *Class Counts: Comparative Studies and Class Analysis*. Cambridge: Cambridge University Press.

Zhang, Y. (2004). "The Attainment of Chinese Social Status: Class Succession and the Intergenerational Mobility." *Sociological Research, 4.*

Zhang, Y. (2005). "The Research of Class Conflict and Consciousness in Cities of China." *Social Sciences in China, 4.*

Zhao, R., & Li, S. (1999). "The Ever Growing Income Gap among Chinese Household and Its Causes." In R. Zhao (Ed.), *Reconsidering Chinese Household Income Distribution*. Beijing: China Financial & Economic Publishing House.

8   Social conflict and class consciousness

Research on contradictions in China today

There are three approaches to understanding and analyzing the social contradictions in the period of socialist construction.

The first approach is the analytic method based on "class struggle." Its fundamental premise and inference is that all social contradictions during the period of socialism are essentially a reflection of the class struggle between the proletariat and the bourgeoisie. Class means equivalent social status and shared interests, whereas the latter further suggests shared social aspiration, attitude, and actions. Along this reasoning, for a long time prior to the reform and opening up, people's class status, political attitudes, and social behavior have been determined by the principle of "class struggle." Once defined as "the other," one can never be redeemed. Whenever events with intensified social contradictions emerge, common steps to solve the problem are to magnify the problem to the level of principle or ideology, catch the bad guys behind the problem, or resort to suppression.

The second approach is the analytic method based on "material interests." Its fundamental premise and inference is that the basic social contradictions during the period of socialism are contradictions amidst the people. Causes to those contradictions are complex, among which are imperfect existing institutions and systems, the work style of state cadres, and more often than not the impertinent, discordant, and unfair distribution of material interests. Consequently, the fundamental solution to contradictions is to coordinate the material interests among a variety of social strata and interest groups.

The third approach is the analytic method based on "social consciousness." Its fundamental premise and inference is that social structure is going through profound changes and social interest groups become diverse, some of which catalyzes the emergence of social contradictions and "social consciousness" of new social movement. The "social consciousness" does not belong to the "objective class" consciousness, but to the "identity" consciousness. Social contradiction and conflict caused by the "social consciousness" are always characterized by "suddenness," "rapid diffusion" and "unpredictability."

History and current social practice have proven that to use the analytic method based on class struggle to solve contradictions among the people and social problems is utterly wrong, if not engenders great social calamities. The "material interests" method is applicable to most of the current social contradiction and conflict.

Although we are not familiar with the "social consciousness" approach, it sheds light on social conflict and problems characterized by modern risks.

There are to perspectives when it comes to examining social contradiction and conflict. One is to chase the causes behind social conflict events – *ex post facto* studies. Most of the current researches fall into this category. The other perspective is to infer results based on the subjective consciousness and behavior disposition – *ex ante* studies, which are largely neglected nowadays.

Our studies presented in this chapter are *ex ante* studies. The basic hypothesis is that the logical connection between the objective of social stratification structure and the economic and social status and people's social attitudes and their choices of social action is established through subjective class identity and consciousness. The main question for this article concerns the rules behind this connection. It also relates to questions like what the factors are that would affect China's future trend and social choices. What kinds of central issues would force Chinese various social forces to reorganize? Which rule does the force reorganization abide by?

The analysis of "Chinese experience" in this article is from a survey conducted by "China Contemporary People's Internal Contradictions" research project that is part of Chinese Academy of Social Sciences major issues project under my supervision. From November to December 2002, we carried out the sample survey concerning urban residents' "social perceptions" in 31 municipality directly under the central government and provincial capital cities.[1] The research participants are urban residents at the age of 18 to 69. There were 15,000 questionnaires distributed. After eliminating invalid questionnaires, there were 11,094 questionnaires left. The effective respondent rate is 73.96 percent. After nearly two years of data collection and analysis, we are here to present the preliminary results of our analysis. To save space, I omit detailed process of data analysis.[2]

Two action logics to explain social conflict

In either the East or in the West, scholars rely on the class conflict framework, before the framework of risk society appears, to understand and explain social contradiction and conflict. In spite of denials from Western scholars, class is the most fundamental social division, as proven by numerous studies, and the most convenient means to position oneself in the society to distinguish between different interests, and to find an identity group. The only difference lies in the fact that the public understanding of the class varies from country to country.

As far as the studies on Marx's class theory are concerned, "class consciousness" is always under addressed. Scholars often focus more on the relations between the class category and the possession of the means of production, wealth, and privilege, inclined to neglect the logic connection identified by Marx between the class and the possible social attitude and action.

In *The Poverty of Philosophy*, the class analysis divides social classes into "class in itself" and "class for itself." A "class in itself" existing as a social group can only gain class consciousness through historical, cognitive, and practical realization. Only in this way is it possible to fight for common class interests through consistent collective actions. Precisely by this token, Marx rejects the idea of peasants as a class in *Louis Bonaparte Eighteenth Brumaire*, believing peasants are "a bag of potatoes" that are homogenous and separated from each other. Because of the lack of a common class consciousness, peasants do not take consistent political actions.

Consequently, the logic connection between the class ascription and the social attitude and action reveals itself only after an intermediate process of building class consciousness. In addition, although class ascription is the basic element for class consciousness, it is the single one, and in many cases not the decisive one. Under specific circumstances, nationality race, social status, oppressed degree would become the major and decisive element. For instance, in the Chinese revolution that overthrew the rule of the semi-feudalism and semi-colonialism, the fundamental force is farmers as China then is a country of farmers. A large number of national bourgeoisie and intellectuals devote themselves to the revolution, however, because reform and revolution start to gain momentum after the introduction of advanced Western thought, even more so when Anti-Japanese and national salvation become the mainstream advanced consciousness after Japanese invasion of China and the ascendance of national conflict to be the main contradiction. However, the proportion of workers among Nazi members in Germany is very high because the pervasive racism in the society points to race as the root of oppression.

With the respect to the class, Max Weber shares Marx's idea in that he also believes that property ownership is the cause for social inequality and the people's market position is one basic dimension of social stratification. However, Weber discovers, from real life, many inconsistences between objective class ascription and subjective class identity. For instance, traditional aristocrats in the Western society have lost their ownership of the property market after the bourgeois revolution but they still identify themselves as among the upper echelon of the society. Therefore, Weber argues that social stratification and the formation of inequality have related not only to class, a dimension distinguished by the amount of wealth and income, but also to "status group," a dimension concerning social status (social prestige and honor), and to political group, a dimension that describes the differences in power. Weber's theory of class conflict is also very similar to Marx's. He attributes class conflict to two factors, one being that the lower social groups refuse to accept the established social relationship and the other being the degree to which the lower social groups can organize politically. Weber figures out four causes to the lower social groups rejecting the established social relationship. The first cause is the correlation among the resource allocation of power, wealth, and social prestige. The second cause is the organization state of social members. The third cause is the frequency of social mobility that helps increase individuals' power, wealth, and social prestige. And the last cause is the gap in the allocation of power, wealth, and social prestige, because the wider the gap is, the harder it will be for individuals to move socially upward, and the more likely it will cause dissatisfaction among lower social groups.

In the study of social stratification, all kinds of measurement methods for social and economic status that develop later on can be traced back to Weber's theory. These methods, along with carefully designed scales of social and economic status, are no more than calculating a unified score to describe the structure of social stratification by taking into account various factors like income, wealth, and professions and utilizing correlation coefficient analysis and the method of weighting. However, these methods fail to capture the real logical relationship between the objective stratification and the subjective class identity. They also fail to reveal the formation process of class consciousness, which has rules and theorems of its own and of the collective actions. The reason to these flaws is social complexity. For in reality, factors that have played roles in determining class consciousness, value orientation, social attitude, preference, expectation, and action choice are intricate. The axis variables for collective social attitude and actions are subject to changes since certain specific social circumstances, key issues at stake, social context as well as the essential social contradictions are not static. In this case, traditional "class determinism" (an analytic method that maintains that class ascription determines the choice of social values, attitudes, and behaviors) may appear inapplicable shedding little light on the social reality. For example, when it comes to the great split on whether embracing the reform and opening up or casting doubt on the direction the reform is taking, people are divided into different groups along the line of collective consciousness, social attitude, school of thought, and action orientation. The class and stratum identifications involved in the split are facing reorganization because new spotlight issues constantly emerge as the reform and opening up is unfolding. "Class determinism" supposedly offers none explanation to the political division on the issue of "Taiwan independence." In the Western society, as the public shift their focus to living and environment issues, Green Party, feminism, and LGBT communities that were once marginalized become significant political forces, whose power have exceeded that of far left or right parties. In many cases, they are the decisive forces for political orders. The fiercest competition for Western political leaders is the general election during which they care about the public opinion trends the most. Candidates and their campaign strategists must also be the masters of psychological analysis of the public. They are more perceptive to the rules of the public opinion formation and change than sociologists. They understand the truth that "water that can carry a boat can capsize it."

The impact of class consciousness on the political order varies from country to country. Sweden is nation that has the strongest consciousness of class and the highest rate of union membership. Until 1980s, more than 90 percent of the employees voluntarily join in the labor union. Working class has also become a lasting supportive force for the left-wing Social Democratic Party, which makes Sweden a unique capitalistic nation (Esping-Andersen, 1985). However, the United States comes with "American exceptionalism" to class politics because the labor party has never become the mainstream political force. The union membership reached its highest level of merely 35.5 percent in the United States in 1945 and dropped to 23.6 percent in 1978 (Goldfield, 1987, p.10).

Some Western New Marxist scholars (e.g., Antonio Gramsci, Georg Lukacs, and the Frankfurt school) simply attribute the declining political influence of the working class in the West to the formation of cultural consciousness and "hegemony" on the part of the ruling class, to the weakening of "class consciousness" and "social critique consciousness" among the working class, or to the demise of proletarian "subjective consciousness." Social conflict theorists (e.g., Ralf G. Dahrendorf, Lewis Coser), however, are aware that a declining legitimacy of "common consciousness," a rising "sense of relative deprivation," an escalating degree of "dissatisfaction," and "block on social mobility" are new causes for contemporary social conflict.

In reality, the inconsistence between the objective "class ascription" and the subjective "class identity" is a norm in modern society. Ever since the 1960s, the greatest change to the relationship between "class ascription" and the "class identity" occurred to the latter, which have made the unclear and controversial category of middle class the mainstream choice for class identity.

Erik Olin Wright is one of the renowned New Marxists who is attentive to middle class studies. Wright's widely adopted theoretical framework of class structure, through constant revisions, resembles Goldthorpe's equally widely adopted framework (Wright, 1979; Goldthorpe & Erikson, 1992). In 1992, Taiwan scholars Xu Jiayou and others conducted a survey investigation concerning "class structure and class consciousness" in Taiwan based on Wright's framework and compared the data with the results from the United States and Sweden. They found among "bourgeois" (defined as employers of 11 or more employees while the employer of 10 people or less is defined as small employer),[3] 66.7 percent in the United States, 75 percent in Sweden, and 57.7 percent in Taiwan identify themselves as "middle class," respectively. However, among "working class" (defined as dependent employees), 54.5 percent in the United States, 34.5 percent, in Sweden, 41.0 percent, in Taiwan categorize themselves as "middle class," as opposed to 36.9 percent in the United States, 63.9 percent in Sweden, and 41 percent in Taiwan categorize themselves as "working class" (Wu, 1992).

These statistics show that even for the groups with divergent objective class status their identification with "the middle class" greatly reduced the objective gap. For the popular psychology verifies that the frame of reference varies from people to people and the most widely adopted frame of reference among the public is based on one's own past and the class of equivalent or similar social status. Under certain circumstances, such as a general improvement in income, the change path of the subjective class identity may deviate from the curve of objective income gap. Moreover, in particular cases, other social factors may exceed the influence of the class ascription and become more significant impact factor on the class identify. For example, in globalization, the disparities between countries, nationalities, and regions will surpass the domestic class conflict and become crucially influential factor for social conflict. On April 1, 1999, Microsoft chairman Bill Gates' personal wealth worth reached $100 billion in a stock frenzy, more than the world GDP with the 18 richest countries excluded and twice the total circulation of U.S. dollars (The Daily Telegraph, 1999). In 1820, the ratio of standard of living between the richest countries and poorest countries in the world was about 3 to 1, but it grew to 11 to 1 in 1913, 35 to 1 in 1950, and now increased to 70 to 1 (Seabrook, 2002, p.97). In addition, according to a report released by the World Bank in 1997, from 1960 to 1989, the share of the world total revenue held by the top 20 percent of the world's richest people increased from 70.2 percent to 82.7 percent, while the bottom 20 percent possessed 1.4 percent of the world total revenue down from meager 2.3 percent in 1960 (Seabrook, 2002, pp. 99–100). Furthermore, according to the second phase of the first "Taiwan social change survey" data under the auspices of Professor Qu Hai-yuan in Taiwan in 1990, native place, education, and occupation are more influential in subjective class identity than class ascription and other objective factors. The survey divides the class identity into lower class, working class, middle class, upper-middle class, and upper class. With not much difference, there are 57.6 percent of employers and 49.7 percent of employees identifying themselves as "middle class." In contrast, a huge difference exists between the non-natives and the aboriginal people as 60.6 percent of the former believe they belong to the "middle class" whereas only 25 percent of the latter believe so. Sixty point four percent of people with a college education and above identify themselves as "middle class" while only 35.4 percent of people with primary education and below believe so. Sixty point four percent of professionals and 35.4 percent of the manual laborers classify themselves as "middle class" (Huang, 2002, p.31). Given the peculiar situation in Taiwan, the remarkable disparity in class identity and social attitude between non-natives and the indigenous people becomes a crucial variable for the politics in Taiwan.

Recent studies on political attitudes in Britain have shown that causes to the formation and changes of the public opinion formation are very complex. It is untenable to pinpoint the class ascription as the single explanation. Interestingly enough, the most steadfast defender of this idea is precisely the upholders of the class conflict framework. A survey result on social attitudes in Britain also shows that the "class consciousness" actually means "social conflict consciousness" in the general perception. The social conflict consciousness is weakest among the bulk "middle class" and the "working class." The groups which have the strongest sense of social conflict are the ones directly involved in it – namely, "the conflict between the managers and the workers" (see Table 8.1). The focal point of the

Table 8.1 What do you think of the conflict intensity between the following social groups? (Britain)

The Conflict Intensity	*Very Strong/Strong*	*Not very Strong/ Not Strong*	*Don't Know*
Working Class and Middle Class	49.8%	44.2%	5.0%
Unemployed and Employed	19.1%	75.5%	5.5%
Manager and Worker	37.6%	55.4%	6.9%
Peasant and Urban Residents	25.5%	66.3%	8.1%
Youth and Senors	35.9%	57.7%	6.3%

Source: Brook, L. (Ed.). (1992). *British Social Attitudes,Cumulative Source Book: The First Six Surveys [WTBZ]*. Aldershot: Gower, p.6.

public "consciousness of social conflict" shifts along with the social hot-button issues (Savage, 2000, pp. 39–40).

Why do inconsistencies occur between the objective class ascription and the subjective class identity?

Inconsistencies between the objective class ascription and the subjective class identity in the Western society can be attributed to the changes in reality, which fall into the following three categories.

The spread of "individualism" in people's life style, value orientation, and behavior choices

Anthony Giddens' publications of *The Consequences of Modernity* in 1990 and *Modernity and Self-Identity* in 1992 reflect a turning point in his analytic methodology. Prior to these publications, Giddens' research of Marx's and Weber's theories in 1971, empirical studies on social elites in 1974, studies on the class structure of the advanced societies in 1973, along with his most influential "theory of structuration" developed from his analysis of the class, all prove his stress on the class analysis. Giddens (1991) argued in *The Consequences of Modernity* that modernity society is going through a significant change regarding "identity politics," which makes a society shifting from the "emancipatory politics" to "life politics." While emancipatory politics is a politics of "life chances," life politics is a politics of "lifestyle." "Lifestyle" differs from the "mode of life" in that it is an individualized choice instead of a group choice. In the past, class politics play a central role in mobilizing people to fight for life chances improvement. However, when the poor living conditions have improved and reflexive modernity (modernity is expected to bring unexpected consequences) appears in the contemporary society, the core issues that people are concerned about have changed to the reflections on the limitations of the dated mode of political participation. This calls for a new kind of politics, the one with more reflexivity, which in turn pushes class politics into the background (Giddens, 1991, p.241). This idea serves as the sociological groundwork of the systematic theorizing of the "third way" offered by Giddens in *Beyond Left and Right* published in 1994.

Ulrich Beck (1986) expressed similar ideas in *Risk Society*, only more articulate. Beck believes that the making of risk society is marked by contemporary individualistic culture deviating from the established class-based culture. Just as social class has taken the place of status group and family as the stable reference frame in the history, now individualism culture has supplanted class culture and autonomous individuals have become the unit of social reproduction in the risk society. However, Beck explains that the ascendancy of individualistic culture does not necessarily mean the weakening in social structural power, but means that individuals become more reflective within contemporary large-scale social changes. Beck even considers the trend of individualization as a new human "Enlightenment movement" since individual is freed from the bondage of social network as a continuation of democratization. He further divides the individualization process into three progressive stages. The first stage is "disembedding" that breaks the historical set of social norms and conventions. The second stage is "losing" in which people discard the established knowledge, faith, and norms, and thus lose traditional security. And the third stage is "re-embedding," which shapes the coming of a new social convention (Beck, 1986/1992, pp. 98, 128, 130).

The accelerating social mobility brings about breakings in social identity

Along with the structural changes of the society, knowledge and technology play an increasingly important role in personal income growth. The pace of knowledge and technology transforming into wealth is accelerating. Large corporate enterprises adopting strategies of "outsourcing" and "order" of parts production to reduce the costs facilitates the development of small and medium-sized enterprises. In modern Western society, two-thirds of the new job opportunities are offered by small business of 20 people or less. The rapid development of the new industries of the Internet, biology, and culture provide ample new opportunities for social class mobility. Flexible work style and the diversification of social service give rise to the appearance of a large number of personalized work. The list goes on. All these factors contribute to accelerating the social mobility and undermining the authority of the traditional organization, hierarchies, and class relations. In addition, the increased market risk and uncertainty of life increase the possibility of social mobility. The individualization of lifestyle and social attitude also dissolves the traditional division between the public and private spheres. Against this background, one's social identity is characterized by "breaking," meaning that one's "self-identity" and behavior choice break from the decisive factors such as traditional class ascription and family background.

Shifts in hot-button social issues engendered by structural transformations cause "fragmentation" in conception and ideology

Many scholars have found that Western societies have experienced profound social changes in the past few decades. These changes shift the social and individual attentions to social issues, and the social conflict stops revolving around traditional classes but erupts in many overlooked respects. Michael Savage, director of the Sociology Department at the University, examines the basic characteristics of contemporary social and cultural transformations in his new book titled *Class Analysis and Social Transformation*. Savage (2000) argued that in the face of new social risk, people's values, ideologies, and social attitudes are changing, and social relations are restructuring. Consequently, the fundamental framework for social analysis needs to change too. Many scholars use the concept "fragmentation" to examine changes occurred to social stratification, conception, and ideologies in the contemporary Western society. "Fragmentation" implies the fact that people's behavioral strategies and social attitudes in the realms of economy, politics, culture, and life are no longer divided by the class as it used to be traditionally, but by specific social issues in question (Clark & Lipset, 1996). Changes in political attitude are a case in point. When Seymour Martin Lipset, American famous sociologist specialized in social stratification, first published *Political Man* in 1960, he emphasized the importance of class politics based on then materials. However, when the book was reprinted in 1981, Lipset revised his argument completely based on newly emerged changes and provided an in-depth analysis in explaining the declining role played by class in electoral politics. According to Alford Index of Class Voting, in the general elections in the 1940s, if three-quarters of the working class voted for the left-wing party, then about one-quarter of the middle class supported the right-wing party. However, statistics from 1980s showed that 50 percent of the middle class voted for the left-wing party, which indicates a blurring line drawn by the class among political voters (Lipset, 1960). Although people still talk about left and right, their meanings are completely different now. A newly emerged new left pays more attention to the problems in the real life and new social issues that people care about, such as unemployment, social security, ecological environment, women's rights, cultural diversity, lifestyle, new social risk, and no longer the traditional political problems like the property ownership (Clark & Lipset, 1996, p.45). The "fragmentation" tendency in values and social attitude is even starker among the new generation that comes of age after 1980s who have become one of basic voting forces.

There is a debate concerning "whether class is dead" in recent years in Western academia, and in European sociological circle in particular. Prestigious sociologists, such as John Harry Goldthorpe, are also involved in the debate. Despite divergent opinions, a relatively accordant idea is that although the impact of the class in the traditional sense has declined, the class analysis remains a valid research and analytic method. However, profound changes in reality cause setbacks in applying the traditional framework of class analysis to many important issues. Therefore, scholars must redefine class analysis and adjust its meanings in accordance with the changes in the reality, and enhance the studies into new influential factors on social attitudes, self-identity, and individual choice of actions.

China is a developing country, facing a different set of questions than Western modern society. The aforementioned transformations in the contemporary Western society may not applicable to China. Structural transformation and profound social changes have also taken place in China, but the path of changes, key issues, and the direction are different. However, given the backdrop of globalization, the development of a nation state can never be immune from the world trend. Particularly for such an unbalanced country as China, varied fields of politics, economy, society, culture, and ideas, lives in urban and rural areas, and the regions with different levels of development in the east, middle, and west of China are subject to the great impact of the globalization.

The number of urban residents in China who self-identify as middle class may well-exceed the objective figure based on social stratification. With regard to its value orientation, social attitude, and ideology, the middle class, which is mainly composed of youth, professionals and technical personnel, and general administrators, becomes a significant force in shaping China's social choice for the future.

In academia, scholars' studies echo the contradiction – namely, the inconsistence between the objective social stratification structure and the subjective class identity. On the one hand, people witness a variety of "ruptures" in different aspects in Chinese social structure, such as in the urban and rural areas, among the new rich and the new bottom of the society, in the developed and less developed regions, and within and outside the system (Sun, 2004). The rule governing social mobility seems to maintain the social reproduction mechanism (Li, 2002). On the other hand, scholars also discover the tendency toward "fragmentation" in social hierarchy, and class consciousness and identity in particular (Sun, Li, & Shen, 1998). This contradiction is also reflected in new waves of thought among intellectuals, such as new left, neoliberalism, neo-conservatism, neo-authoritarianism, new nationalism, and new democracy. It is difficult for a layman to distinguish one from the other, because each one of them shifts their position depending on the issue in question. This school of thought may appear drastically different from each other, but their perspectives may be identical on certain problems. However, they tend to provide different remedies for the social issue. The complicated situation of this kind has put an end to the clear-cut political divisions as we know it.

Seven findings on social conflict consciousness in contemporary China

According to the sample survey of more than 10,000 urban residents in 31 big cities (municipality directly under the central government and provincial capital cities) in China, the main results inferred from various statistical analytics and models are summarized as follows.

Class identity defines social conflict consciousness and behavior orientation

People tend to think that one's income and social status determine one's identity and consciousness, and the latter further determines one's social action. This reasoning is based on the assumption that "poor people would revolt." However, our investigation and study results present a different picture, not completely supporting this inference.

Our study confirms that a common class identity is easy to form a common class consciousness and behavior orientation. Class identity is the most influential, among all explanatory variables for social conflict consciousness. People with the same class identity tend to concur, more or less, on the severity of social class conflict.

Our survey shows that the higher one self-identifies his/her social class, the more likely one would believe that social class conflict is slight both now and in the future. The lower one self-identifies his/her social class, the more likely one would believe that social class conflict is severe both now and in the future. Especially for those who identify themselves as one of the social bottom, they are more prone to extreme behavior. For instance, when we ask about a respondent's individual attitude toward "participating in collective petition invited by colleagues or neighbors in particular cases," our survey shows that 37.4 percent of respondents who self-report from the social bottom are positive, which sets this group apart from the rest social class. This also means that this segment of the population is more inclined to induce all kinds of unexpected incidents whose behaviors have great potential for social risk.

This finding suggests that it is not true that in modern society the poor people in the objective stratum are more likely to participate in and support the social conflict. People often develop a sort of bias that the poor stratum of the population as demarcated by objective indicators are most likely to be dissatisfied with the existing society and resort to furious social confrontational actions. However, our study finds that when it comes to explaining "the severity of social class conflict" happening now and in the future, the objective indicators of the social bottom have limited statistical significance. What matters more is the explanatory variable "class identity" which is more indicative of social class conflict consciousness in an accelerating process of industrialization and marketization.

The finding that class identity determines social conflict consciousness and behavior orientation implies that during China's new stage of development, the inducement to social conflict as well the threat to social stability may not come from the objectively defined social bottom, but from those who self-identify as lower class in the reference groups. Our analysis shows that class identity is also closely associated with one's perception of the severity of the conflict between the rich and the poor, cadres and the mass, and managers and ordinary workers in the state-owned enterprises, and labor-management strife.

One possible explanation is that factors that determine social conflict consciousness vary at different stages of social development. When the society as a whole lives below the poverty line, the poverty-stricken population is a large social group. As the sense of being poor is pervasive, the objective poor population exerts significant influence on one's awareness of social conflict. However, after being lifted out of poverty and living in society in a well-off state, social class would become more indicative of one's attitude and behavior. In reality, one is subject to the influence of social values, and once identifying with a social class, one tends to consider the relationship between social classes from the standpoint of the class they identify.

Findings on social reproduction in the making of class identity

What on earth affects subjective class identity? Our survey and analysis show that objective index for stratification such as income, education, occupation and consumption are correlated with subjective class identity, although the correlation is weak. Multivariate statistical analysis finds that the factor determining one's subjective class identity is "parents' social status" among various factors.

The results of this study show that, despite remarkably accelerating social mobility since the reform and opening up, the social reproduction mechanism that the parents' social status determines class identity still exists. One possible reason is that parents' life circle has greater impact on their offspring's subjective assessment than factors like income and education attainment of their own. This indicates that the intergenerational effect is still prevalent in family social status, which has a crucial impact on subjective class identity.

The results also show that "the region" and "the largest expenditure in life" also have significant impact on one's subjective class identity. This means "the sense of relative deprivation" and "the sense of relative gains" play important roles in shaping one's subjective class identity. The reference frame that one chooses and the relative position one situates one's in inside the chosen reference frame greatly affects one's subjective class identity. The fact that people from "western region" and "the disadvantaged regions" are more likely to identify with the lower class shows that in an ever opening society, the scope of comparison is expanding and the selection of reference groups is no longer restricted to the neighboring communities. Living in an increasingly open society, people from the rural and disadvantaged regions are more likely to have the sense of "relative deprivation," which would influence their subjective class identification.

In addition, it is noteworthy that the difference in the big-ticket consumer items also affects subjective class identity to a large extent. When the society shifts from a thrift-oriented era to a mass consumption era, consumption becomes symbolic behavior of value and power. Consumer behavior may engender "epochal" changes, which means that not only income but also values would influence consumer behaviors.

The inconsistence between objective class and subjective class consciousness is not unique to China, but rather a pervasive phenomenon across the world. There are many complex causes leading to this phenomenon, but the major ones are as follows. The first cause is an undermined class "lifestyle" convergence and an intensified tendency toward "individualized" "life tastes." The second cause is the "breaking down" of social identity resulted from the accelerating social mobility – that is, subjective class identity is not determined merely by objective status such as income, education, and occupation. The third cause is the immobilization of objective social stratification concurs with the fragmentation of subjective class identity in contemporary China.

Findings on "downward" subjective class identification

From a transnational comparison of subjective class identity, we find that even for Chinese residents in the big cities there is a "downward" tendency when it comes to self-identified class. This downward drift is not structural, however. It manifests in a disproportionately shrinking self-identified middle class but a growing self-identified social bottom. For example, in the developed countries like the United States, Germany, Italy, Australia, Canada, and Japan, people who identify as "middle class" are all exceeding 55 percent of the total population, with the highest rate nearly 69 percent. In great developing countries like Brazil and India, the proportion of middle class is also more than 55 percent, with a higher end of more than 70 percent in Australia and Singapore and a lower end of 51 percent in South Korea. However, in Chinese big cities, the rate is 46.9 percent. Meanwhile, as compared to its international counterpart, Chinese urban residents identify remarkably more with the social "bottom." The self-identified social bottom in the developed countries is generally below 5 percent, with a lower end of less than 3 percent in Australia and Canada and a higher end of about 9 percent in South Korea, 8 percent in Italy, and 7.5 percent in India, respectively. However, 14.6 percent of urban residents in China self-identify as "lower class," a rarely seen high rate.

The "downward" tendency in class identity among Chinese urban public suggests that a society dominated by the middle class has not yet come into being even in the urban China. This outcome may be explained by China's trajectory of income gap changes that differ from the general international development experience. Namely, after the per capita GDP reaches $1,000, the income gap, instead of shrinking, continues to expand. Among Chinese special factors are unlimited supply of non-technical labor and an accelerating accumulation of wealth. However, the spread of globalization demands a rapid income raise for Chinese senior managers and professional and technical personnel. Plummeting information cost leads to decentralizations of organizational structure and further differentiations among mid-level management.

The middle class is often regarded as the social "stabilizer" – that is, a large middle class acts like a "buffer" between the upper class and the social bottom, thus alleviating intense social conflicts. When the middle class dominates a society, its mainstream ideology is stable to the extent that it is less likely to be inflicted by extreme ideas. Consequently, a relative lack of "middle" class identity among the Chinese urban public and a relatively high rate of self-identified lower class are likely to induce social conflict and contradiction, which poses a potential threat to social stability and security. This is noteworthy and calls for further investigations.

Findings on social conflict consciousness caused by new clashes between values

In reality, especially when the society is at a lower level of development, the main social contradiction concerns with the interest conflict. The difference in material interests is the root for all kinds of social conflicts. As far as social conflict analysis is concerned, scholars use to examining the conflict of material interests.

However, our study has found that in the current stage of development, urban China is witness the rise of a new type of social conflict and contradiction, the one that is caused by social value differences.

Through path analysis, we find that one's position in a changing interest pattern does not directly impact one's propensity for conflict. There are some intermediate steps from interest loss to actual conflicting action. According to the inference from statistical analysis, changes in interest pattern per se are insufficient to cause conflicting behavior. Perceived injustice and a declining degree of life satisfaction resulted from changes in interest pattern are direct causes for conflicting actions. The perceived reasons to the income gap that is distorted by the "feeling of injustice" would "amplify" the feeling about the income gap psychologically. Those who believe that their current standard of living is low, those who think their future living standard is hard to improve, those who believe that the current income distribution is unequal, and those who consider the current property possession as unfair share their opinions on a stronger tendency toward class conflicts both at the present and in the future.

In this case, it is more important policy-wise to enhance the effort to crack down various forms of illegal income, standardize income distribution order, and maintain social justice. Additionally, initiatives to give appropriate compensations to groups impaired by the reform preventing their standard of living from dropping and lifting their satisfactory degree are also indispensable content to reduce social conflict and maintain social stability.

A stronger social conflict consciousness on the two poles of social stratification

From statistical analysis, we also find that those who experience "rapid richness" and "rapid poverty" believe the class conflict is and will become worse in the future. Scholars once pay more attention to the social conflict psyche of those "who are struck by sudden poverty" because of the belief that people having "a sense of relative deprivation" are more inclined to form class conflict consciousness. A significant finding from our study is that those "who are on the expressway to being rich" – "whose living standard has greatly improved in the past five years" – also believe "the class conflict tends to be severe."

Compared to middle class, lower middle class, and upper middle class, the self-identified lower class is more likely to believe that the class conflict is getting more severe at the present and in the future. On the other hand, the upper class is also pessimistic about the harmony of social relations at present and in the future.

That people who are getting rich fast also have a strong consciousness of social conflict is primary because the upper class is insecure about their own wealth. For although nearly half of the respondents agree or very agree with the idea that allowing for small group of people getting rich first benefits the society, a majority of the population is discontent about the existing income distribution hoping to improve the distribution order that allows for a more reasonable income gap. This form is a prevailing public opinion that results in the upper class's insecurity. The second reason lies in the divergent solutions to the problem of income distribution. Our survey shows that 35.4 percent of the upper class does not agree to levy taxes on the rich to help the poor, and if combined with the 13.6 percent of the people who do not care, roughly half of the social upper class does not support paying more taxes to help the poor.

Noteworthy opinions of the urban public toward cadres

When asked about "which group benefits the most from the reform and opening up" in a nationwide survey in the 1990s, most people answered private business owners or entertainers. However, the answer from the respondents to the same question on our 2002 survey is the party and government cadres. Our study shows that two out of ten group categories are believed by a majority of the respondents to have benefited the most since the reform and opening up. One is the party and government cadres, and the other is private enterprises owners. The party and government cadres are believed by 59.2 percent of the respondents to be the greatest beneficiaries since the reform and opening up – that is the highest percentage, followed by private enterprises owners whom 55.4 percent of the respondents think benefit the most since the reform and opening up.

Moreover, this seems to be a consensus across social classes. The survey results stratification by objective social class and by subjective identity arrive at almost the same conclusion that approximately half of the top and upper class believe that the party and government cadres are the greatest beneficiaries since the reform and opening up. This perception is shared by approximately 70 percent of the bottom and the lower class.

In search for collateral evidence for this unexpected result, we further analyzed another set of data from a survey in 2001 on contemporary social structure changes in China, only to reach a similar conclusion. When asked "which three categories of people do you think are most likely to have high incomes in contemporary China," respondents who think "bureaucrats," "highly educated," and "people who have assets" are more likely to earn high incomes are 50.7 percent, 28.8 percent, and 7.1 percent, respectively.

Urban public's perception that the party and government cadres are the greatest beneficiaries since the reform and opening up contradicts with the actual income comparison among different occupations. There are mainly two explanations for such a perception. First, as the market competition is increasingly fierce lately, many enterprises face difficulties in business operation, and with a growing market risk, "taking an entrepreneurial plunge" is no longer synonymous with "making a fortune." In contrast, public servant is an occupation with a stable income, a prospect of income improvement, and often associated with a mature social security system (pension, medical care, and employment). Second, serious corruptions among some officials and the exposed amount of money involved in corruptive crimes inflict baneful influence on the public's perception of the cadres. The survey result also shows that a majority of the respondents consider unemployment and corruption as the most intractable social problems. There are 70.4 percent and 54.7 percent of the respondents, respectively, think that unemployment and corruption are major social problems currently facing the cities.

This finding, it is safe to say, shows a thought-provoking and alarming betrayal of the mission that the party should represent the fundamental interests of the broad masses of the people.

The urban public feels strongest about the labor conflicts in private enterprises

The survey results show that the majority of the urban public believes that the labor conflict is serious at present in China. There are two outstanding findings. First, people have the most intense feelings about the labor conflicts in private enterprises. When asked to compare labor relations in four types of enterprises – namely, state-owned enterprises (SOEs), private enterprises, foreign-funded enterprises, and joint ventures, more respondents believe the hostility between capital and labor is fiercest than otherwise. This perhaps has a lot to do with the non-standard employment and management system deployed in the private enterprises that fail to protect labor rights properly. Second, the perception of labor relations in the state-owned enterprises has the greatest impact on people's consciousness of social conflict. Multiple regression analysis shows that the judgment of the conflict between "the managers and workers of SOEs" is the most influential factor on people's overall feeling of social conflict. It is perhaps because the SOEs play an important role in the social and economic life, and the public is less tolerant of the labor conflicts happened in SOEs than in any other types of enterprises.

We also find that many factors are at play when it comes to shaping people's perception of labor conflict. It is common sense that people with low occupation status, low income, and lower class identity and people who recently have encountered a fall in the living standard are more inclined to believe that the current labor conflicts are serious. There are also some noteworthy yet neglected new factors. For instance, people with higher education, of a younger age, and living in a relatively disadvantaged region, are more sensitive to labor conflict problems.

The survey result also indicates that the more intense people believe the labor conflict is, the less they are satisfied with work and life, the more likely they think that the society is an unfair place, and the more severe they believe the overall social conflict is. When it comes to actual action propensity, they are also more likely to resort to violent behaviors to deal with contradictions and disputes.

We can expect that as the quality of education and the awareness of rights continue to strengthen, the public will pay more attention to the labor conflict problem. In reality, the fierce market competition forces some of the owners of the private enterprises to reduce labor cost at the expense of worker's interests, which exacerbates labor conflicts. Consequently, how to effectively mediate labor relations and reconcile the conflict between the capital and labor will be important issues to maintain social stability for China's future development.

Notes

This chapter was originally published in *Society*, 2005, issue 1.

1 The research project is funded by "China Contemporary People's Internal Contradictions" project as part of the Chinese Academy of Social Sciences major issues project under my supervision and Social Conflicts and Consciousness in China's Social Transformation, part of Shanghai City Board of Education E Institute Construction Project.

2 For those who are interested in detailed statistical analysis, please see Li (2005).
3 The item on the survey asks: "Many believe that they belong to working class, middle class, or upper-middle class. Which category do you think you belong to?"

References

Adam, B., & Beck, U. (Eds.). (2000). *The Risk Society and Beyond: Critical Issues for Social Theory*. London: Sage Publication.

Argyle, M. (1994/1997). *The Psychology of Social Class* (L. Lu, Trans.). Taipei: Juliu Publishing Company.

Beck, U. (1986/1992). *Risk Society: Towards a New Modernity*. London: Sage Publications.

Beck, U. (1999). *World Risk Society*. Cambridge: Polity Press.

Bian, Y. (Ed.). (2002). *Market Transformation and Social Stratification: American Sociologists' Examination of China*. Shanghai: SDX Joint Publishing Company.

Bian, Y., & Logan, J. (1996). "Market Transition and the Persistence of Power: The Changing Stratification System in Urban China." *American Sociological Review, 61*, 739–759.

Bian, Y., & Lu, H. (2002). "Reform and Socioeconomic Inequality: A Shanghainese Perspective." In Y. Bian (Ed.), *Market Transformation and Social Stratification: American Sociologists' Examination of China*. Shanghai: SDX Joint Publishing Company.

Cantril, H. (1943). "Identification with Social and Economic Class." *Journal of Abnormal and Social Psychology, 38*, 74–80.

Caplan, P. (Ed.). (2000). *Risk Revisited*. London: Pluto Press.

Centers, R. (1949). *Psychology of Social Class: A Study of Class Consciousness*. Princeton: Princeton University Press.

Clark, T. N., & Lipset, S. M. (1996). "Are Social Class Dying?" In D. J. Lee & B. S. Turner (Eds.), *Conflicts about Class: Debating Inequality in Late Industrialism* (pp. 42–48). London: Longman.

Coser, L. A. (1956). *The Functions of Social Conflict*. London: Free Press.

Coxon, A. P. M., & Davies, P. M. (Eds.). (1986). *Image of Social Stratification*. London: Sage Publications.

Dahrendorf, R. (1959). *Class and Class Conflict in Industrial Society*. Palo Alto, CA: Stanford University Press.

Dahrendorf, R. (2000). *The Modern Social Conflict* (R. Lin, Trans.). Beijing: China Social Sciences Publishing House.

Esping-Andersen, G. (1985). *Politics against Markets: The Social Democratic Road to Power*. Princeton: Princeton University Press.

Giddens, A. (1991a). *The Consequences of Modernity*. Cambridge: Polity.

Giddens, A. (1991b). *Modernity and Self-Identity: Self and Society in the Late Modern Age*. Cambridge: Policy Press.

Giddens, A. (1998). "Risk Society: The Context of British Politics." In J. Franklin (Ed.), *The Politics of Risk Society* (pp. 23–34). Cambridge: Polity Press.

Giddens, A., & Held, D. (Eds.). (1982). *Class, Power, and Conflict: Classical and Contemporary Debates*. London: Macmillan Press.

Goldfield, M. (1987). *The Decline of Organized Labor in the United States*. Chicago: The University of Chicago Press.

Goldthorpe, J. H. (1980). *Social Mobility and Class Structure in Modern Britain*. Oxford: Clarendon Press.

Goldthorpe, J. H., & Erikson, R. (1992). *The Constant Flux: A Study of Class Mobility in Industrial Society*. Oxford: Clarendon.

Gouldner, A. (2001). *The Future of Intellectuals and the Rise of the New Class* (W. Du, Trans.). Beijing: People's Literature Publishing House.

Gurr, T. R. (1970). *Why Men Rebel*. Princeton: Princeton University Press.

Huang, Y. (2002). *Social Class, Social Network, and Subjective Consciousness: The Continuation of Unfair Social System in Taiwan*. Taipei: Juliu Publishing Company.

Jackman, M. R., & Jackman, R. (1973). "An Interpretation of the Relation between Objective and Subjective Social Status." *American Sociological Review*, 38, 569–582.

Jaeger, C. C. (Ed.). (2001). *Risk, Uncertainty and Rational Action*. London: Earthscan Publications.

Japanese National Committee on Social Stratum and Social Mobility. (1985). "The Dynamics of Class Consciousness in 1985." *Survey Report on National Social Stratum and Social Mobility, 2.*

Kluegel, J., Singleton, R. Jr., & Starnes, C. E. (1977). "Subjective Class Identification: A Multiple Indicator Approach." *American Sociological Review*, 42, 599–611.

Lee, D. J., & Turner, B. S. (Eds.). (1996). *Conflicts about Class: Debating Inequality in Late Industrialism*. London: Longman.

Li, L. (2002). "Institutional Transformation and Changes in Stratification Structure: Dual Reproduction of the Pattern of Relative Inter-strata Relations." *Social Sciences in China, 6.*

Li, P. (2001). "Social Factors Leading to the Disparity between the Rich and the Poor in China and Countermeasures." *Journal of Renmin University of China, 2.*

Li, P., Li, Q., & Sun, L. (2004). *China's Social Stratification*. Beijing: Social Science Academic Press.

Li, P., & Zhang, Y. (2003). "From Life's Adversity: Studies on "Human Capital Malfunction" in Re-employing Laid-off Workers." *Social Sciences in China, 5.*

Lipset, S. (1960/1997). *Political Man* (S. Zhang, Trans.). Shanghai: Shanghai People's Publishing House.

Lipset, S. (1995). *Consensus and Conflict* (H. Zhang, Trans.). Shanghai: Shanghai People's Publishing House.

Liu, X. (2001). "Strata Consciousness of Urban Residents in Mainland China during the Transformation Era." *Sociological Research, 3.*

Liu, X. (2002). "Relatively Deprived Status and the Cognizance of Class." *Sociological Research, 1.*

Mannheim, K. (2002). *Man and Society in an Age of Reconstruction* (L. Zhang, Trans.). Shanghai: SDX Joint Publishing Company.

Marx, K. (1972a). "Louis Bonaparte Eighteenth Brumaire." In *The Complete Works of Marx and Angle*. Vol. 1. Beijing: People's Publishing House.

Marx, K. (1972b). "The Poverty of Philosophy." In *The Complete Works of Marx and Angle*. Vol. 4. Beijing: People's Publishing House.

Marx, K. (1972c). "Labor and Capital." In *The Complete Works of Marx and Angle*. Vol. 1. Beijing: People's Publishing House.

Masao, W. (1998). *The Class Stratification in the Modern Japan and its Fixation* (Z. Lu, Trans.). Beijing: Central Compilation & Translation Press.

Matras, J. (1984). *Social inequality, stratification, and mobility* (T. Ding, Trans.). Taipei: Taipei Guiguang Publishing House.

Parrillo, V. N., Stimson, J., & Stimson, A. (2002). *Contemporary Social Problems* (B. Zhou, Trans.). Beijing: Huaxia Publishing House.

Rosenberg, M. (1953, October). "Perceptual Obstacles to Class Consciousness." *Social Force, 32*, 22–27.

Savage, M. (2000). *Class Analysis and Social Transformation.* Buckingham: Open University Press.

Schultz, T. P. (1998). Inequality in the Distribution of Personal Income in the World: How It Is Changing and Why. *Center discussion papers* 784. Yale University Economic Growth Center.

Seabrook, J. (2002). *Class: Unveil the Myth of the Social Label* (T. Tan, Trans.). Taipei: Taipei Shulin Publishing House.

Sun, L. (2004). *Transformation and Rupture: Changes in Chinese Social Structure since the Reform.* Beijing: Tsinghua University Press.

Sun, L., Li, Q., & Shen, Y. (1998). "The Recent Trend and Hidden Perils in the Social Structural Transformation in China." *Strategy and Management, 5.*

Thompson, E. P. (1963/2001). *The Making of the English Working Class* (C. Qian, Trans.). Nanjing: Yilin Press.

Venneman, R. & Pample, F. C. (1977). "The American Perception of Class and Status." *American Sociological Review, 42.*

Worchel, S., & Morales, J. F. (Eds.). (1998). *Social Identity: International Perspective.* London: Sage Publications.

Wright, E. O. (1979). *Class Structure and Income Determination.* New York: Academic Press.

Wright, E. O. (1999). *Class Counts.* Oxford: Oxford University Press.

Wu, N. (1994). "Class Cognizance and Class Identity: A Comparative Study on Two Class Structures in Sweden, the United States, and Taiwan 1992." In J. Xu (Ed.), *Collection of Comparative Studies on Class Structure and Class Consciousness.* Taipei: Institute of European and American Studies, Academia Sinica.

Xu, J. (Ed.). (1994). *Collection of Comparative Studies on Class Structure and Class Consciousness.* Taipei: Institute of European and American Studies, Academia Sinica.

Zhang, Y. (1997). "Urbanization, Stratification, and Living Status." In L. Zhang (Ed.), *Taiwanese Society in the 1990s.* Taipei: Institute of Social Studies, Academia Sinica.

Zheng, C. (2001). "Class Identity Consciousness and Its Causal Analysis – A Study on Residents in Guangzhou, China." *Zhejiang Academic Journal, 3.*

Zunz, O., & Schoppa, L. (2002). *Social Contracts under Stress: The Middle Class of America, Europe, and Japan at the Turn of the Century.* New York: Russell Sage Foundation.

9 Problems on China strengthening and innovating social management[1]

Social management, in general, refers to the process in which agents that are dominated by the government but still include other social forces act in accordance with the law laws, regulations and policies to organize, coordinate, provide service, supervise, and control various social fields through a variety of means.

After the foundation of the People's Republic of China (P.R.C.), under the leadership of the Communist Party of China, China has taken a series of measures to eliminate all kinds of hideous social phenomena and vile practices, purifying the society in a prompt fashion. These measures also help establish a new nationwide social order through stabilizing price, implementing full employment, providing the public with the living necessities, and strengthening social safety and security. After the reform and opening up, with the further development of the socialist market economy, the whole society has changed. To accommodate the needs of the socialist democratic politics and the market economy, China has carried out a series social management reforms with respect to employment, income distribution, social security, education, health care, housing, and the urban-rural relationship, out of which a vibrant and relatively orderly social management situation takes shape.

However, the rapid economic and social development has posed new situations, problems, and challenges for China's existing social management undertakings, which, in many cases, lag behind in accommodating the emerged demands of recent development. This requires us to deepen our knowledge about social management, bring our social management theory to the date, integrate social management resources, and innovate the institutions of social management, so that we can bring into being a new social management order. Under the current new circumstance, strengthening and innovating social management endeavors has become a prominent task for economic and social construction in China and a new focus in the economic and social reform.

On February 19, 2011, General Secretary Hu Jintao delivered an important speech at the social management and innovation seminar at the Central Party School for the main leading cadres at provincial and ministerial levels. General Secretary Hu called on the entire party to grasp the new changes and characteristics of domestic and international orders, focus on strengthening and innovating social management mechanism in view of the outstanding problems, work on the thinking and practices of mass work in new position, in order to promote social harmony and gather a strong force to achieve the economic and social development goals set for the twelfth five-year-plan period. On May 30, General Secretary Hu Jintao chaired a meeting of the Central Political Bureau, focusing on how to strengthen the social management and innovation. The meeting noted that as the actual situation changes, China's social management thinking, the system and the institution, laws and policies, means and approaches are largely ill suited. It is extremely urgent yet takes long-term efforts to solve the problems in the social management. Strengthening and innovating social management concerns the consolidation of the ruling status of the party, the national stability in the long run, and whether the people live and work in peace and contentment.

I will discuss how to strengthen and innovate social management in the following aspects.

The basic characteristics of China's social management system and its achievements

The basic characteristics of China's established social management system

In modern history, China has repeatedly been ravaged by great powers and war after war, in spite of its large population. One of the causes of the national poverty and weakness is that the society is disunited, like a heap of loose sand. Therefore, the first and foremost task for the newly founded China is to "unify." On September 30, 1949, as Chairman Mao declared at the closing session of the Chinese People's Political Consultative Conference, "Fellow countryman, we should further unify and organize ourselves. We should overcome the desultory and disorganized state that prevailed in the ancient China and unify the overwhelming majority of the Chinese people in the political, military, economic, cultural, and other organizations." By this token, after the foundation of P.R.C., under the planned economy system, China has arranged all the people in sort of work unit and built a highly centralized social management system in which the government takes over and takes care of everything. The characteristics of this kind of social management systems are as follows.

First, the government-led social management is omnipotent. The government implements uniform plans, takes the sole responsibility for balancing the budget, directly control the purchase and sale, and is in full charge of generating revenues and expenditure, so that a highly centralized planned economy is set up. Moreover, government puts itself at the center of an omnipotent social management system by unifying the management concerning cadres deployment, professional identity, personnel placement, and social affairs and putting every social activities under centralized organization. It deprives a stand-alone room for the society to grow.

Second, the employment management is based on "work unit." What we need understand about "work unit" is that it is not a general workplace but a work organization that is built to be omnipotent. "Work unit" is more than a work organization in that it is part of a grassroots organizational system to solve all kinds of social affairs where social management and control is carried out. Be it administrative unit, institution, enterprise, or the rural people's commune, they are all affiliated with concerning governmental departments, and all sorts of social organizations are subordinate "unit" to the government. "Work unit" is both an organizational unit for Chinese society and the foundation for the social management in the planned economy system which makes state organs, enterprises and institutions, and the people's commune "big or small comprehensive" unit organization. It helps establish a mechanism that solve all kinds of social problems at the grassroots level.

Third, the urban idle personnel management system is based on the "neighborhood." Through neighborhood residents committee, government manage the unemployed, idlers, and the recipients of civil relief and social special care. Indeed, since a vast majority of the population are affiliated with a work unit, neighborhood residents committee complements the role of the work unit.

Fourth, the social mobility is managed through the work unit system, the household registration, the professional identity system and the personnel archives system. The goal of social management under the planned economy is to make the society highly organized and in order and make employment and residence of general social members as fixed as possible. Social mobility management that is based on the work unit system, the household registration, the professional identity system and the personnel archives system restricts the freedom of social members to move between the rural and urban areas, change workplace and jobs. All the population flow and migration needed by the country are organized in accordance with central plans.

The making of the omnipotent social management system in the planned economy has transformed China's loosely organized state in the past and established a highly centralized social order, which has greatly enhanced the nation's capacity for mobilization and social control. This plays a positive role in mobilizing all the possible resources to accomplish the construction industrial system when China's economic foundation was extremely feeble. Nonetheless, this kind of social management system also has its inherent drawbacks. On one hand, the government becomes omnipotent directly supervising the economy and the society and taking full charge of all social affairs. By doing so, not only the administrative cost is very high, but the responsibilities concentrate in the hand of the government with the centralization of power. The society thus lacks the mechanism of self-organization, self-management, and self-regulation. On the other hand, all social members are restricted to relatively isolated work unit, which hinders the natural social mobility and deprives the society of vitality and creativity.

The achievements of social management since the reform and opening-up

Since the reform and opening up, in order to adapt to changes from the planned economy to the socialist market economy, China has carried out a series of reforms in the social management system and made remarkable achievements. The achievements are characterized in the following aspects.

First, a series of social management system reforms have changed social members' state of working and living in relative isolation, greatly boosted the social mobility between urban and rural areas and between different workplaces and jobs, which have mobilized the masses' potentials, creativity and enthusiasm for work. The efficiency of human resources allocation has been significantly improved, and the whole society is vibrant.

Second, reforms in social contradiction management changed the practice that politicizes social contradiction and treats internal contradictions among the people as that with the enemy. In the reform and development, China has paid attention to intermediating the interests of various social strata and interest groups, taken full consideration and recognition of the fundamental interests of the overwhelming majority of the people and the relationship between the common interests of the masses and the special interest groups at present. China has handled the internal contradictions among the people in a decent manner and maintain the basic social harmony and stability.

Third, reforms in household registration, employment, social security systems and so on have amended the security and management system of the floating population, the disadvantaged population and the unemployed, and thus improved the people's living standard.

Fourth, reforms in education, health care, culture and other institutions have increased the supply of public goods and public services, largely catching up the growing demands from the people for education, health care, and other aspects of cultural life.

Fifthly, China has reinforced its comprehensive administration with the respect to food and drug safety, production safety, and public safety, ensuring a good production and social order wherein China's rapid development.

Sixthly, the establishment of a national emergency management system has greatly improved the responsiveness to emergency. China has revealed its strong emergency and social management capacity in an array of major events such as "SARS," Wenchuan earthquake, the disastrous blizzard that devastated the southern regions, the Olympics, and the World Expo.

Challenges posed by dramatic social transformations since the reform and opening-up for social management system

Since the reform and opening up, with the further development of the socialist market economy, Chinese society has went through a great deal of changes. The dramatic change taking place in China is unprecedented in the modern world history with the respect to its magnitude, pace, scope, repercussion, and momentum. Under the new situation, China's social management system is facing challenges from the social changes left and right.

The first challenge is engendered by the changes in social stratification. The initial social class structure that consisted of working class, farmers, cadres, and intellectuals is morphing into a complex and diverse class structure of many different interest groups. New social class and strata come into being, including the self-employed, private entrepreneurs, the executives of foreign-funded enterprises, the scientific and technical professionals at the private enterprises, various intermediary agents, and freelancers, many of whom have split from the ranks of workers, farmers, cadres and intellectuals. Even within the same social stratum, people differ in their economic status and pursuit of interests. For instance, among working class are workers in monopolistic industries and in foreign-funded enterprises, and urban workers in general industries and migrant workers, and so on. How to integrate and coordinate interests of different clustering in the new situation becomes an important task for the social management in the making of competitive but harmonious order.

The second challenge concerns the changes in the urban-rural structure. Since the reform and opening up, 200 million farmers have left the soil that generations of their ancestors have cultivated, and even left the villages they live, turning themselves into workers engaged in secondary and tertiary industries. They collectively have precipitated the largest wave of industrialization and urbanization across the world. Massive and rapid social mobility has raised a series of new problems for social management. How to shape the new system of integrated development of urban and rural areas by encouraging farmer-turned migrant workers to adapt to the new urban living becomes a major challenge for current social management.

The third challenge is posed by structural changes occurred to the income distribution. In the recent 30 years or so, China, which was once an egalitarian society, has become a country with great income disparity with reference to the international context. The expanding income gap, unfair distribution, and the related corruptions are the underlying causes for dissatisfactions among cadres and the masses as well as for many of the social problems. How to adjust the income distribution structure and establish a fair and reasonable income distribution order become deep-seated problems to be solved in order to maintain social harmony and stability.

The fourth challenge is about demographic and family structure. Profound changes in China's demographic structure accelerate the miniaturization of the family and the aging of the population. Problems that used to be solved by families and intergenerational help, such as providing for the elderly, supporting the single parent, psychological barrier, disability, and intergenerational conflict, are now gradually socialized. Widely adopted traditional practice of providing for the aged by the families that has existed for thousands of years is put into jeopardy by changes resulted from changes in family structure, intergenerational relations, and social mobility. These are the new missions facing China's social management undertakings.

The fifth challenge comes from the changed mode of social organization. Along with the deep reform of the economic system, the organization of social life in China has changed from being a "unit person" to being a "social man." On one hand, as some of the work units largely implement reforms in "privatizing housing ownership, marketizing employment and logistic service, and socializing social security," "the work unit organization" plays a lesser role in solving social problems than it used to be serving as the foundation for traditional social management system. Some of the work unit organizations have broken up completely. On the other hand, social mobility speeds up because of employment diversification. A large number of new employment organizations emerged after the reform and the opening up manage in a "non-work unit" style. They are no more than workplaces, rather than work units that take care of everything. More and more social members are becoming "social person" instead of "unit person." "Unit person" used to make up more than 95percent of the urban employees, but now the proportion drops to about a quarter.

The sixth challenge is the changes in social norms and values. Market transformation has promoted economic development and has greatly improved the people's livelihood, but also brought about the changes in social behavior norms and values. Individual's pursuit of self-interest becomes legitimate and rational practice, but social norms that restrain and inspect such behaviors are not yet in place. Social management and monitoring and surveillance technologies fail to keep up with the growing complexity in social lives and production behaviors. The construction of corresponding social morality and credibility system lags behind the profound changes to people's mind-set triggered by the market economy.

A sea change posing various challenges to China's social management system urge China to strengthen social management and innovation and blaze a new trail of social management that dovetails with socialist democratic politics and market economy.

New situation and problems facing Chinese social management

New situation and problems facing Chinese social management at present are related to both international and domestic issues, which are intertwined together under the sway of globalization of social life and the information networks.

From the international perspective, after the international financial meltdown, the confrontation between the unemployed college graduates and the policemen at the end of 20120 led to an accidental self-burning incident in Tunisia, which triggered a domino effect in the Middle East and North Africa of social upheaval, political unrest, civil war, and regime changes, to the world's astonishment. Among those countries that were caught in political turmoil in the Middle East and North Africa, some have developed fairly quickly in the past decade. A majority of the GDP per capita is also at the upper-middle level across the world, and some countries are relatively rich. However, long-standing social problems like wealth disparity and high rate of youth unemployment are at the root of social unrest.

From the domestic perspective, after more than 30 years of reform and opening up, China's economic and social development has entered a new stage which is characterized by sustainably fast-growing economy, overall political stability, and prominent social issues. Many factors catalyze the current prominence of social problems. As far as the management system is concerned, one of the important reasons is that the existing social management system fails to fully keep up with the rapid process of industrialization, urbanization, marketization, and internationalization. This urges for strengthening and innovating social management techniques. New situation and problems facing China's social management system at present fall into the following categories.

Arduous task of managing massive floating population due to the accelerating social mobility

The accelerated industrialization since the reform and opening up has resulted in a massive floating population in China. However, slums that pervaded Brazil and India in their industrialization and urbanization process do not surface in China, which should be regarded as an accomplishment for China's social management. The migrant population from the rural region to the cities found it difficult to merge fully into the urban life because of the barriers with respect to household registration, employment, housing, children's education, social security, and so on. Most of the migrant population concentrates in the rural-urban fringe zones and underground architectures. The social management and public service system that was always correspondent to the urban population in the past has failed to evolve in accordance with the newly added population. This failure significantly undermines the management capacity in the rural-urban fringe zones where migrant population tend to concentrate, and leaves social problems unchecked in the areas such as theft, robbery, drug trafficking and abuse, and underworld prostitution. It is an arduous task to manage such a large-scale floating population with due attention to all aspects of the social management system.

Escalating conflict and confrontation triggered by land requisition and housing demolition in the midst of the new force of urbanization

China's urbanization process is accelerating since the new century, which is the inevitable trend of economic and social development. Urbanization has become a powerful driving force for China's economic and social development after industrialization. Dismantling the dual urban-rural structure and integrating the urban and rural areas has become an important development goal from the top to the grassroots. However, the problems are extraordinary that urbanization lags behind industrialization and the population urbanization lags behind the land urbanization. Agricultural added value accounted for only 10 percent of the GDP in 2010, while agriculture workers made up of 38 percent of the total population of the employees. There were still 52 percent of the farmers living in rural regions, even when the statistics of the urban resident population included farmers who have lived in the cities for more than half a year. Given the stimulus of the enormous facial revenue generated via land-added value for the local economy and the government, a new wave of "land replacement" comes into being. Massive enclosure of farmland and forced eviction arises more and more social issues. Frequent occurrence of malignant evens and mass disturbances harms social stability and harmony. According to statistics, from 2006 to 2008, despite the state requirement of the balance between the arable land requisition and compensation, the actual net cultivated land in China has reduced by 124.8 million *mu*, decreasing by nearly 42 million *mu* annually, which is a rate much higher than an annual decrease of 226 million *mu* during the tenth five-year plan period. China must pay great attention to the relationship between the development and stability in the process of population urbanization and land nonagriculturalization as to prevent and put an end to the occurrence of serious damage to the interests of the masses.

Strained labor relations in the non-public labor intensive enterprises stand out due to changes in the supply-demand of the labor force

The supply-demand relationship in the primary labor market is undergoing profound changes; the amount of new labor is declining year by year and expected to drop below zero during the thirteenth five-year plan period. At the same time, although there are more than 200 million in labor force who need to be transferred out of the rural regions, "the recruitment problem" that intermittently occurred since 2004 is now normalized and deteriorating because a serious aging agricultural and rural labor force is ill suited to the demand for the youth labor in the primary nonagricultural labor market. Against this backdrop, the wages for the migrant workers are experience an upward spiral, and the consciousness of labor protection and rights protection is strengthened remarkably among the new generation migrant workers, for whom the dilemma is the reluctance to return to the rural life and the difficulty to stay in the cities. Increase in labor costs, rise in the raw material price, and the appreciation of RMB all contribute to squeezing the profit margins for the labor-intensive export enterprises and impacting the interests of the owners. At present, the strained labor relations in the nonpublic-owned labor-intensive enterprises are drastically stark, which throws labor conflict into relief. In 2010, strikes for pay raise, as represented in the event occurred at the Honda factory in Nanhai, produced a "butterfly effect," spreading to other coastal areas and dozens of large-scale strikes taking place nationwide. Suicides committed by the new generation migrant workers at the Foxconn shock the whole society. These incidents reflect a strengthened awareness of right protection among by the new generation migrant workers and the desire for harmonious and decent labor relations. Consequently, how to coordinate the labor relations in the new situation and legalize the rules, intermediation, and handling of the labor conflict is the urgent problem at the present.

A weak fiscal basis at the rural local level and the need to sort out the relations between the masses and the grassroots cadres

Since China adopted the tax sharing system in 1994, it witnessed an overall fiscal upturn. However, the fiscal foundation below the county level in the majority parts of the nation remains relatively weak, and a considerable number of towns and villages operate in high debt. After the abolition of agricultural tax, for some agricultural production areas the primary finance mainly depends on transfer payments, but the fiscal situation is even worse. In some areas, the grassroots financial power fails to accommodate the needs of administration. All kinds of the social affairs are in the need of correspondent appropriations from the local financial department. Defying repeated bans on "arbitrary charges" from the central government, some of the local governments that are facing the problem of financial insufficiency collect random charges in all kinds of names. Grassroots government tends to focus on the political performance in a myopic fashion, following the principle that "the current reign ignores [problems] passed from the prior reign," which has caused many tensions in the relations between grassroots cadres and the masses, or even public resentment because of the accumulation of social problems in the transition of local administrators since the reform and opening up. Surveys on the public satisfaction with the government in recent years have shown that the satisfaction declines from the central government to the grassroots level. Some rural areas have seen rural hollowing and decaying, as the rural industries go empty, young people leave the areas, the rich buy houses and move to the city, and cadres do not live in the villages and towns any longer. How to handle the relations between the grassroots cadres and the masses in the new situation in the endeavors to build a new socialistic countryside is an important issue of social management concerning China's governance and stability in the long run.

Changes in grassroots management and a weakened mechanism to solve social problems

China's social management system was once built on the "work unit," and the "unit organization" used to be the grassroots place where social problems got solved. Nowadays, the vast majority of urban employees are "social people" rather than "unit people." This means that the government often has to face a large number of scattered individuals directly, and the friction cost of governance rises sharply in that both the implementation of social policies from the top down and the reconciliation and the settlement of social problems from the bottom up would meet with great resistance. For instance, social affairs like tax, law and order, social security, employment, sanitation and anti-epidemic, as well as conscription and blood donation, cannot be carried out solely through the "work unit." In addition, some of the social disputes and social contradictions occurred at the grassroots now can no longer be "solved at the grassroots." The cost of "lawsuit" is too high for the ordinary people, quite a few of whom "trust appealing to the higher authorities for help more than laws" and whom would often resort to the local governments for justice. Given that now the government functions are set apart from the enterprise management and social regulation, leapfrog petitions and appeals to Beijing become more and more prominent. Mass appeals for help pose sharp conflicts with the local governments that attempt to intercept the appeals. In some places, many social problems pile up causing public grievance, which are likely to trigger inadvertent mass incidents. Therefore, how to reduce the cost of social management and build a mechanism that effectively copes with problems at the local level is a new problem worth exploring for social management system.

Expanding income gap and unequal distribution: underlying causes for social problems

The ever-expanding income gap at present has become a major problem affecting China's development and stability and an underlying cause for several social problems. The characteristics of current income distribution pattern that distinguishes China from other countries are as follows. First, as China outgrew from a country of planned egalitarian distribution into a country of a wide income disparity, tremendous changes have taken place regarding the distribution and the policy orientations, which are not made or implemented without public resistance and controversies. Second, in addition to the disparity caused by the market distribution, there is a huge difference caused by fiscal redistribution. For instance, civil servants at the same level may earn differently depending on the regions where they work. Not only the public but also the cadres are complaining about the current distribution order. According to investigations, Chinese are much more dissatisfied, on subjective terms, with the income distribution, as opposed to countries and regions where the objective income gap is comparable. Third, China is facing a dilemma in some of the income distribution situations. There is a strong public outcry against the fat salaries of the executives at the state-owned monopolistic enterprises, on one hand. On the other hand, the talents at the state-owned monopolistic enterprises are in the global market for head-hunting companies' to grab, which works for internationally monopolistic enterprises. Fourth, power-for-money deals and corruptions have intensified the psychological feeling about the wealth disparity, which might have caused an "anti-rich" complex. Reform practices have to come to terms with the relationship between the fairness and the efficiency, straightening out the income distribution order and establishing a reasonable and fair income distribution system. These practices affect the established interest order inevitably, which takes courage and foresight as well as wisdom and social management techniques. If the greatest accomplishment of the reform and opening up is the rapid economic development and a significance raise in people's living standard, then the most significant problem yet unsolved is perhaps the income distribution inequality.

Outstanding problems of mass incidents and be closely attentive to various kinds of new social risks

Mass incidents have caused great repercussions among the public lately. There are many reasons for the mass incidents, but a majority of them reflect appeals concerning people's livelihood and economic interests, such as improving labor welfare and treatment, raising the standards for land acquisition and relocation compensations, protesting corporate-led environmental pollutions, ascertaining the accountability of medical accidents. There are "mass incidents of direct interest conflicts" caused by infringing the interests of the employees and the mass; there are also "mass incidents of non-direct interest conflicts" serving as vents for the widespread public resentment. The latter, in particular, is unpredictable and prone to spread very quickly and cause large-scale chaos. These risk characteristics of the modern society are especially noteworthy. China must also be closely attentive to frequent occurrence of food safety and environmental safety incidents in recent years, which are also characterized by unpredictability and the proneness to public panic.

Increasingly perplexing problems in keeping public order with an accelerating the social transformation

With the acceleration of social transformation and social mobility, social security issues tend to be multiple and social management is facing many difficulties. Although the public security agencies at all levels have taken a series of measures to crack down on all kinds of crimes, the total amount of the criminal offense is still running high and the new crime continues to grow. Crimes committed by underworld Mafia-like gangs, violent crime, Internet fraud crimes and all kinds of property-seizing crimes, in particular, pose serious harm to the public safety and social order as well as people's lives. Comprehensive management of social security is a long-term task in the social transition period.

Some of the aforementioned new situations and problems are caused by structural conflict, system friction, the vacuums in social norms, and inadequate laws and regulations in the process of social structural transformation and system transition. Others are left over by history yet unsolved for various reasons. Still, others come into being because of the management deficiency, improper handling techniques, and errors. China has to tackle these problems gradually while strengthening and innovating the social management system.

Major steps toward strengthening and innovating social management

Improve social management and give full play to the power of the society in all respects

When it comes to strengthening and innovating social management, China shall shape and improve the formation of a social management pattern in which the party committee wields overall authority, the government is in charge of execution, and various social parties coordinate and implement concerted actions with wide public participations. In practice, however, there is no consensus on the understandings of social management pattern. Some government officials maintain that the power of the government must be enhanced in order to strengthen social management in the challenges of prominent social problems. Otherwise, the government has their hands tied in front of social problems, ineffective in taking mild measures but fearful of taking tough measures. Some scholars, however, argue that China is now characterized by a powerful government, strong market, and weak society, and that the most important thing for innovating social management is to balance the power, control the market, and foster social development through promoting the development of social organizations.

When national conditions are taken into consideration, China can no long follow the traditional approach toward social managements – that is, by centralizing power in government's hands and allowing the government to take care of every social issue. China cannot follow the path advocated by some Western nations that solely depends upon the civil society to foster social development, either. In the process of building socialism with Chinese characteristics of social management system, China must allow the grassroots party organizations to play their due roles, speed up the classification reform of public institutions, guide and stress the social responsibility of enterprises, establish a set of "social enterprises" that are willing to shoulder more social responsibilities, develop and expand social organization to undertake the government purchase of social services, and transform community into a new basis for social management by strengthening the construction of communities. Special attentions should be given to fostering the roles played by organizations of workers, youth, and women, as well as trade associations in social management and public service provision. These institutions have mature bottom-up organizational structure and are equipped with the talents who have ample experience in mass work, ideological and political work, and social work. They not only bridge the mass and the party and the state but also play a unique role in reflecting the demands of the masses, resolving social contradictions, providing public services, and participating in social management.

Integrate and coordinate all interests groups and balance the relationship between protecting rights and maintaining stability

China should further strengthen and improve the government-led mechanism of safeguarding the rights and interests of the masses, coordinate the fundamental interests of the people, current common interests of the masses, and special interests of special groups. China need form scientific and effective coordination mechanism, the appeal expression mechanism, conflict mediation mechanism, and rights protection mechanism. Properly handle all kinds of contradictions among the people, resolutely correct the unhealthy tendency to harm the public interests, and earnestly safeguard the legitimate rights and interests of the masses. In the process of reform and development, China should always insist on balancing the relationship between safeguarding the rights and interests of the masses and maintaining social stability, not allowing the slogan of "stability" to trump the appeals of "rights" nor letting people harm social stability and harmony in the name of "protecting rights."

China must make breakthroughs in establishing a fair and reasonable income distribution system. Spare no efforts to rectify the income distribution order, to combat all kinds of illegal profit-making activities, to ban all kinds of illegal income, to tackle the problem of corruption at its roots, make an overall plan to close the income gap between the general competition industry and the monopoly industry, standardize the civil servants wage system, coordinate the relationship between the labor income and capital gains, be determined to reverse the trend of a widening income distribution gap, and maintain social fairness and justice so that the people can share the fruits of reform and development.

Fortify the infrastructure construction at the local level and turn the urban and rural community into a new foundation for social management

In the new social management order, it is of significance to let grassroots communities play their roles in social management. Community is an autonomous organization, but at the same time, it also shoulders the responsibility for self-management and self-service. Many "community service centers" provide dozens of different services, including tax, law and order, employment, social security, social welfare, social assistance, health, epidemic prevention, and the spiritual civilization construction. The mass describes such an extensive service provision as "community as a needle running through thousands of threads of the society." Community plays an increasingly important role in the grassroots social management. With the development of socialist market economy, people's consciousness of safeguarding their own rights and interests has been enhanced, which will bring about disputes over rights and interests. Consequently, community work has to become specialized and professionalized from the community level, which will help build a new system to "solve the problems at the grassroots." Proper regulation of the relationship between the community committee, the owners committee, and the property committee would form a joint force for the construction of grassroots infrastructure.

Professionalize the social management team and manage the mass work under the new situation

The sixth Plenary Session of the sixteenth CPC Central Committee has made the resolution to build a talented social work team. Just like the third Plenary Session of the eleventh CPC Central Committee is committed to fostering and training managerial professionals in the economic management, we must, with equal devotion, foster and train social management talents. Connect social management to social service, as to subsume social management under social service provision through which the former can be improved continuously. Social management is not restricted, rather simplistically, as to "control, stop, and suppress." Nor can it be understood as merely solving problems such as petitions and mass incidents or to keep social stability. Instead, social management relates to everything about the social construction, including employment, social security, income distribution, education, medical care, housing, and other livelihood issues. Advocate the professionalism and work ethic of social management that is people and livelihood oriented. Vigorously improve the professional level of mass work under the new situation, and create a new order of social management and mass work. Form a healthy social ethos that promotes self-help, mutual help, dedication, and integrity by making arduous efforts to develop volunteer terms and organize volunteer activities.

Establish robust public safety systems and alerts to guard against new social risks

It took China thirty plus years to accomplish the development transitions in modernization that once took many countries hundreds of years. Compression of the development length also encapsulates problems into a single space and time that otherwise emerge at various stages of development. Social problems before China not only include those traditional security issues, such as fire, traffic accident, mine disaster, drought and flood, earthquake, labor dispute, and the conflict between the rich and poor, but also include new social risks that are unpredictable, prone to spread rapidly, and panic-eliciting, such as chemical pollution, nuclear pollution, food safety, unknown infectious diseases, financial crises, and terrorism. These security problems, with distinct characters, are intertwined sometimes, which complicate the handling process. China should further establish and improve the public security system, enhance the government and the people' capacity to respond to the emergency, universalize public safety education, boost its competence to keep away, withstand, and control new social risks, and improve the public safety system and its legal system.

Highlight the current prominent contradictions and solve a batch of social problems left from the history step by step

In the process of reform and development, because institutions in transition are disconnected and imperfect, and because the development is realized at the expense of social management endeavors, a number of historical problems concerning people's livelihoods have accumulated. There are problems of holding compensations for the employees of the restructured enterprises, of the social security of workers in collective enterprises, of the way-too-low wages for the enterprise retirees, of land compensation for farmers, and of proper placement of the returned veterans, and so on. As China's financial situation has improved, the ability to solve these historical issues is also greatly enhanced. China should take a responsible attitude, determined to solve these social problems left from the history in the next ten years. The last thing China wants is the persistence of the attitude that "disguises disaster as incident and treats incident as triviality" for the sake of economic development. China has to prevent the outbreak of social problems caused by historical accumulation.

Develop and expand social organization and mobilize the enthusiasm of the masses to participate in social management

In social management practice, China should let the community, trade organizations, and intermediary organizations and other social organizations play full roles in providing services, reflecting the public demands and setting the social norms. Strengthen and improve the management and the supervision of all kinds of social organizations, improve the social service network, and strive to form a joint force of social management and social services by actively fostering the development of all kinds of social organizations. By doing so, China can constantly meet the growing material and cultural needs of the people. Currently, and in the near future, the goal is to allow social organizations to facilitate economic development with an emphasis on improving the social organization abilities so that China can push forward innovations in management system and the establishment of social organization management system that builds on mature legal institutions and standardized management procedures – a system of classified management and graded responsibilities. Adapt to the development of the socialist market economy and the need to transform governmental functions. Foster the development of economic associations for public welfare and rural professionals and the nongovernmental community organizations. Support and guide the development of new social organizations in realms of science, education, culture, education, and health to improve people's living standards. Meanwhile, it is necessary to strengthen the supervision of social organization activities by law and to allow the social organizations to operate in a self-developing, self-managing, self-educating, and self-disciplinary fashion. Intensify the efforts to investigate illegal and undisciplined social organizations, fight against cult organizations, gangland, illegal pyramid selling organization, and social hostility organizations to ensure the healthy development of social organizations.

Perfect the social management legal system and strengthen social management practice by law

After the reform and opening up, China's legal system construction has made great achievements in that governance the country by law is realized on the whole. However, the legislations in the social realms lag behind those in the economic field. Particularly with the respect to social management, it is quite common in some regions that there is a legal vacuum, or nominal laws are ignored in practice, or administrative decisions override legal governance. Social management laws and regulations are important components of the socialist legal system with Chinese characteristics. This requires meeting the needs for building a socialist harmonious society and of placing social construction in a prominent position, to speed up the pace to improve the legal and regulatory system of social management, especially regarding labor relations disputes, land requisition, housing demolition, social order, production safety, food and drug safety, and environmental protection. Further, strengthen the social management in accordance with the law and maintain social harmony and stability.

Strengthen the construction of moral and credit system and improve the soft power of social management

When innovating the social management system, China should pay attention to constructing not only hard power but also soft power. Strengthen the value system with a the socialist with the respect to democracy and the rule of law, harmony and justice, common prosperity, bring the concept of social management up to date, and ameliorate the moral order, credit system, and the behavioral norms of the new social management system. Strengthen the construction of citizens' morality that is based on the social morality, professional ethics, and family virtues, and advocate traditional ethics of patriotism and law-abiding, work ethics of integrity and professionalism and family virtue of mutual help and love. Guide ethics and public opinions to curb the spread of money worship, hedonism, extreme individualism, deception and fraud, power abuse, and corruption and to bring about a social atmosphere and mechanism that awards justice-holding and penury-alleviating behaviors, the willingness to contribute, and actions to maintain social justice and fairness.

Conscientiously sum up the experience of local government and improve the top design for the social management innovations

Local specificities in China vary drastically from place to place. It is proven effective by the reform practices to sum up local experience. There are many great practices in strengthening and innovating social management all over the country. For example, Beijing has the experience in setting up social work committee and "hub-type" social organization work systems. Shanghai has plenty of experience strengthening and innovating the management of communities. Nantong municipal government in Jiangsu Province set up a "large-scale mediation." Hangzhou municipal government in Zhejiang Province has utilized democratic measures to improve people's livelihood. Liaoning Province has MXWZ, a website to solve problems and deal with petitions for the public. The list of experience continues. Summarize and refine the local experience, improve the top design for the social management innovations, and break a trail of social management with Chinese characteristic socialism.

Note

1 This chapter is based on a lecture delivered at the seminar before the 11th Session of the National People's Congress Standing Committee on June 30, 2011.

10 Mass consumption stage and social reform[1]

My topic for today is "mass consumption phase and social reform." Let me start with concepts. So what does "mass consumption stage" mean? American economist Walt Rostow proposed the stage of "mass consumption" in the 1960s. He theorized a famous model of economic growth in which he divided the national development into five stages and later extended it into six stages, as we know it today, in *Politics and the Stages of Economic Growth* published in 1971. The six stages are traditional society, preconditions for takeoff, takeoff, drive to maturity, high mass consumption, and transcending mass consumption. However, in the descriptions of the six stages, what impresses the scholars the most is description and analysis of the takeoff stage, for which Rostow used ample materials and experience to prove right. Therefore, the theory of economic growth is known as the "Rostovian takeoff model." Rostow argues that the takeoff stage +is characterized by: 1) a large number of labor transferring from agriculture to manufacturing; 2) remarkable increases in foreign investment; and 3) the emergence of a regional growth pole and the comparative advantage shifting from agriculture to labor-intensive products. Based on empirical materials, he examined the takeoff stage in a number of countries, including, for example, the United Kingdom from 1783 to 1802, France from 1830 to 1860, the United States from 1843 to 1860, Germany from 1850 to 1873, and Japan from 1878 1900. What Rostow refers to as the takeoff stage is actually the process of industrialization, although the preconditions for industrialization are different from country to country. China has long been considered a traditional society. As a result, some scholars from domestic or even international economics circle reckon that China's takeoff stage is from 1977 to 1987. Nonetheless, one flaw in Rostow's theory is the lack of equally detailed documentation of characteristics and empirical proof for the rest of the stages for the maturity stage; in particular, his description is rather simple. So when China completely takes off, which stage are we heading for?

I would argue that China has entered the stage of mass consumption after taking off. This is a brand new stage of development, which differs from the previous stages in fundamental aspects. In more than 30 years since the reform and opening up, the main analytical framework we adopt is to draw comparison before and after the reform. Two significant changes set post-reform stage from the previous stage. The first one is what we call institutional transition, or market transformation.

Many foreign scholars apply the analytical framework and model for transitional countries to the case of China and argue that China, like Eastern European countries and Russia, is one of the market transition countries. However, from the economic growth perspective, China is different from those countries in that when they begin market transformation those countries have completed industrialization process so they encounter no significant structural changes. The other one is to put China into the model of economic takeoff. For instance, comparing China with the Asian Tigers, some have examined China using the flying-geese model and maintained that these countries, including China, are in a Confucian cultural circle, and they belong to the yellow race and the oriental culture. However, the reality is that China is also very different from these East Asian countries and regions. While they experienced a structural transition and industrialization without a simultaneous transformation from planned economy to the market economy, China's economic takeoff have involved both economic transition and social structural transformation at the same time – that is, two T's changes.

Now more than 30 years later, the old comparison between before and after the reform and opening up is insufficient in many fronts to explain new changes. As a result, now the reform has entered a midterm stage, which not only differs from the pre-reform state but also calls for significant shifts in reform and development agendas set in the initial stage of the reform. The shifts fall into categories as follows, which might as well be called "new stage characteristics."

First, the country shifts from shortage economy to inadequate supply of public goods and public services. What was the circumstance like at the initial stage of the reform and opening up? That is shortage economy, meaning everything is in short supply. The main task is to expand the economy at great scale and provide consumer products in great numbers, in order to meet the basic needs of the people, so at that time there was market for any produced goods, even for some counterfeit and shoddy products. However, since 1990s, we have turned to be a buyer's market from a seller's market, which means our production has reached a supply-demand balance, if not a state of oversupply. Up to now, according to the National Bureau of statistics of more than 300 kinds of products, there is a basic balance between supply and demand, some oversupply, and even excessive production in some sectors. In other words, it is difficult to sell products, and sometimes to the extent that it still fails to sell even at a price below the cost. Meanwhile, new shortage is taking shape. As the economy grows, people's material and cultural needs also rise. According to Maslow's hierarchy of needs, the satisfaction of the lower layer of need produces the demand for needs at the higher layer. Now we are mainly in need of public goods and public services. Current livelihood issues cover clearly different range than that in the initial stage of the reform and opening up when the major livelihood issue is food and clothing. Now the livelihood issues are mainly employment, education, health care, social security, income distribution, and environmental protection. What exactly is in short supply? The commonplace in these livelihood issues is that they belong to public goods and public services, which cannot solely rely on the market competition. Consequently, we now propose to establish public finance, equalize public goods and public services, change the government functions, and build a service-oriented government. This set of proposals is to respond to the problems China is facing at this stage.

The second fundamental change is from "equalitarianism to a widening income gap." What was the circumstance like at the initial stage of the reform and opening up? That is equalitarianism – eating from "common rice pot." Later on, the party's main literature from the Twelfth and Thirteenth National Congress considered equalitarianism is a major obstacle in our system. Reform, for that matter, is to smash the egalitarianism, widen the income gap by introduction competition mechanism, and improve the efficiency of resource allocation. This is the direction of the reform. In addition, Comrade Deng Xiaoping mentioned many times that it is a great simulative policy to allow some people and some areas to get rich first. Under the auspices of this policy, China has revitalized and mobilized the enthusiasm in all respects. In the mid-1990s, however, the income gap gradually passed over a reasonable range and into the state of an overlarge income gap. Hence this second fundamental change. When we attempt to reverse this trend and take a series of measures to control the income gap, the gap continues to expand regardless of people's will. Our policy has changed gears to solve this problem and have achieved fundamental improvements. It is not to say that the common rice pot practice has disappeared, but the foremost problem in income distribution is the ever-growing income gap.

The third change is from "the era of food, clothing, and durable consumer goods to the era of large consumer goods." We have experienced three waves of consumption in the last 30 years. The first one is to provide the public with enough food and adequate clothing. The clothes with different styles and different colors did not appear until mid-1980s. It took us less than ten years until 1990s to have home appliances spread to millions of households, which is much shorter that many years in the world. We entered a new era of consumption in the new century – namely, large consumer goods era. This era is characterized by the entry of automobiles and housing into the consumption list for the household. This era, which not only involves monetary consumption but also credit consumption, is in sharp contrast to the old days of consumption.

Fourth, China begins the stage of rapid upgrading of industrial structure from the stage of cheap labor production. We all see that in the more than 30 years after the reform and the opening up China has encountered a great opportunity of demographic dividend – an unlimited supply of labor force – and a declining total burden coefficient of the elderly and the children. This endowed China with a period of cheap labor, which is our major comparative advantage. However, the situation has changed. We thought we would have encountered difficulties in employment after the international financial meltdown, but now it recovered fairly quickly, and many people are talking about how to manage the new prosperity. In 2010 when I participated in writing the report in "social blue book," I maintained that China's development has entered a new stage. The annual 10 percent or so growth rate in the last 30 years as we know it has come to an end. According to the experience in other countries, it is impossible to keep such a high growth rate, but China has miraculously maintained such pace since the beginning of the new century. However, what accompanies is the end of an era of cheap labor and the anticipation of a rising wages. Intermittently incidences of "migrant worker shortage" and "recruitment difficulties" and the changes in the international trade market since 2004 forced our industry to transform from "made in China" to create "Chinese brand," to upgrade our native brands and produce high value-added products.

The fifth change occurred to the mode of our nation's growth and development, meaning that economic growth starts to "depend more on domestic consumption than on investment and exports." China's growth used to rely heavily on investment and exports. The investment rate used to be always more than 30 percent, and the dependence on foreign trade hovered around 60 percent before the financial crisis and once reached 70 percent. However, nowadays, we see the rise of trade protectionism in that many countries filed far more trade litigation cases against China to protect their domestic jobs. Since China is a vast nation, such a high dependence on export to maintain economic growth means a great risk. It is also risky to have excessive investment. We put four trillion RMB worth of investment to retain the growth rate, but if China chooses not to gradually withdraw when it is appropriate, it will give rise to problems of redundant construction and overcapacity, inflations, and falling investment efficiency. Consequently, we will have to depend on domestic consumption as for an ultimate shift, which requires a fundamental assessment on whether domestic consumption is robust enough to support the rapid development of our economy in the future, and whether we are at the threshold of mass consumption. Perhaps some people would believe this perspective is too optimistic. However, some key indicators show that the era of mass consumption is upon us. The first key indicator is the growth of per capita GDP. At the beginning of the reform and opening up, the per capita GDP was more than $200. In 20 years leading up to 2000, the per capita GDP reached more than $800 and exceeded $1,000 for the first time in 2003. Three years later in 2006, the per capita GDP was $2,000; it rose to more than $3,000 in 2008; and this year (2010), we expect it to reach $4,000. At the same time, we also noticed a huge regional disparity. According to a recent report on regional competitiveness, which compares the economic level of different provinces with their equivalent in the developed countries, there are five or six provinces reached the level of G-20. Although the average figure is still very low, few percentage point increase in China's vast market means enormous increase in the consumer market. Therefore, every seven RMB increase in consumption for each 1.3 billion Chinese is a gigantic consumer market of $1.3 billion. This is exactly why major international business focuses on China. The second key indicator is the level of urbanization. The level of urbanization is closely associated with the level of consumption. For instance, urban consumption and rural consumption is a completely different concept. The level of urbanization in China is close to 50 percent, though there is much controversy over the number because the statistics of urban population from the National Bureau includes permanent residents who stay in the cities for more than half a year but whose household registrations remain in the rural areas, such as migrant laborers. These populations have not urbanized technically speaking. We also notice that many rural areas in the coastal economically developed regions are urbanized by the international standard, alas, a place where more than 2,000 people live can be called a city in Europe. Indeed, the countryside in Europe is relatively developed, so there is no difference in housing and living level. The difference lies in business and financial sectors. Now our country is speeding up the process of urbanization by lifting the restrictions on entering small and medium-sized towns and medium-sized cities and setting in motion the urban and rural integration in which we anticipate a rapid development. The third indicator is the employment share of the second and the third industry is close to 70 percent. This is symbolic of the stage of mass consumption according to the international standard. However, the figure lags far behind the structure of economic output. Agriculture makes up only 10 percent of the GDP, but the number of workers employed in the agriculture remains high because the population outnumbers the land and villages are scattered, which makes it difficult for farmers to get rich. Some sociologists even claim that there is a gap worth of 15 years of development between our country's social structure and the economic structure. The fourth key indicator is mass higher education, which is also one of the benchmark in the international standard. By 2010, the gross enrollment rate of higher education in China was about 25 percent. This is largely resulted from the enrollment expansion in recent years, which also invites many controversies. Some question whether the enrollment expansion causes the difficulty in getting a job. With the respect to the actual numbers, there is nothing to be proud of about our country's figure because there is still much room between China and a country with huge human resources despite a rapidly increasing enrollment rate. The enrollment rate in Taiwan region has reached more than 90 percent and in the general developed countries, it is about 60 percent. With a rate of 25 percent, China needs to continue its endeavors in cultivating highly educated talents. The fifth key indicator is that the Engel coefficient is nearly 30 percent. The Engel coefficient describes the proportion of food expenditure in total consumption. The lower the number is the higher the living standard is. However, according to National Bureau of Statistics, the Engel coefficient is 42 percent and 37 percent in the rural areas and the city, respectively. However, I believe these figures are overrated in that we underestimate the share of housing in the total consumption, meaning that underrating other aspects is to overrate the share of food expenditure. The sixth indicator is that the third wave of consumption is upon us. After the stage of fulfilling the basic needs of food and clothing and the stage in which durable consumer products spread to every household, here comes the stage of big-ticket consumption. I believe the greatest factor on consumption is the disparity in the urban and rural development because the urban consumption patterns and habits differ from that in the rural areas. The added value created by agriculture only accounts for about 10 percent of GDP growth. Generally speaking, the proportion of labor involved in agriculture should drop to 25 percent or so, but now it is 38 percent in China contradicting the economic structure. From the perspective of residential pattern, rural residents make up 42 percent of the population wherein the urbanization level in

China remains at 48 percent. There ought to be a balanced ratio among these three structures – the industrial structure, employment, and urban-rural structure – but deviations occur in practice. The deviation is emblematic of the problem that the pace of social structural transformation is out of line with an economic transition, which inhibits our consumption from growing fast.

As China consumption is now in a new era, in addition to the mass consumption of automobiles and housing, some newly emerged consumption is increasing rapidly, such as information and communication, education, health care, leisure, and tourism and so on. The total amount of consumption has long been lower than the growth of investment, but a new order of rapid growth of consumption surfaced since 2004. In 2009, total retail sales of consumer goods increased by about 16 percent – almost double the growth of GDP – which is unprecedented in China. At present, the rate of consumption growth is getting close to the investment growth rate. When it surpasses the latter, our development is said to be built on the dependence on domestic consumption. At the same time, however, we see a contradictory phenomenon. Take housing price as an example. We often say that the consumption is insufficient. Under normal circumstances, insufficient consumption leads to housing and consumption downturn – that is, insufficiency caused by consumption oversupply. However, the reality is a different picture in that the housing price keeps rising and so many people are eager to buy a house or an apartment. Is it necessary to put efforts in bring down the housing price when the consumption is insufficient? Why can't the high demand for houses never be met? Housing is a peculiar product, the consumption of which differs from general products such as clothing, home appliances, and automobiles. What is law of prices for these general products? Once in the mass consumption stage, there will be various competing manufacturers on the market. The fiercer the competition is, the lower the price is going to be. When one needs to buy a home appliance, or a computer, or even a car, what is his/her expectation? If one is not in an immediate need of the product, he/she can wait for a couple of years when the price will be lower and the quality will be higher. One can buy more cost-effective products at the same price in the coming years. When it comes to housing, one's expectation is completely different. Everyone is expected to buy immediate, otherwise he/she would not be able to afford it because the price is soaring. The reason why people have such an expectation is that residential housing is a consumer good and also an investment good. House purchasing sometimes is consumption demand but sometimes is investment or even speculation. There are many contradictory characteristics concerning Chinese consumption pattern. Many people's living condition is extremely difficult in the western and rural regions but at the same time, we are among the top of the world in large number consumption of luxury goods and cosmetics, including the so-called Remy Martin, brand-name cosmetics, and designer bags. This is self-contradictory in sense that it is difficult to judge if China is a rich country or not. China is not rich because the GDP per capita is merely over $4,000, while the GDP per capita of developed countries is about $20,000 to $30,000. However, if China is not a rich country, how comes each member in our overseas tour groups would purchase a dozen of designer bags as gifts? On one hand, the statistics indeed proves that the urban income is growing faster than the rate of GDP growth, but why does the average people feel that he or she is "out-grown?" People's mean income is different from the average income of the whole society. If the income gap is wide enough, 60 percent to 70 percent of the population is likely to be below the average income. Never think the average line is equal to the day-to-day standard. Balance of urban and rural residents' savings grow faster than the income due to many reasons, among which is the off-payroll income. In China, income is the most obscure figure that is also most difficult to grasp because we do not have a strict property and income declaration system. As far as the growth of savings is concerned, technically speaking, the remainder of the national income minus consumption, handheld cash, and set-aside investment goes to savings. However, the increase in the savings year by year is greater than the amount of income minus consumption. In other words, a good part of the income cannot be explained away by knowledge and statistics. The perplexity of this kind is even more palpable on housing. If we take a look at the improvement and growth of present consumer goods, housing has witnessed the fastest, greatest, and most profound changes since the reform and opening up and particularly late 1980s. We notice that the per capita living space of rural residents is now more than 30 square meters, rising from less than 5 square meters in the past, and the per capita living space of urban residents is now 27 to 28 square meters, compared to a little more than 3 square meters in the past. The average house ownership rate in China is 90 percent – almost the highest in the world. One possible reason is the large population of farmers who normally would own their houses. Another reason is the housing reform. Prior to the reform, the welfare housing distribution system owns many houses, which are sold to the resident household at a discounted price thanks to the housing reform. Therefore, almost every household owns their house. However, in foreign countries, about 50 percent to 60 percent of the population is renting. Let us imagine what our household housing was like ten years, or 15 years ago. It was unthinkable to own an apartment of more than 100 hundred square meters 15 years ago. Now we make this dream true but you will find that what the public are least satisfied, grumbling and denouncing the most is about housing. What leads to this situation? Different from other commodities, housing is associated with land. Since the population outnumbers the amount of land, the scarcity of arable land forces us to strictly control the land, which ultimately pushes the housing price high. New land kings constantly emerge. The price of the land king is often counted into the housing price and distributed to each household. How can we expand the access to housing? One may say, for instant, that there are so-called social security housing, economical housing, and low-rent houses in Singapore and Hong Kong so China should follow suit. But let me say this, China is a vast country, not like Singapore or Hong Kong with millions of residents, so it can rely on the government to solve the housing problem for so many people. Our past experience in the development of a market economy tells us that we need to rein in the market supply. How wonderful it is if there is a way to meet the housing needs of the masses so that the government can collect the tax and there is a new momentum for the economic growth. For example, what if we allow farmers' houses to enter the consumer market since a great majority of them are countryside houses. Now the urban land belongs to the government but one has the property right over his/her housing meaning he/she is able to rent it out, sell it, or even survey the house for the mortgage. Farmers housing is built on a collective land that is under a collective ownership, so only the house above the homestead belongs to the owners. Farmers only have use permit, instead of property right certificate, which deprives them of the right to sell or mortgage. If farmers' houses were allowed to enter the market, it would be of great benefit to stabilize prices and increase farmers' property income. This is by no means without drawbacks because the demolition cost would be higher. The government needs weigh the pros and cons before making the best choice.

However, we also feel that many of the present problems run counter to our anticipations. For instance, why on earth is consumer spending weak now? Weak consumer spending is evident in statistics, which shows that from 1985 to 2008, Chinese household consumption rate dropped from 52 percent to 35.4 percent. Household consumption rate refers to the proportion of all household consumption in GDP. The number 35.4 percent is very low if compared to any other nations. The household consumption is close to 70 percent in the United States and 65 percent in Japan, while our consumption rate declines as the income grows. Three hundred million Americans spend over $10 trillion on consumer goods in one year, whereas 1.3 billion Chinese only spend $1 trillion. Now you see that the size of the consumer market is not defined by population, but by the disposable money. From 1990 to 2008, the average propensity to consume decreased from 85 percent to 72.7 percent. The average propensity to consume is the proportion of the income that is used for consumption expenditure – namely, how much money you would spend on consumption out of $100 income. In addition, from 1991 to 2008, the ratio of China's total retail sales of social consumer goods and household savings showed a gradual downward trend, decreasing by more than a half from 1.02 in 1991 to 0.5 in 2008. These are three key indicators.

Weak consumer spend should be attributed to the lack of money, but that seems to be not the case for our country. From 1994 to 2008, our total revenue jumped from 500 billion RMB to 5.4 trillion RMB, with an annual growth rate of 18 percent, much higher than the pace of GDP. The total government expenditure made up 21.6 percent of the total consumption expenditure in 1980s, and the share grew to 24.2 percent in the 1990s and is now about 27 percent. Ordinary people seem to have money, too. From 1994 to March 2009, Household savings deposit increased from 2 trillion RMB to 24.7 trillion RMB, with an annual growth rate of 18 percent and equivalent to three-quarters of GDP. The general measure to simulate consumption is for the country to lower interest rates. Nowadays, the one-year deposit rate is merely 2.25 percent, lower than the price increase rate, which means that the deposit is not inflation proof or appreciation, but depreciation. Therefore, low interest rate is one way to force the public to consume. Why doesn't the public consume? The fundamental cause is related to our distribution structure. Although the total amount of savings is on the rise, the distribution is uneven, so the rich people do not necessarily tend to consume and those consumers are not necessarily rich.

China's Gene coefficient of income distribution is relatively high in the world. Besides the income gap, the social stratification structure is still the shape of a pyramid, and it takes years of effort to change it into the olive-shaped structure that is dominated by the middle-income class. This can only be materialized when farmers are few and a majority of rural residents is no longer engaged in farming. How to enable farmers to get rich is a hurdle to achieve the transformation of social stratification structure and expand consumption. The scale of land management for farmers is too small. Even in the vast Northeastern region, each household has up to 20 to 30 *mu* of farmland. However, in some developed countries such as France, Canada, and Australia, farmers have 30 to 40 hectares of farmland on average, not to mention the United States where farmers have more than a hundred hectares of land. One who has reached such a scale can reach the middle-class living standard. There is an admittedly huge difference between China and those countries. Since we don't have enough land and it is impossible for an outward expansion, we have to develop inwardly with massive investment of money, human resource, and time. After all, the land is limited, so unit area yield increase is not sufficient, and planting flowers and growing vegetables is not good enough to raise the income. Only through the scale economy can the nation become a middle-income class society. Given this context, we realize that the restriction on consumption lies in the small size middle class. The definition of the middle class is fuzzy. While economists tend to treat assets, income, and housing as indicators for the middle class, sociologists emphasize occupations. Against the benchmarks in occupation, income, and education, 12 percent of the population belongs to middle class by estimation, and 20 percent borderline middle class who are yet middle class but would be in the future. It will be fairly fast if the number increases to 30 percent in the coming 20 years. Indeed the percentage of middle class is too low because the rural population is too high. If we exclude rural areas and count only urban population, the proportion of the middle class is expected to reach 25 percent in 2006, still lower than that of South Korea where middle class makes up 46 percent of the population.

Why are we saying that income gap affects consumption? There is one rule in consumption, which may not applicable to every nation but is particularly explanatory in China. That is, the household consumption rate decreases as the family income rises, and the higher the income, the lower the consumption rate. So, what does this mean? Household consumption rate refers to the proportion of household consumption in the household income. If we divide the family into five types: low income, middle and low income, middle income, middle-high income, and high income, then we would find that the consumption rate of the low income family is 90 percent but for high income family less than 60 RMB is spent out of 100 RMB income. This suggests that if one wants to expand the entire domestic consumption, one has to channel the income increase more toward middle and low-income family. Moreover, three main factors affecting household consumption are education, health care, and housing, which exert great influence on our consumption behaviors and expectations. Why so many people choose to put so much money into savings account? Many American take on cultural factors. They would say they are credit consumption, borrowing money from future for now and use them up. Why Chinese choose to do the opposite, they would ask, saving money for the second half of their life or even the next generation. How stupid is that? However, I would argue that this is something that can be explained by cultural difference. Anything, for that matter, if one attempts to explain it from a cultural perspective, would become vague and obscure. In reality, you will notice that a high savings rate among Chinese is a rational behavior in its own right. A family needs to avoid future risks by asking themselves, what we are supposed to do for our children's education, when I am sick but without a health insurance, and when I am getting old, and we have to save money to buy a house or an apartment. According to the surveys on the purposes of savings conducted by many banks, children's education, medical needs, and housing are perhaps among the top three. We need to expand the coverage of social security, provide better public services, and give people stable expectations. With stable expectations, the public is willing to spend money on consumption.

From the aforementioned analysis, we learn that it is not a pure economic question to expand domestic consumption, but it is associated with many social institutional problems. We need establish a normal growth mechanism for wage and income, adjust income distribution structure, expand the coverage of social security, equalize the access to public goods and public service, eliminate the urbanrural dual structure, and accelerate the pace of urbanization, and so on. Reforms in social institutions involve employment, social security, income distribution, education, health care, and other fields. Among them, the extremely crucial is the income distribution system, which shakes the established interest order. When at a critical period reforms benefit some people at the cost of others, reforms would encounter difficulties and resistance. However, we should hold a firm confidence, be steadfast in reforms, and provide new impetus to social development. Meanwhile, we need come to terms that industrialization and urbanization are at a new stage in the midst of structural transformations. The development in the next ten to 20 years will have to rely more on the domestic consumption. We not only will make our country strong but also let ordinary people get rich since prosperity is the foundation for a powerful state.

Note

1 This chapter was adapted from a lecture delivered at the twelfth lecture series of the Luojia Forum at the Wuhan University on March 28, 2010.

11   Radical changes

The end of the village: studies on the villages in the city

When I translated *La Fin Des Paysans* (the end of peasants) ten years ago, now a classic book by Henri Mendras, the celebrated French rural sociologist, the topic of village seemed in a distant future for such a vast agrarian country as China. Mendras (1991, p.6) wrote, "two billion farmers standing at the threshold of the industrial civilization is the major issue for the social science raised by the contemporary world in the second half of the 20th century." For prior to that, "the slowness in the agricultural development makes people feel stable and secure, a balance lasting for thousands of years, as opposed to the rapid development in the industrialization. In shape contrast to the industrial enthusiasm, peasant's worldly wisdom and moderation seems to be eternal. City and industrialization attract all energy, but villages always nurture the idyllic dreams of happiness, safety, and timelessness." However, industrialization and urbanization broke the original balance, having shaken up and changed the whole social structure. For China as a whole, this kind of "radical changes" might last for a long period of time. Thanks to the regional disparity, in some of the developed regions in China, the "radical change" is accelerating. Scholars once thought that the process of village demise coincides with the end of peasant – that is, the transitional process of nonagriculturalization, industrialization, and household registration changes. However, in reality, the process in which village, as a living system and a form of social network, comes to an end is lagging behind and more difficult than the occupational identity of farmer coming to an end. Urbanization is more than an obbligato to industrialization, which has its own development pattern.

The problem, method, and hypothesis

"Urban villages" are pervasive in the entire Pearl River Delta region. It is also a heated topic recently, around which there are a variety of stories told in town. The Pearl River Delta has witnessed a dizzying pace of industrialization and urbanization in the past 20 years. This unique "urban village" seems to be a direct outgrowth of this rapid expansion. However, the problem is much more complicated in that the phenomenon of "urban village" has never appeared in other countries urbanization. Along this line, the emergence of "urban village" must have related to certain peculiar factor in China. Off the top of one's head, one might think of the household registration system that has divided the urban and the rural regions for decades. However, the household registration system is a commonplace for all villages in China, so there must be else mechanism at work. It leaves us "in suspense" to find out what this mechanism is.

Before the start of our investigation, we initially thought that the so-called urban village refers to the village-turned business region that appears at the urban fringe where the city meets the countryside. It is part of the natural expansion of the urban region, similar to the "Zhejiang village" and "Hancunhe village" in Beijing, which that is much urbanized in terms of life and work except lower houses and lesser commercialization. Nonetheless, when we conducted the field-work in the "urban villages" in Guangzhou, the economic, political, and cultural center in south China, the jaw-dropping observations leave us speechless despite our preparation by reading relevant literature. The "urban village" in reality differs stark from our imagination. Every "urban village" is like manmade "cement giant" of more than 20 meters high in a radius of a few kilometers of bustling downtown and skyscrapers. Shock does not stops here: the "cement giant" is not built by a single company or an economic collective, but by individual one household after another. The building, however, has completely lost the aesthetic significance of individual variations to the profit from the land and rentals. The iron rule of the economy has also crushed "the cultural significance" of the traditional Chinese village that is symbolic of harmonious living space (Liu, 1998). Between the linked and identical seven- to eight-storied buildings is the street of about 1.5 and 2 meters, the width of which is determined by the original homestead intervals. The second floor and above are stretched out toward and over the street for the purpose of maximizing the residential construction areas. To the extent that they almost occupy all the open space, local people call them as "check-to-check buildings," "kiss buildings," and "a thin strip of sky." Most of the households in the urban villages need lamp lightings during the daytime, and the streets in the villages feel like "tunnels." Despite this kind of environment, the villages are popular and business oriented. Shops, grocery stores, and service outlets are lined with the narrow and dark streets. In addition to rural residents, there are thousands of migrant works living in the rental houses.

The "urban villages" in the big cities are like relics of ancient history, but also like the newborn in the process of rapid urbanization. All kinds of stories happened in the "urban village" attract rather simplistic criticism from some media and scholars. A scholar writes, "the plan, construction, and the management of the 'urban villages' are extremely chaotic. The expansion of migrant population has made the rental houses hotbed for pornography, gambling and drug abuse and trafficking and a hidden haven for 'a gorilla of children born beyond the birth quota' . . . These contradict the ecology, tidiness, and comfort afforded by modern cities" (Ma, 2000). Another reporter comments on the farmers:

> who wash the mud off their feet and leave the field" that "they need not work for the village dividends and rents are enough for them to lay aside all anxiety and rest content . . . They become a unique group of urban residents – in and

out of urban public space without decent outfit or corresponding temperament. The entire village is permeated with the worship of the clan ideology and the homage for God and Buddha. Cities are evolving, villages are disappearing, but the 'village' people caught in between are disintegrating. The elderly spend their rest lifetime on the Mahjong table, and the middle-aged in the low cultural level who are outdated by the advanced industries in the society tend to stick to the status quo, to the extent that any newly unveiled policy about the 'urban village' would make them worry about their living conditions.[1]

On September 6, 2000, the city of Guangzhou held a "working meeting on urban construction management," determined to accelerate the process of urban-rural integration and establish a metropolitan urban system with overall coordination in five years. One of the important tasks is to complete on basic terms the restructuring and transformation of "urban villages" in the central city within five years. In the planning area, it fully implements the plan to build farmers apartment complex so that farmers who have no land or are not farming can be turned into urban residents and put under the urban management system (Zheng, 2000). However, the unexpected prudence and calmness expressed by the major in an interview with reporters are in sharp contrast to this optimistic plan. He thought that it takes longer, maybe one or two generations rather than three, five, or even ten years to complete the transformation of "urban villages"(Zheng, 2000).

From a macro perspective, urbanization is the inevitable way to transfer the rural surplus labor force, improve farmer income level, and transform the social structure of the village. We normally consider that urbanization would be full of celebrations, joys, and dreams of farmers. However, at the last stand of the urbanization, the finish post for villages, why do we see the fission of a millennium village civilization and the hardship for its rebirth? The questions we raise and attempt to address are, why "urban villages" only appear in the most prosperous Pearl River Delta in China in the world history of urbanization? Are they a rational choice made by farmers or an irrational construct? What kind of mechanism or function is at play in the persistence of the "urban village?" Where should we start for the project of "urban village" transformation?

To study the subject of the process in which villages come to an end, the appropriate sociological method is perhaps participatory observation. As for the diachronic "process," there are great limitations in synchronic questionnaires. Although using survey data to study the life course has made great breakthroughs, the "process" reflected by statistics still lacks "fullness" and "texture." Case studies based on participatory observations, however, often are restricted by the case specificity but lose applicability to general cases. Perhaps our goal is too grand since through our research we attempt to build an ideal type that is universally applicable to explain the end of Chinese villages. As far as the chain of urbanization process since the reform and opening up are concerned, there are all kinds of scattered sociological studies, including Zhou Daming's (2001) study on "Nanjing village" in the urban areas in Canton Province, Wang Chunguang (1995), Xiang Biao (1998), and Wang Hansheng's studies (1991) on "Zhejiang village" in Beijing where migrant workers and small business owners concentrate, Zhe Xiaoye's (1997) study on the mega-village "Wangfeng" in the highly industrialized southeastern region, Lu Xueyi and others' studies (2001) on "Xingren village," which is at the incipient stage of industrialization in north China, Wang Mingming's studies on agricultural villages in the developed regions like "Meifa village" and "Tangdong village," and Huang Ping and his college's study (1997) on eight villages in four disadvantaged provinces from which workers migrate out, and the list continues. Through establishing ideal models for each one of the development link in the chain of village urbanization, we are able to reproduce the entire vivid and rich process of Chinese village urbanization in theory.

The empirical materials for this chapter are from the investigations into nine "urban villages" located in Guangzhou in October 2001. They are Shipai village, Tangxia village, Yaotai village, Sanyuanli village, Tongde village, Xian village, Yangji village, Linhe village, and "Liede village." We interviewed government administrators, village cadres, villagers, and migrant workers who are living in the "urban villages." By doing so, we have a more in-depth and nuanced interview-based framework. According to statistics, there are a total of 139 "strips" of "urban villages" in Guangzhou City. That they are "strip-shaped" is emblematic of the way in which "urban villages" merge into the cities. The 139 "strips" of "urban villages" largely fall into three categories. The first type of village is located in the downtown area, which has no agricultural land. The second type is located in the suburban areas with a small amount of agricultural land. The third type of village is far away from the city with plenty of land. The "urban village" in study is largely limited to the first type for they throw into relief the characteristics of the village coming to an end. This type of village makes up about one-third of the 139 strips. The term "urban village" used throughout this chapter refers to this type of villages as well.

The birth of "urban village": the impetus from land and rentals

To understand the birth of "urban village" and the reasons to it, one has to approach "urban village" as representative of a mixture of the urban and the village. If there is such a thing as "mixed economy" existing between the market economy and the redistributive economy, then the "urban village" is the "mixed community" existing between the city and the village. Life in the "urban village" is completely urbanized; "villagers" who reside in urban areas, even in downtown, basically do not engage in agricultural work, if not completely, and even a vast majority, if not all, of their households are registered as urban residents. However, do we still define them as a "village" or "villagers" in their respective terms? Aren't the aforementioned aspects the most common criteria to distinguish "city residents" from "villagers?" Isn't it true that the label "migrant work" signifiers more than their "rural" households registration?

Characteristics of the "urban village" may reveal some of the more profound institutional factors that we tend to overlook yet contribute to urban-rural disparities. These factors can be summarized as the following three aspects. First, the land system is different. According to the law, all the property right of the urban land is owned by the state, and the property right of the village land belongs to the village collective ownership. The state may acquire lands that are farmers' production materials in the urbanization, but is hard to acquire the homesteads that are farmers' means of substance. Hence, the urban residential land and part of the village collective property land where "urban villages" embedded into the urban areas still belong to the village collective ownership. We will find the significance and great impact of this difference in the analysis that follows. Second, the social management system is different. According to the law, urban communities are managed by the "street committee," a branch of the local government, whose cost is covered by the local government, while village communities are managed by the self-organized "villager committee" whose cost relies on the shoulders of the village collectively. This is a fundamental cause to the "system of village work unit," which we will examine next. Third, there is a system of "village membership" associated with the land system and the management system. We tend to consider that the main hurdle for urbanization is the household registration system, so the identity change for farmers is from a rural household register to an urban household register. However, for farmers, "village membership" is more important than "household registration," since the "village membership" is the ticket of shareholders of the strong village collective economy. Precisely because of this, their economic status is greatly different from the migrant worker renters in their houses and the ordinary urban residents, and they are willing to maintain the "village membership" instead of becoming "city resident."

The problem is, however, the macro rules and institutions apply to the entire nation, why the agglomeration of village buildings appear so intensively in Pearl River Delta region that make the most of land value? Aren't farmers aware that the alienated architecture "monsters" have violated the rules for the urban living space to the extent that from the date of their birth, it foreshadows a "short life" and an "ultimate destruction?" Even from the perspective of the economic profit, why can't farmers build "nicer" houses so that they may raise the rent, just as what real estate developers do to the residential areas? Is it because farmers lack the capital and the discernment that developers possess? Many scholars attempt to address these questions from the angle of institutional changes. They attribute these problems to the abyss caused by the high-speed urban expansion in the developed regions and the serious lag in the village institutional changes. The huge gap sets in motion the contradiction and conflict between the social rationality of urbanization and irrationality of individual farmers, and the "urban village" emerges as the "alienation" of this kind of contradiction and conflict. In this chapter, we are inclined to adopt a contrary approach of individual rational choice to examine the causes of the "urban village" for by so doing it enables us to pinpoint the real difficulty in transforming "urban villages" better.

Seen from the perspective of the individual rational choice, the "urban village" taking shape as a special building group and village institution is resulted from farmers' pursuit of maximum land and rental profits when land and housing rentals experience a rapid appreciation. Although, whether farmers have the economic rationality, or are able to, pursue maximum profit on their own is a long-standing controversy in academics. Most of sociologists and anthropologist who value the "small tradition" and "local knowledge" maintain that petty farmers lack modern economic rationality and tend to be caught in the irrational "deep game." Even if one cannot arbitrarily claim that they are irrational, petty farmers are "rational" in an "alternative" sense to the "rationality" defined by "utilitarianism." For relatively affluent farmers, the alternative rationality reflects farmers' attitude to maintain "comfortable self-sufficiency" and "wise moderation" in the absence of the momentums from external capital accumulation and appreciation. But for poor farmers, it reflects a "survival rationality" to evade living risks (Chayanov, 1925; Geertz, 1973; Scott, 1976). Instead of believing petty farmer's "alternative rationality," many economists and historians have verified the "applicability" of "economic rationality" to explain petty farmers' economic behaviors. They argue that farmers have no different potentials than real estate investors. Once responding to new external economic stimulus, farmers would also overcome the "survival logic" that dominates their lives and make the choice to search for maximum profits (Schultz, 1964; Popkin, 1979; Huang, 2000). When it comes to process analysis, these two arguments do not contradict each other and there are no fundamental differences between them. The contradiction and difference lies in the hypothesis that whether there would be "radical changes" leading farmers "survival rationality" to "economic rationality." This "radical change" has actually occurred to "villagers" in the "urban village" at the beginning of "the end of villages."

We learn from out surveys that the villagers' household homestead is on average more than 70 square meters (approximately one tenth of one *mu*) – that is, about ten cents of mu according to the Chinese calculation system. The "ten-cent land miracle" created by farmers maximizes the value of the land, expanding the possessed residential areas to 400 to 600 square meters by building the house to six or eight stories and the building stretching from the second floor and above that occupy the public space without occupying the territory of the street. "Villagers" in general live in the first floor and lease rooms with a shop front and the rest spare rooms in the house. While the rentals for the shop front rooms may vary much from each other depending on the location of the house, rents for other rooms normally range from 10 to 15 RMB square meter per month, which is very cheap for the downtown area. There are generally two units every floor, and since most of the tenants are single migrant workers, several of them may share a unit. Interestingly enough, the rent for one unit in the "urban village" is not fixed. For instance, if a unit were shared by one family, the monthly rent would be 600 RMB; if it were shared by four single persons, the monthly rent would be 800RMB in total and 200 RMB for each person; if shared by five people, then it would be 900RMB in total and 180 RMB for each person; if there are six people, then it would 1,000RMB in total and a little more than 160RMB each. However, this line of reasoning cannot continue in this way, because the "villagers" have come to understand what housing depreciation means and have developed the consciousness to avoid congestion risk. They have their own conventional ratio of the tenant numbers and the living areas that maximizes the utility.

The "story" of "urban villages" reminds me of the famous "theory of share tenancy" put forth and applied by Steven Ng-Sheong Cheung to the Asian context. Western scholars once in general believed that the fixed rent system for the land is more conducive to a maximum output than the revenue sharing system, as the fixed rent provides more incentives for tenant farmers to invest labor and capital than the system that raises the rent if the output increases. Based on theoretical reasoning and empirical statistics, Steven Ng-Sheong Cheung, however, argues that certain degree of revenue sharing for the cultivated land is also a reasonable arrangement to maximize the output when constrained by competitions and a peculiar circumstance of sufficient labor supply by farmers outnumbering the amount of the land. His argument is summarized in a simple and hypothetical "story" as follows. If the owner has a large piece of land and rents it to one tenant farmer, the dividend revenue rate will be higher, because the profit of the scale of the economy makes the tenant farmer stay. However, if the owner wants more and rent the divided land to two tenant farmers, although the dividend revenue rate declines, the total income for the owner would rise because the total output increases thanks to the increased unit investment after the scale of the farmland gets smaller. Nonetheless, if the owner continues to divide the land and rent out divided land to more people, the logic that the dividend rate falls while the total income rises cannot last forever. Once passing the tipping point, if the owner continues, his/her total income would fall. In other words, there is only one point where the maximum profit meets the competitive equilibrium without conflict on the curve of cultivated land renting. The land reform in some areas of Asia determines that the rate of dividend for the landlord not exceeding 37.5 percent of the land revenue. The sharing rate in the neighborhood of this percentage shows the land reform success made possible by government regulations and a type of contractual success of competition (Cheung, 1969/2000).

"House rental story" in the "urban village" is analogous to Steven Ng-Sheong Cheung's "land rent story." Indeed, there is an equilibrium price for the revenue rate of urban land based on free competition. Under certain systematic constraint and control, we might see a fell in the revenue rate may and even "the disappearance of the rent" except that the "rent" does not really disappear but manifests itself in other forms of compensations or the government cost. The residential building in the "urban village" is not constructed without any institutional constraint. The government stipulates that villager housing cannot be more than 3.5 floors, and fines incur if the house surpasses the limit. However, villagers build six- to eight-storied houses violating the rule for the profit they gain from the rent increases are far more than the fines. As the urban land price is rising, the general distribution of the six- to eight-storied residential houses falls short in reaching the profitable equilibrium price. However, six to eight may be the maximum number of floors that the government would tolerate with the respect to illegal constructions by "villagers." In this case, "villagers" have to make the most of the disposable areas and space in order to make up the price difference between their land income and the equilibrium price set by the competition. This is the fundamental reason to the intensive building "monsters" in the "urban village." Consequently, to transform "urban villages," if the "villagers" are reluctant to lose part of the rental income and the government is also reluctant to pay extravagant compensations, the only solution is to allow residential buildings to be constructed even higher, replacing the revenue made from the higher space with that of the current space. Only this solution can largely ensure that it will reach or get close to the competitive equilibrium price of land revenue.

From "village unit system" to "village corporate system": symbiotic, sharing, and dividends

The "work unit system" refers specifically to the organizational mode of the urban state sectors in the Chinese redistribution economy. There have been numerous studies about it (Walder, 1986; H. Li, 1998, 1993; Lu, 1989; Li, 1992; Li & Zhang, 2000). In the "work unit system" the state organs, the state-owned enterprises, and institutions, are not only workplace or business unit but also management unit for social living and politics, wherein unit members strongly depend on the unit organization regarding identity, employment, pension, health care, welfare, and many other aspects. We find an analogous organizational mode in the "urban village" – "the village unit system" – in that "villagers" who have land and a majority of whom are not working in the villages remain highly dependent on their own "villages" for income, living, emotion, social communication, psychological identifications, and so on.

"The village unit system" comes into being because of two reasons: the social network that lives together under the same village management system for one and the dividends from the village collective economic property for the other. "Urban village" is like isolated islands spotted in the vast ocean of cities. While the ocean represents a strange world, the island is a society of acquaintance thanks to the "village unit system."

Village management differs greatly from the street management. Under the management of street community, the neighborhood committee is only responsible for limited affairs, and the social service provision, such as education, health, security, water and electricity supplies, road and environmental constructions, and military conscription, rests directly on the shoulder of relevant agencies. As for village community management, however, the village committee is in charge of almost matters related to "village life," and the village head is like the patriarch in the extended family of the entire village who shoulders unlimited responsibilities. While street community construction and management costs are part of the national fiscal expenditure, the village community construction and management costs are paid by the village collective. There are more than 6,000 indigenous "villagers" and more than 30,000 migrant workers living in Tangxia village. In order to manage the village community, the village collective employs more than 100 security personnel, more than 30 cleaners, 15 market managers, 6 family planning management personnel, and more than 20 people to transport garbage. Moreover, the village collective is also responsible for the pensions of more than 1,000 elderly villagers, the health benefits of the villagers, welfare allowance in addition to the wages for the village primary school teachers, the construction of infrastructure in the elementary schools, the road and pipelines in the village, subsidies for the villagers who serve in the army, who donate blood, and who attend higher education institutions. The village collective economy of Tangxia village generates a net profit of about 100 million RMB in a given year, of which 12 percent to 15 percent would be used as public expenditure for the aforementioned community management, construction, and service provision. This proportion of public expenditure is similar in other "urban villages." Take Shipai village as an example. More than 9,000 indigenous "villagers" and more than 40,000 migrant workers live there. The village collective earns an annual net income of more than 90 million RMB on average. It pays five to eight million RMB taxes, spends a few million RMB on daily administrative operations and more than 10 million RMB as public expenditure on social affairs. The remaining 40 to 50 million RMB is dividend profits. That village collective is in full charge of the community lives in the "urban village" paves the way for "villagers'" dependence upon "the village unit system," but this dependence is also derived from another cause at a deeper level – that is, the village collective economy is exclusive and outsiders in the community cannot get a share of the dividend.

"Urban village's" early collective income came from certain collectively owned labor-intensive industries, such as spinning, brewing, papermaking, brickmaking, tea manufacturing, stonework, and garment processing and so on. As the urban labor cost and land price rise and labor-intensive industries decline in the cities, the "urban village" has went through the process of "deindustrialization." Now the village's collective income comes mainly from the village's collective property. The village collective economy is managed by "economic union," with which a number of "economic cooperatives" are affiliated. They are all independent accounting units, integrative with the administrative village committee and villagers group. Here we can still find the traces of "the three-level management based on teams" – the organizational mode of the commune, brigade, and production team in the rural people's commune system. As for the "urban village," the disintegration of the rural people's commune leaves behind it the organizational legacy of brigade and production team, which pave the organizational foundation for "villagers" to form "join stock partnership." "Villagers" are shareholders of both "economic cooperatives" and "economic union."

"Economic cooperatives" and "economic union" adopt the "join stock partnership," which differs from the "shareholding system" and the "partnership system." In fact, it is the outcome of the integration of administration and economy in the villages. "Shareholding system" allocates "one vote per share," while the "join stock partnership" allows for "one voter per person" and "partnership" means every partner is the owner and is able to withdraw their capital from the enterprise. However, the "join stock partnership" for ordinary villagers does not mean voting rights, and they are not allow to withdraw either. The only commonality is the distribution of profits according to shares.

There are two principles for the allotment of shares. The first one is "based on rural membership," meaning that all villagers have equal shares, regardless of ages. Generally speaking, every person gets five shares, also known as "head stocks." There is additional allotment "based on the length of service" – each year of service accounts for one share, also known as "seniority stocks." The limitation to the sum of "head stocks" and "seniority stocks" is about 25 to 30 shares. Shares are inheritable, but cannot be transferred, withdrawn, and used to pay a debt. Because the "urban village" earns mainly from property not industries, basically no "capital stocks," "technology stocks," and "relationship stocks" appeared in the urban village as they did in other developed industrial villages.

In the recent two years, two institutional changes have already occurred, or is about to occur to, the "urban village." The first one is a proactive choice of contractual change made by "villagers" shifting the economic system from "economic union" to "group company." The second one is initiated by the government in terms of new arrangement of the system transforming administrative management from the "village committee" to the "street committee." These two changes are taking completely different process. While the substantial change is outpacing the formal change for the former, the latter is the opposite; the formal change is outpacing the substantial change.

As far as the economic systematic changes are concerned, from 1994 to 1995, "urban villages" implemented the property right reform known as the "rigid uniformity," driven by "villagers'" appeals and government support. The purpose of the reform is to avoid the ownership dispute caused by mobility and migration and thoroughly solve the problems of internal blurry boundaries in the collective economic property right and unclear main body of the property right. From a given point of time when the "rigid uniformity" is carried out, there is "no increase from new birth, no reduction from death, no increase from influx, and no reduction from outflux." Specifically, it means the shares will not go up because of the added village population and labor force, and they will not go down because of the reduced village population and labor force. Hence regardless of the increase or reduction in the assets of the collective economic organization, the shareholders own them collectively. After this reform of "stock holding fixation," "villagers" almost obtain complete property rights in that they have the usufruct and a free hand in handling the property, the shares are not only inheritable but may be transferrable and pledged. However, there remain restrictions on withdrawal. So property operation is no longer abide by informal conventions in the village but by formal laws. Along this line, it is a natural step forward to "corporatization." However, because the "corporate" revenue mainly comes from the property income that has close to "zero cost," the possession of the property as well as the income are collectively "closed" in terms of preventing external capital from flowing in and shifting the structure of property right and profit sharing.

Another transformation concerns the administrative management system. In 2000, to accelerate urbanization process, the government unveiled "renovation and construction plan for 'urban village,'" demanding that the "urban village" need separate the government from the enterprise, the village collective economic organization practice corporate governance, the street committee take the place of the former village committee and function to manage the social affairs. Nonetheless, as the time of our investigation, the changes in the mode of management have not brought about any substantial transformation. All social affairs, except that they are in charge of registering temporary population from other places, are still the responsibilities of the village. The village "group company" becomes the "shadow cabinet" thanks to the fact that neither can the government afford nor it is eager to pay for the enormous public expenditures of social affair management on behalf of the former village committee. The original device to induce fundamental changes to the village system by replacing the "village" with the "street committee" seems to fail in materializing substantial changes.

"Village unit system" and "state-owned unit system" are actually facing the same problem – the exclusivity of the unit interest and the pursuit of internal benefits that have enhanced the internal cohesion have restricted the flow of resources and increased the cost of social management. The key to reforming the "work unit system," be it the "village unit system" or the "state-owned unit system," lies in finding the means to make up or clear off the "social transaction cost" of the "work unit system," rather than changing the institutional forms.

In the transformation of "urban village" from the "village unit system" to "village corporation system," it is assumed that the operation would be more efficient and effective if the "social affair cost" were covered by the government public expenditure. However, the cadres from the "urban villages" in our investigation are not particularly optimistic about this prospect, unclear if it is because of the loss of administrative power or because of the fact that it is difficult to develop the village economy without the support from this power.

Social stratification structure in the "urban village:" the established and the generated

Identity and property, organizational power, capital, and knowledge and technology are the four categories of factors playing in the social stratification in the "urban village."

First, the distinction is made between those with "village membership" and those without. While almost all of the income of "non-members" comes from business and labor, the "village members" have three sources of income: dividends, rental income, and income from business and labor. Since the first two sources generate far more income than the last, the economic status of "village members" is not only higher than "nonmember" migrant workers but also is at the level no ordinary urban workers can match. As a result, many "villagers" in the "urban village" lead an idle life depending entirely on the dividend and income from house rentals, becoming the new "class of rent and interest." More often than not, they also lease out the shop fronts in their own house, because they feel it is beneath their dignity to do such a laborious business with "marginal profits." "Villagers" consider themselves as the upper class in the "urban village." Some rich "villagers" have purchased houses elsewhere and lived in quiet and elegant environment because they think mingling with migrant workers is "detrimental to their children's development and character."

Second, among those with "village membership" the stratification is made possible by the possession of the "organizational power." The "urban village" is a small society, but there are many hierarchies in its management system. The "economic union" has its own ministries of finance, property management, labor and human resource, office administration, and legal counsel office. Its subordinate "economic cooperation" also has many agencies. In addition, administrators for law and order, health, market management, family planning, education, and providing for the elderly are all "villagers" who enjoy different organizational power resources. "Villager-turned" administrator means a fat salary. For instance, the annual salary for village-level leadership position is more than 10,000 RMB. The organizational power in differentiating the urban village is not restricted to this for the power-holder is more likely to have their property getting higher income and turn their savings into "living capital."

Third, among the outsiders who don't have "village membership," there is a division between those "with capital" and those "with no capital." The tens of thousands of outsiders who live in the "urban villages" can be classified into two categories. One includes those "with capital" who lease the shop fronts for various business and service – namely, commonly referred to as the "self-employed." The other is the wage-earner workers who have "no capital." The gap is not as huge as one would normally think perhaps because the self-employed living in the "urban villages" is engaged in small business. Many of them hire family members or self-employed. With rent for the shop front and tax deducted, their remaining revenue actually is slightly higher than the ordinary working class. Here we notice the so-called complicated "tertiary industry." In the "urban village," both native "real estate holders" and external "small business owners" belong to the tertiary industry, but their economic status and social status have great differences, even greater than the differences between agriculture and industry. We also observe a lot of "invisible economy" within the active economy of the "urban village." The massive transactions from "villagers'" leasing business exist are counted out by the calculation of GDP, for instance. Contrary to places where GDP might have been inflated, the GDP of "urban villages" ought to be lower than its actual value due to the "invisible economy."

Last layer of stratification is caused by the possession of "knowledge and technology" among "workers." Not all workers have capital, but the demarcation between the "white collar" and the "blue collar" is generated by "knowledge and technology." The "white collar" living in the "urban village" is normally employed as enterprise technicians, salesperson, teachers, doctors, taxi drivers, editors, reporters, and company clerks and the sort. The "blue collar" is normally engaged in the processing manufacturing industries, and working as construction and decoration employees, waiter or serviceperson in catering shops, transportation stevedores, and casual workers. There are also "pink-collar workers" at the "hair salons" and "black collar workers" who engaged in illegal activities. We find a new trend among the migrant "workers" of the recent years. Migrant workers from other places are not all from rural areas. More and more of them are migrating from small cities to big cities, from disadvantaged regions to developed regions, and from the city of the economic downturn to the city of vibrant activity. This may reflect a precursor to a new wave of employment mobility.

The social hierarchy structure listed earlier is "established" in the "urban village," but the structure is not fixed. In the mechanism of individual rational choice, the stratification process that is "generated" or "constructed" is not a "reproduction" of the original structure. The "small business owners" and "white collar workers" in the "urban village," relying on their spirit of entrepreneurship or taking advantage of their own "knowledge and technology," have a promising prospect in the stratification process. There have already been waves of successful entrepreneurs from the "urban village." However, for "urban village" upper "class of rent and interest," they do not have enough "knowledge and technology" advantage to secure a satisfactory job. Their enterprising and pioneering spirit die out in the comfortable and idle live, so they are like to experience a downward mobility in the social stratification. Some of them, without making any progress, may eventually become the safeguard of agricultural civilization heritage.

Social network in the village: divide up family property and from rags to riches and back again in three generations

Village is a living community composed of social networks based on bloodline, kinship, clan relatives, and geographical proximity, with no exception to the "urban village." In previous attempts to "organize" villages, people tried to break up the social network of this kind and substitute it with administrative system or economic organization of modern corporate, but in vain in most cases. These modern constructs from the outside have been subtly yet thoroughly transformed after being implanted into the village social networks. Even for those "migrant farmers" who have already entered and worked in the city, they are like the "new Hakka" transplanting their social networks from their villages to the city, such as the living community of "Zhejiang village" in Beijing. It is difficult to comprehend why the traditional social networks from the village are so powerfully persistent.

In the "urban village" that is located in downtown, the living standard and lifestyle, although they are comparable to the urban level, have not disrupt the original social networks. The "village community" in the "urban village" differs significantly from urban "street community" and "unit community," because it is not a living community composed of strangers (e.g., street and residential community), or an acquaintance community bounded by business ties (e.g., unit dormitory compound), but a society of people who know everybody else who are connected by blood affinity, kinship, clan, and geographical proximity.

What all "urban villages" have in common is the existence of three luxurious buildings in the crammed building complex with spatial "privileges" that disregard the logic of "rent maximization." They are the ancestral hall, the primary school and kindergarten, and the entertainment center for the elderly. These buildings are symbolic of the common values held by villages to worship for ancestors, respect the elderly, and care for the young. There are in general three to five leading families in each "urban village." Different leading families have their own ancestral halls, whose style are associated with the position of the family in the village. Only when the village power allocation dovetails with the clan structure can things "be made right." Clan relationship is far more entrenched in villages in south China than in north China, perhaps because communities that are uprooted collectively tend to be more attentive to their "roots."

From our interviews, due to complex social relations bounded by kinship and marriage, every villager household is linked to at least 20 villagers by blood ties and kinship. The number expands to 50 or a hundred for large families. Family position in the village is defined by the position of the clan community. The clan is like the subordinate "branch company" in the village "group company," and families are "subsidiary companies" under the "branch company." The social network at the deep level is the foundation for the structure of economic and organizational property rights.

The cohesive power the "leading big family" in the village has is closely related to the relative closeness of the social network in the village, which ensures that the collective who "makes the pie" is the same as the collective who "carves up the pie." The collective interests maintain its equilibrium since girls marrying out are offset by outside girls marrying into the native villages. However, since 1990s, the equilibrium protected by the relative closeness began to tilt as increasingly "inter-marriages" between younger villagers and urban youth threatened the collective economic interests, the foundation for village social network. Because the more people "carving up the cake" the less each share is going to be, "urban villages" largely have carried out the policy of fixed stock that won't increase or decrease according to new birth, death, or marriage, since the mid-1990s.

An old proverb from the Chinese history says, "From rags to riches and back again in three generations." This can also be dubbed as "the law of family rise and fall." The moral explanation of this "law" is that children of the wealthy family are often prodigal and good-for-nothing. This reasoning is not universally true for it is easier to verify the hypothesis of reproducing family human capital. It is more convincing to explain this "law" from the perspective of the inheritance system. The inheritance system of Chinese traditional families is different from that in Europe and completely different from the Chinese rule of throne-succession because it is "dividing up the family property among brothers" that disperses wealth and power rather than concentrating them as done by "primogeniture." The system of "dividing up the family property among brothers" functions similar to "inheritance tax" in modern states, seemingly the outcome of a national design, which prevents the power of a single family from expanding infinitely to the degree of challenging the imperial power and the state. In the rise and fall of the family, "dividing up the family property" upon the death of the business-starter, a moment of internal strife, often is the turning point of downturn. We notice from the tragic rise-and-fall history of some families that the "law" is still at work. Consequently, big families always refuse to "divide up the family property," the ultimate means to evade and resist the risks of falling into a decline, for "dividing up the family property" means reorganizing property rights and social relationship.

The "urban village" is actually an "extended family" connected by social networks based on blood ties, kinship, and clan relatives. The village social network of this kind facilitates the concentration of wealth and capital, and the village joint-stock system generally has strict provisions disallowing share-withdrawal. Farmers retain their strong reliance on the village social network even after their occupational identity changes because they find themselves in need of withstanding risks and external pressure while facing a new and strange society. That the traditional social networks from the village are so powerfully persistent in the "urban village" is the outgrowth from the decisions made by "villagers" not to "dividing up the family property" for the sake of sustaining the prosperity of "the big family." This is a rational choice made out of their intuition to keep the "big family's" fortune destiny.

The reasoning of transforming "urban village": policy and property replacing funds

Village system is the rule for generations of villagers in the "urban village" where all kinds of "invisible economy" are in full swing, which can never be accommodated by the modern cities but which shapes the "prosperity" in the "urban village." "Villagers" wish the profits from the invisible economy to continue. However, in the eyes of the urban administrators, "urban village" is likely to become "new ghetto" and "den of vice." In addition, the ultra-dense building groups in the "urban village" indeed is like an "alienated body" in the rapidly developing cities. Thus, the clash between the iron rule of urbanization and the "resistance" against the iron rule from the village community is worrisome.

In fact, a thorough transformation of the "urban village" is much more difficult than establishing street committee system in the "urban village" because the transformation implies not only relocation and renovation but also redefining property rights and restructuring the village social network. Transforming the "urban village" is on the right side of the history, and it is only a matter of time. Some leaders of the "urban village" have sensed the inevitability, and they have begun the economic accounting of the transformation project of their own "urban village." According to Shipan village's estimation, it takes two billion RMB to purchase all one million square meters of construction areas that cover a variety of the properties with an acceptable price of 2,000 RMB per square meter. By this rough estimation, it costs 80 billion RMB to buy out all 40 "urban villages" in downtown, more expensive than the massive relocation caused by the "Three Gorges Migration" (which cost about 60 billion RMB). However, different from Three Gorges Migration, the land in the "urban village" is the "living capital" that makes money. In many "urban village" household or at the entrance of the household, there is the dedication to the God of the Land, with the couplet saying, "The land makes money, and the soil yields gold."

In the game of transforming "urban villages," there are three players – namely, the government, real estate developers, and "villagers." The ultimate transformation plan is going to be made in a contractual arrangement balancing the interests of three players. In the transformation project, "villagers" want to protect their rent profits or to be compensated for the lost rent profits, real estate developers want to gain at least the average profits from their investment, and the government hopes to avoid financial pressure and ensure market and social stability. Under this circumstance, the real challenge of transforming "urban village" is the source of funds. What the government concerns is that the interest conflicts given rise by the relocation may cause social instability. Although the government cannot afford to develop the land on its own, involving developers in through preferential policies may also lead to excessive housing supply, which will affect the near-saturated real estate market so that a large number of state-owned bank loans cannot be recovered from the existing real estate development. What worries real estate developers is multiple interest conflicts and uncertainties in the demolition and development. High transaction costs will engulf and eat up the normal profits from the real estate development, and the strict governmental controls on height would eventually make the development unprofitable. "Villagers" are worried that in the development no one protects the real estate rental income that is already in their pocket at the expense of a promising prospect of property appreciations in downtown (the rent for shop front have increased about five time in the past five years). They fight for every penny of their vested interests on the grounds that they have been living in the area generation after generation for hundreds of years.

From a pure development business point of view, the problem is quite simple. It is no more than developing higher space to substitute the congestion in the lower space as to change the long-derided "ultra-density" of the buildings and the disorder state in the "urban village." In terms of the sources of the funds, some proven successful experience include land lease exchanging for fiscal revenue and development funds in Hong Kong and construction funds gathering through house options in Pearl River Delta. However, the complexity lies in development process, which is also an interest game, whose success depends on a contractual arrangement that creates a win-win for all parties involved. The government, an obvious dominant play in this game, can allocate another piece of residential land to interchange the real estate in the "urban village," loose the restriction on the building height for the developers involved in the "urban village" transformation project, and reduce or remit some of the additional costs incurred in the development enabling real estate developers to replace the existing housing in a specific location at a given time with the new residential house option. Meanwhile, the government may also allow "villagers" to change the use permits of their existing village residential housing for the property permits of urban housing, granting "villagers" complete property permits for the new housing, which allows sales and mortgage, in return for "villagers" in the residential relocation compensation price concessions. To prevent excessive supply of housing and the fluctuations in the real estate market caused by the "urban village" transformation, the transformation project is obviously better to carry out in a gradual, stage-by-stage manner, than on a large scale. One cannot expect it to be completed in the short term. Urban construction is a fundamental task crucial for generations to come, and by no means can be accomplished in the herd manner of "a few years" of impulse.

Nonetheless, the government must determine immediately what the "urban village" that must be transformed is and make public the scope of transformation, as well as the timing and location of the compensated buildings. For in our investigation, some of the "ultra-dense" buildings that must be torn down in the transformation are still renovating, which further increases the transformation costs.

Prior studies on village urbanization focus on the problem of household registration system, reckoning that once the household registration system is thoroughly reformed the urbanization will have it way. However, we find in the process of the "urban village" coming to an end, the household registration system plays little role but the village urbanization is yet to complete. The end of the village still need go through a difficult process of redefining the property rights and restructuring the social network. What "urban villages" in Guangzhou have revealed in terms of various conflicts in the process of the end of village, with many particularity passing over the developmental stage, has universal bearing.

For a village soil society that is constituted by deep level social networks of blood ties, kinship, geographical proximity, clan relations, fold faith, and local rules and norms, the ultimate problem cannot be solved by nonagriculturalization or industrialization. The fission and rebirth in the process of the end of village makes the journey uneasy and unpleasant. It not only is full of interest friction and cultural clash but also accompanies loss from radical changes and difficulties hard to surmount.

Note

This chapter was originally published in *Social Science in China*, 2002, issue 1, with appropriate adaptations in the citation style.

1 Translator's note: farmers "who wash the mud off their feet and leave the soil" is a common description of the rural surplus labor force that is no longer engaged in agriculture but moves to cities for jobs or doing business. The quotation is from Commentary. Fission in in the Cracks of the City (2000).

References

Cao, Q. (2000). *China along the Yellow River: Reflections on Rural Society*. Shanghai: Shanghai Literature and Art Publishing House.

Chayanov, A. V. (1925/1986). *The Theory of Peasant Economy*. Madison: University of Wisconsin Press.

Cheung, S. N. (1969/2000). *The Theory of Share Tenancy: Agriculture in Asia and Land Reform in Taiwan*. Shanghai: The Commercial Press.

Chow, Y. (1966/2000). *Social Status and Mobility in China Careers among the Gentry in a Chinese Community*. Shanghai: Xue Lin Publishing House.

Coase, R., & Alchian, A. A. (Eds.). (1990/1994). *Property Rights and Institutional Evolution* (Z. Hu, Trans.). Hong Kong: SDX Joint Publishing Company.

Commentary. Fission in in the Cracks of the City. (2000, September 6). *Southern Metropolis Daily*.

District Party Committee of Tianhe District in Guangzhou. (1994). *Some Provisions on Further Improving the Rural Stock Cooperation System*.

District Party Committee of Tianhe District in Guangzhou. (2001). *Basic Provisions on Rural Joint Stock Cooperative Economic Organizations.*

Duara, P. (1988/1994). *Culture, Power, and the State: Rural North China, 1900–1942* (F. Wang, Trans.). Jiangshu People's Publishing House.

Fei, X. (1943/1985). *From the Soil: The Foundations of Chinese Society.* Hong Kong: SDX Joint Publishing Company.

Files from the Investigated Villages. (1988, 1995). *Statutes of Village Cooperative Economy Joint Stock System.*

Geertz, C. (1973). *The Interpretation of Cultures.* New York: Basic Books.

Geertz, C. (1983/1999). *Local Knowledge* (H. Wang & J. Zhang, Trans.). Beijing: Central Party Literature Press.

Guo, Y. (1996). "Traditional Affinity Relationship in the Rural Modernization." *Sociological Research, 6.*

Huang, P. (Ed.). (1997). *In Search for Survival: A Sociological Study of Contemporary Migration Population from Rural China.* Kunming: Yun'nan People's Publishing House.

Huang, P. (2000). *The Peasant Family and Rural Development in the Yangzi Delta, 1350–1988.* Beijing: Zhong Hua Book Company.

Interview with the Mayor. (2000, September 6). Transform Urban Village According to the Plan. *Southern Metropolis Daily.*

Ke, L., & Li, H. (Eds.). (2001). *Villagers in the City: The Floating Population in China's Big Cities.* Beijing: Central Compilation & Translation Press.

Li, H. (1993). "Chinese Work Unit Phenomenon and the Integrated Mechanism of Urban Community." *Sociological Research, 5.*

Li, H. (1998). *Seeking New Coordination: A Sociological Analysis of the Development of Chinese Cities.* Beijing: Surveying and Mapping Press.

Li, P. (1992). *Chinese Enterprises in Transition: The Theory of Organizational Innovation of State-Owned Enterprises.* Jinan: Shangdong People's Publishing House.

Li, P. (1996). "Social Network and Social Status of Migrant Workers in China." *Sociological Research, 4.*

Li, P., & Wang, C. (1993). *The Growth Point of the New Social Structure: The Social Exchange Theory of the Village and Township Enterprise.* Jinan: Shangdong People's Publishing House.

Li, P., & Zhang, Y. (2000). *Analysis of the Social Cost of State-Owned Enterprises.* Beijing: Social Science Academic Press.

Liu, M. (2001). "Study on the Concentration Areas of Floating Population in Shipai: And a Comparison with 'Zhejiang Village' in Beijing." In L. Ke & H. Li (Eds.), *Villagers in the City: The Floating Population in China's Big Cities.* Beijing: Central Compilation & Translation Press.

Liu, P. (1998). *The Ancient Village: Harmonious Living Space.* Shanghai: SDX Joint Publishing Company.

Lu, F. (1989). "Unit: A Special Social Organization." *Social Science in China, 1.*

Lu, X. (Ed.). (2001). *Village with Internal Development: Xingren Village.* Beijing: Social Science Academic Press.

Ma, G. (1999). *Family and Chinese Social Structure.* Beijing: Cultural Relics Publishing House.

Ma, Z. (2000). "The Need of Constructing Modern Cities to Transform Urban Village." *Guangdong Spiritual Civilization Newsletter, Special Issue,* 87–88.

Mendras, H. (1984/2005). *La Fin Des Paysans* (P. Li, Trans.). Beijing: Social Science Academic Press.

Olson, M. Jr. (1980/1996). *The Logic of Collective Action: Public Goods and the Theory of Groups* (Y. Chen, Trans.). Shanghai: SDX Joint Publishing Company.

Polanyi, K. (1958). *The Great Transformation*. Boston: Beacon Press.

Popkin, S. L. (1979). *The Rational Peasant: The Political Economy of Rural Society in Vietnam*. Berkeley: University of California Press.

Research Group of Migrant Workers. (1995). "The State of Migrant Workers in the Pearl River Delta." *Social Sciences in China, 4*.

Schultz, T. W. (1964). *Transforming Traditional Agriculture*. New Haven: Yale University Press.

Scott, J. C. (1976). *The Moral Economy of the Peasant: Rebellion and Subsistence in the Southeast Asia*. New Haven: Yale University Press.

Tang, C., & Feng, X. (2000). "Stratification of Migrant Workers in 'Henan Village.'" *Sociological Research, 4*.

Walder, A. G. (1986). *Communist Neo-traditionalism: Work and Authority in Chinese Industry*. Berkeley: University of California Press.

Wang, C. (1995). *Social Mobility and Restructuring: A Study on the "Zhejiang Village" in the National Capital*. Hangzhou: Zhejiang People's Publishing House.

Wang, H. (1991). *Contemporary Rural Community and Clan Culture in China*. Shanghai: Shanghai People's Publishing House.

Wang, H., Liu, S., Sun, L., & Xiang, B. (1997). "'Zhejiang Village': A Special Way for Chinese Farmers to Blend into the City." *Sociological Research, 1*.

Wang, M. (1997). *Culture and Power from the View of the Village: Investigations into Three Villages in South Fujian Province*. Shanghai: SDX Joint Publishing Company.

Wang, X. (1993). *Blood Relationship and Geography*. Hangzhou: Zhejiang People's Publishing House.

Wang, Y. (1996). *New Collectivism: Re-organization of the Rural Society*. Beijing: Economic Management Publishing House.

Wei, A. (2000). "Spotlight on 'Urban Village.'" *Civilization, 10*.

Xiang, B. (1998). "What Is Community? A Study on the Concentration Area of Floating Population in Beijing." *Sociological Research, 10*.

Zhang, J. (1999). *Informal System in Marketization*. Beijing: Cultural Relics Publishing House.

Zhang, L. (1998). *Farewell to the Ideal: A Study on People's Commune System*. Taipei: Oriental Publishing Center.

Zhe, X. (1997). *The Reconstruction of the Village – Social Change of a "Super Village."* Beijing: China Social Sciences Press.

Zheng Y. (2000, September 6). Goals Settled for the Transforming "Urban Village" Project in Guangzhou. *Southern Metropolis Daily*.

Zhou, D., & Gao, C. (2001). "A Study on Community between Rural and Urban Area: The Social Changing for 50 Years in Nanching Village of Guangzhou City." *Sociological Research, 4*.

12 Examining the "urban village"

My methodology to studing "the end of village"[1]

China is currently in the middle of rural racial changes. In less than 20 years from 1985 to 2001, thanks to urbanization and village mergers, the number of Chinese villages plummeted from 940,617 to 709,257. In 2001 alone, the Chinese villages that have lasted for thousands of years, reduced by 25,458, about 70 per day on average. One once thought that the process in which the village demise coincides with the end of peasant – that is, the transitional process of nonagriculturalization, industrialization, and household registration changes. However, in reality, the process in which village, as a living system and a form of social network, comes to an end is lagging behind and more difficult than the occupational identity of farmer coming to an end. Urbanization is more than an obbligato to industrialization, which has its own development pattern (see Li, 2003).

The current situation of the "urban village" I focus on

I select the "urban village" in the metropolitan areas in south China as the subject for this study. "Urban villages" are pervasive in the entire Pearl River Delta region. It is also a heated topic recently, around which there are a variety of stories told in town. The Pearl River Delta has witnessed a dizzying pace of industrialization and urbanization in the past 20 years. This unique "urban village" seems to be a direct outgrowth of this rapid expansion. However, the problem is much more complicated in that the phenomenon of "urban village" has never appeared in other countries urbanization. Along this line, the emergence of "urban village" must have related to certain peculiar factor in China. Off the top of one's head, one might think of the household registration system that has divided the urban and the rural regions for decades. However, the household registration system is a commonplace for all villages in China, so there must be else mechanism at work. It leaves us "in suspense" to find out what this mechanism is.

Before the start of our investigation, we initially thought that the so-called urban village refers to the village-turned business region that appears at the urban fringe where the city meets the countryside. It is part of the natural expansion of the urban region, similar to the "Zhejiang village" and "Hancunhe village" in Beijing, which that is much urbanized in terms of life and work except lower houses and lesser commercialization. Nonetheless, when we conducted the fieldwork in the "urban villages" in Guangzhou, the economic, political, and cultural center in south China, the jaw-dropping observations leave us speechless despite our preparation by reading relevant literature. The "urban village" in reality differs stark from our imagination. Every "urban village" is like manmade "cement giant" of more than 20 meters high in a radius of a few kilometers of bustling downtown and skyscrapers. Shock does not stops here: the "cement giant" is not built by a single company or an economic collective, but by individual one household after another. The building, however, has completely lost the aesthetic significance of individual variations to the profit from the land and rentals. The iron rule of the economy has also crushed "the cultural significance" of the traditional Chinese village that is symbolic of harmonious living space. Between the linked and identical seven- to eight-storied buildings is the street of about 1.5 and 2 meters, the width of which is determined by the original homestead intervals. The second floor and above are stretched out toward and over the street for the purpose of maximizing the residential construction areas. To the extent that they almost occupy all the open space, local people call them as "check-to-check buildings," "kiss buildings," and "a thin strip of sky." Most of the households in the urban villages need lamp lightings during the daytime, and the streets in the villages feel like "tunnels." Despite this kind of environment, the villages are popular and business oriented. Shops, grocery stores, and service outlets are lined with the narrow and dark streets. In addition to rural residents, there are thousands of migrant works living in the rental houses.

The "urban villages" in the big cities are like relics of ancient history, but also like the newborn in the process of rapid urbanization. From a macro perspective, urbanization is the inevitable way to transfer the rural surplus labor force, improve farmer income level, and transform the social structure of the village. We normally consider that urbanization would be full of celebrations, joys, and dreams of farmers. However, at the last stand of the urbanization, the finish post for villages, why do we see the fission of a millennium village civilization and the hardship for its rebirth?

From the perspective of research subject, it is easier to enter village compared with enterprises, agencies, and urban communities. First, the village is at the most peripheral node of the Chinese society, so outside investigators, often seen as someone from the top, or at least in the sense of institutional structure, are generally received with respect and conscientiousness. Second, the village is an acquaintance society; it is easy to blend in through personal relationships. Farmers are also earthly and hospitable, different from respondents at urban communities and enterprises who often show vigilance and suspicion. Third, there is no clear-cut distinction between living and production and operation, home and workplace, private sphere and public sphere. One can easily set foot in through a mundane realm and shift the attentions to the one of his/her wants to focus on. Lastly, there is basically no secret in the village. Every aunt in the village is a "Holmes" who has strong capacity to decipher secrets of the village. Neither is difficult to borrow documents and archival materials and have them copied.

Our investigation went smoothly because of the administrative introduction and the arrangement made through private relations. Our first investigation occurred in October 2001, and we focused on nine "urban villages" located in Guangzhou. They are Shipai village, Tangxia village, Yaotai village, Sanyuanli village, Tongde village, Xian village, Yangji village, Linhe village, and "Liede village." We interviewed government administrators, village cadres, villagers, and migrant workers who are living in the "urban villages." Then we designed a more detailed outline of structured interviews and invited college students to join us after they finished proper training. We sorted out more than 400,000 characters of materials from the first round of interview. Unfortunately, we found that students followed the outline too strictly, hoping to capture everything, to dig deeper for some of the cases. Along this line, we modified the interview outline and asked them to focus on the "stories" happened in the everyday life, turning interview into "life story" collecting activity. From this second batch of interviews, we sorted out about 800,000 characters of materials, and the interview scope has also expanded to more than 40 "urban villages." I select and compile some of the interview materials concerning 22 villages.

Methodology and accomplishment of others

How to handle and use case study and interview materials – the so-called qualitative research method in sociology – is always a puzzling problem. In this respect, there are two methods to process the raw materials seen in the past studies on Chinese village.

The first method was used by Fei Xiaotong, and I call it "text summarization." This method is used to contemplate on the survey materials and the respondent's words before expressing them in a more refined and structured language and text. This kind of language is straightforward, not like inference that is full of academic concepts. It is not like literary language, either, because what it expresses is "fact" instead of fiction or logic. The text is like the tree of reality after trimming off excessive leaves and flowers in that the appearance may not be appealing but the text audience is mainly for professionals read. The general readers may find it difficult to follow for the lack of stories. Fei Xiaotong's *The Economy of Jiang Village* and Li Jinghan's *A General Investigation of the Society in Ding County* are case in point for this method.

The other method is used by Lin Yueh-Hwa, and I call it "literary summarization." This method refine the raw materials from the investigation into literary language, or to be more specific, the fictional language. The method does not discard the freshness and liveliness in the everyday language, but rather make a complete story out of fragmented, at odds, and miscellaneous materials. It is like a novel in that the original meaning of the novel is stories in the town that differ from "text meta-narrative." A representative work of this method is *The Golden Wing*, an anthropological monograph written by Lin Yueh-Hwa in the genre of fiction. This writing approach has attracted endless questions in the academia in the past decades. Is this a fictional story, or scientific research? Mr. Lin has repeatedly stressed that the stories in the book are true, they are the epitome of the oriental village society and family structure, which have revealed all kinds of social networks, and the book is the research outcome based on socio-anthropological investigation. Raymond Firth, an internationally renowned economic anthropologist, wrote the preface for Lin's book in which he acknowledged the value and significant intellectual contribution made by Lin. In spite of these, Lin's ingenious "literary summarization" method has always considered an "outlier" in today's academic world where scholarly research, like artisan's craftsmanship and industrial assembly line, is "standardized" in terms of "rules" regarding how to conduct survey investigation, how to collect and process materials, and how to examine research questions and so on.

In the Western sociology world, valuing the method of interview and the fieldwork materials can be traced back to the Chicago School in the United States. From 1918 to 1920, William Isaac Thomas and Florian Znaniecki published a five-volume *The Polish Peasant in Europe and America*, which have shaken up the entire academia. Thomas and his colleagues dismissed the historian tradition that tends to focus on political leaders, major events, and significant themes such as politics and war, and sought to write the history "from bottom to the top" by turning to problems like "ordinary people's" unemployment, poverty, social unrest, crowdedness, and rootless wandering and so on. They called their new approach "the life study method" which lets migrants tell their life stories and focuses on collecting primary documents where research subjects express their life experience, such as letters. The five volumes of *The Polish peasant in Europe and America* collect many live materials of this kind. The authors have their own hypothesis – while migrating out, people leave behind a cohesive, family-oriented traditional culture and strive to adjust to a more individualistic and competitive society, whether they are young men and women who leave American farms for jobs in the cities, or African Americans who leave the agricultural South for Harlem or Chicago, or a Polish peasant comes to a steel factory in Pittsburg, or an Italian family leave home to make a living in a canned food factory in Buffalo. The authors hope that this universal character can be expressed through life stories on their own. They reject compiling statistics in the method of "social census" and the morally didactic "common sense sociology." For instance, in the "Investigation in Pittsburg," they wrote, "there you will see how irresistible the power to crumble the society is and how progressive power keeps at bay the social doldrums and selfishness." According to Thomas's "life study method," what really counts is the "life materials" from these immigrants rather than the interpretation and analysis by the authors.

William Foote Whyte, another member of the Chicago School who is deeply influenced by Thomas and others, attempts to adopt an original approach toward handling the investigation materials in a more literary fashion. He is known as the senior Whyte because his son Martin K. Whyte is a sociologist who is best known for his research on contemporary problems in China. *Street Corner Society* published by the senior Whyte in 1943 focused on a slum inhabited by Italians in Boston. He is not a loyal observant of all research rules and regulations but has been a bit unruly in the style of narratives which read as something between academic works and novels. While narrating the story, Whyte constantly cites materials from the interviews no differently from the way scholars quote from classic academic works. He once dreamed of becoming a novelist and sent the first draft of *Street Corner Society* to a non-fiction book contest. Meanwhile he successfully had the department of sociology at the Chicago University that is known for its rigorous academic tradition accept *Street Corner Society* as dissertation, and audaciously stroke back the harsh criticism of his dissertation for "the lack of clear definition and systematic literature review." *Street Corner Society*, later on one of the representative works of the Chicago School, became a standard "storytelling method for the outside world" and the exemplary text imitated by the future scholars of case studies and interview-based investigations.

The literary approach sets *Street Corner Society* apart from earlier classic works on community studies such as *Yankee City* by W. Lloyd Warner, *Middletown* by Robert Staughton Lynd and Helen Merrell Lynd, and *Greenwich Village, 1920–1930* by Caroline Farrar Ware. The last book shares the theme of this chapter, which described how Greenwich Village was incorporated into the New York City in the rapid expansion of the city in 1930s. However, Ware is interested in how Greenwich Village prevented its unique characteristics from being engulfed by the urbanization process. When it comes to narratives, these classic works on community studies tend to be along the logical line instead of the story line. For instance, *Middletown* is structured by the general themes of working, home and family, child care, and leisure time.

Indeed, how to utilize interview materials from case studies is a confusing and strait question, which is also the so-called confusion and predicament of "qualitative" research. On the one hand, many scholars hope that this kind of interview data can also be "representative" and of statistical significance, so when it comes to the community in question, they often use stratified sampling and a unified outline of interview questions. However, it turns out that the unified outline of interview questions limits the conversation topics making the interview documents bald and repetitive. To researcher's greater embarrassment, the attempt of "scientific" interview not only fails to bring scientific character to the interview data, but also deprives the study of its liveliness. On the other hand, interview data is from living language, which has the duality of discourse/ontology, symbol/ meaning, and signifier/signified and as a metaphor by itself represents the interpretative process of decoding meanings. However, interpretations by researchers may vary from one researcher to another, and at times contradictory to each other. In other words, the relationship between the researcher and the research participants is not subjective-objective but intersubjective – that is, the meanings of interview materials will change according to different intersubjectivity. By this token, can researchers self-righteously believe that they are superior to the research participants so they have the power to dismember, dissect, screen, and reinterpret the latter's living language? Is it possible that interpretations made by researchers "conceal" rather than "revealing" the true meanings of the living language? For the meanings of the words in the interview highly depend on the interview "context," which is different from data from questionnaires, and researchers are not able to reproduce and repeat the "context" after all. The problem with questionnaire data is that it discards and forgets about the investigation "context" completely and assumes that the latter is irrelevant to data explanation. Therefore, data measurement and analysis is repeatable "scientific work," while the interpretation of interview materials is unrepeatable "artistic work."

At present, we still fall short to solve the methodological dilemma and embarrassment of this kind. In my study, I adopted a compromised method, not turning interview materials into text language and arranging them along logical clues like in the *Middletown* and *The Economy of Jiang Village*, nor telling a complete story in the living language like in the *Street Corner Society* and *The Golden Wing*.

The first half of *The End of Village* covers my personal interpretation, understanding, perception, and knowledge and judgment, which are the endeavors I have made in terms of the academic framework to extract the rules and reasoning from the numerous and disorderly phenomena and stories. The second half, however, includes authentic interview records, in which I surrender the interpretative power to every attentive reader. Through their own interpretation and comprehension, readers may confirm or disprove my argument in the first part of the book.

According to statistics, there are a total of 139 "strips" of "urban villages" in Guangzhou City. That they are "strip-shaped" is emblematic of the way in which "urban villages" merge into the cities. The 139 "strips" of "urban villages" largely fall into three categories. The first type of villages is located in the downtown area, which has no agricultural land. The second type is located in the suburban areas with a small amount of agricultural land. The third type of village is far away from the city with plenty of land. The "urban village" in study is largely limited to the first type for they throw into relief the characteristics of the village coming to an end. This type of village makes up about one-third of the 139 strips. The term "urban village" used throughout this chapter refers to this type of villages as well.

Village life is in different postures and manners, and every village has its own unique constraints. Although the case study on the village can be very profound and subtle, the specificity of the case may compromise its universal applicability. However, the village survey data on the macro scale often miss and even conceal part of flesh and blood of the real life. Especially when it comes to studying the diachronic "process" in which the village life and the system have changed, a synchronic questionnaire survey is obviously insufficient. Although using survey data to study the life course has made great breakthroughs, the "process" reflected by statistics still lacks "fullness" and "texture."

Fei Xiaotong is among the early scholars who are aware of the limited applicability of the case studies on the village. From comparing the forms of village industry, to comparing the types of small towns and cities, to comparing the patterns of regional development in rural areas, Fei has been exploring the comparative method for studying the actual rural community types with the hope to step out the confinement of case studies by so doing.

Nevertheless, the comparative approach toward actual types still falls short to overcome the limitation in the case study's applicability, only finds itself extending the limited scope. The limitations of actual types are manifested mainly in two respects. First, the compared types in question are not based on abstract ideal type, and thus they lack the universal explanatory power beyond the individual experience. They are not the prototype after reduction and thus lack the significance of historical roots. Due to the numerously different types in reality, the ultimate classification needs certain basic criteria, but one may find that different types are distinguished by one prominent aspect, and that they there are more common among different types. On this ground, one may propose to establish an ideal type to strengthen the applicability. In addition, existent comparison among actual types of villages are more often than not cross-sectional or synchronic, which lacks the comparative interpretation of in-depth or diachronic process. These limitations confine the spread of conversations on the village types in reality.

In order to surmount this kind of limitation, some scholars have also tried to abstract an ideal type or quadrant diagram of village for the sake of comparison. In 1988, Prasenjit Duara published *Culture, Power, and the State: Rural North China, 1900–1942*, having utilizing the materials collected by the research bureau of the South Manchuria Railway Company (commonly abbreviated as Mantetsu) on six villages in the Hebei and Shangdong provinces from 1940 to 1942 (the six-volume *Investigation of Customs in Chinese Villages*). The materials held by Mantetsu are also important sources for other works written by foreign scholars, such as Ramon Myers's *Chinese Peasant Economy: Agricultural Development in Hopei and Shantung, 1890–1949* and Philip Huang's *Peasant Economy and Social Change in North China*. Duara's book (1994) reinterprets the investigation materials and he is obviously unwilling to be confined by the case materials and with the hope to explore in-depth meanings of these materials. Duara has drawn a quadrant diagram of village categories, which is rarely seen in domestic scholarly works. The x-axis marks the relative well-off-ness or poverty of the village and the y axis has religious community close to urban center and lineage community distant from urban center its two poles. The six villages are grouped into four ideal types in the four quadrants (Duara, 1994, p.10). With the regard to the three criteria for the categorization, whether the villages are relatively well off or poor or the level of development has always been an important dimension. The criterion of the distance to from a major city is clearly influenced by the market system theory put forth by G. William Skinner (1964, 1965) who distinguishes himself from a majority of Chinese scholars in that he particularly stresses that the degree and means of Chinese villages connecting to the cities and market determine many of the village characteristics. It seems implausible to bring religion and lineage together into one single criterion, but it provides a whole new dimension. By connecting the problem of lineage to religion, Duara has greatly broadened the horizon of the village research and raised the dialogue ability of the village research.

In 1990, Wang Hansheng and his colleagues tried to summarize the explanatory model for village changes against the backdrop of rural industrialization. They argue that the differentiation of the rural society since the Chinese reform can be categorized into four types of village or rural regions, which are divided by the two intersectional lines of the degree of "industrialization" and "collectivization," respectively. Therefore, on the coordinate diagram, the four types of village or rural regions are high collectivized and low industrialized type, low collectivized and low industrialized type, low collectivized and high industrialized type, and high collectivized and high industrialized type. The degree of "collectivization" is tantamount to the degree of "social differentiation," meaning that the higher the degree of collectivism, the lower the degree of social differentiation (Wang, Yan, Cheng, & Yang, 1990).

There is no way to know if Wang and his colleagues are inspired by Duara in terms of the ways of village ideal types categorization, since many of the contemporary Chinese scholars have not been exposed to Duara's work. It is more likely that they drew the insights from the analytical framework used by Daniel Bell in *The Coming of Post-industrial Society*, which was quite popular in China then. In the foreword to the 1976 edition of the book, Bell (1973/1997) constructed a coordinate with the horizontal axis of technology representing productivity and the vertical axis of property relations representing social relations. While the horizontal axis indicates the industrialized degree (e.g., industrial, pre-industrial), the vertical axis shows the degree of collectivization (e.g., capitalism, collectivism). By this division, there are four combinations: industrial capitalism (e.g., the United States), industrial collectivism (e.g., the Soviet Union), pre-industrial capitalism (e.g., Indonesia), and pre-industrial collectivism (e.g., China). Bell maintained that there is no single explanatory framework for social changes, but different schemas for thee social development: such as feudal, capitalistic, and socialistic; or pre-industrial, industrial, and post-industrial; or patriarchal, hereditary, and legal-rational bureaucracy according to Weberian political authoritarian structure. "Within a given historical period, it may well be that a specific axial principle is so important that it becomes determinative of most other social relations" (Bell, 1973/1997).

Wang Xiaoyi (1991) proposed a very similar hermeneutic framework for the ideal types of villages in which he relies on two dimensions of "the degree of centralized power" and "the development level of the commodity economy" to divide the social stratification of the village into four ideal types. They are the homogeneous society of low-level commodity economy and highly centralized power, the heterogeneous society of high level commodity economy and centralized power, the homogeneous society of low-level commodity economy and decentralized power, and the heterogeneous society of high level commodity economy and decentralized power. On surface Wang's categorization is almost identical to Wang's, but after careful examination, one can find some distinctions. For villages with a low level of collectivization does not necessarily have centralized power as, the centralization of power is related to the collectivization and to patriarchy. By the same token, the development level of commodity economy is related industrialization and to marketization. In this sense, Wang's framework indeed adds two new perspectives.

Li Guoqing designed a classification scheme for a research project on hundreds of villages, in which he set the lineage and administrative power and the influence of market and administrative power as two axes for eight coordinates (Lu, 2001). The economic, political, and cultural factors are all taken into consideration, and the quadrantal diagram also becomes more complicated and farther away from the reality. As I have discussed with Li, as the diagram becomes complex and seemingly more inclusive the ensuing problem is that it is difficult for us to find exemplary villages that fit the diagram hermeneutically.

It seems to be a theoretical progress to construct the analytical framework of the ideal types by intersecting different perspectives, when compared to plain cross-sectional comparison of the actual types. However, the complexity of the quadrant diagram also brings about new problems in that it increasingly resembles the dry skeleton without blood and flesh. The original intent to search for more applicable hermeneutical framework is reversed because it becomes studies of "models" and loses its hermeneutical power when applied to reality. No one is more successful than Duara so far in applying the quadrant diagram of the ideal types to examine villages.

The sources of my methodology

With these in mind, when weighing on the methodology for my own research, I hope to open a new path and construct an ideal type that has universal bearings to explain the end of Chinese villages. This thought is certainly affected by Max Weber's original discussions on the ideal type, but the applied meanings are quite different. Weber, like many German thinkers under the influence of German philosophy, believe that the more "formal" the subject is, the more it is in line with logic, the more revealing of the essence of the subject. This is in stark contrast to the idea of "social facts" put forth by French sociologist Émile Durkheim who is under the influence of empiricism. While Durkheim insists that empiricism disclose the reality, Weber argues that the essential quality is transcendental, which is only comprehensible through the mind-set in line with the causal relationship in reality.

What I mean by the ideal type is not the abstract skeleton constructed by philosophers, but something of blood and flesh, something like the story and characters in novels, which comes from real life, but it cannot be restored to the original life. It is the extraction and summation of life experience as there may not be identical characters in the real life but one may still find many resemblances. From a research point of view, Lao She's *Teahouse*, Lu Xun's *New Year Sacrifice*, Cao Yu's *Thunderstorm*, Ba Jin's *The Family*, and Shen Congwen's *Border Town* and the like are all extracted ideal types with universally explanatory bearings.

I give a formal name to the constructed village type as "Yangcheng village" that represents the process of the village coming to an end in the suburban areas of Pearl River Delta. In reality, there is a village serving as the construction plate for "Yangcheng village" and many prototypes. I select the most representative characteristics and stories from those prototypes and raw life experience, which I then compress into the "Yangcheng village" and the stories around "Yangcheng village" analogous to manufacturing hard tack. These stories are true and reliable, not groundless make-believe or fabrication, but they are not in their original state since many irrelevant details are removed and clues close related to the theme are thrown into relief.

Since the reform and opening up, as far as the chain of urbanization process is concerned, there are all kinds of scattered sociological studies. It is not to say that every scattered studies on the village types have their own ideal type, but all together, the spots can be connected and lined up to form a process or a clue. These studies include Zhou Daming's (2001) study on "Nanjing village" in the urban areas in Canton Province, Wang Hansheng's (1991), Wang Chunguang (1995), and Xiang Biao (2000) studies on "Zhejiang village" in Beijing where migrant workers and small business owners concentrate, Zhe Xiaoye's (1996) study on the mega-village "Wangfeng" in the highly industrialized southeastern region, Wang Mingming's studies on agricultural villages in the developed regions like "Meifa village" and "Tangdong village," Lu Xueyi and his colleagues' studies (2001) on "Xingren village," which is at the incipient stage of industrialization in north China, Yu Jianrong's (2001) studies on rural village of Yue village in Hunan Province, Xiao Tangbiao's (2001) study on nine rural villages in Jiangxi and Anhui Province, and Huang Ping and his college's study on eight villages in four disadvantaged provinces from which workers migrate out, and the list continues. Through establishing ideal models for each one of the development link in the chain of village urbanization, we are able to reproduce the entire vivid and rich process of Chinese village urbanization in theory.

It should be said that my approach to construct "Yangcheng village" is similar to the "case study" taught in the business school in that the significance of the case lies in the laws it reveals instead of the story per se.

In the past, when my friends from social science and economics got together, they always "ridiculed" each other. Economists often "ridiculed" sociology for its detailed description without a conclusion, for its lack of finely extracted materials, and for its "hodgepodge" words full of sympathetic tears and indignation and nothing else. Sociologists answered back in sarcastic tone that what economists care about is how to reduce costs but the cost is too high to conduct research thanks to the profits gained beyond producing economic knowledge. And that is why, it continues, views, ideas, opinions, and comments from economists on macro issues are everywhere, nowhere is seen in-depth analysis of micro cases, and the so-called insights are like "bones with piecemeal meat," tasteless but too wasteful to toss.

Later on, the Unirule Institute of Economics in Beijing launched a grand research project focusing on case studies to examine institutional changes. With plenty of research grants, a large number of economists jumped on the bandwagon of case studies like the way they teach MBA classes. The research outcomes from this project are compiled and published titled *Case Studies in China's Institutional Change*, one collection after another.

What strikes me the most is not the analytical difference between these case studies and those in sociology, but what Professor Zhou Qiren has defined as the problem of "economics of transcending empiricism" in the commentary "Studying Economics in the Real Life" he wrote for the first collection of the case studies.

Zhou argues that one of the most prominent characteristics of the first collection of case studies is the systematic application of many of the new developments in the institutional economics since Ronald Coase to the institutional changes occurred to China lately. Coase's methodology stresses that the premises for theories not only have to be manageable but also realistic. Throughout his life, Coase preferred to use cases and even more so the cases he investigated – for instance, the question of whether the lighthouses in the British history were built by the government or private sectors, how the U.S. Federal Communications Commission consolidated power by allocating channel resources, and of the integration degree between Ford Motor Company and its parts manufacturing factories. In these notable questions, Coase takes advantage of numerous primary or secondary materials to figure out the sequence of events on one hand, and on the other hand, he "reduces" the facts to cases "qualified" for economic research. Nevertheless, Professor Zhou holds that the nine case studies from the Unirule in the first collection are fascinating, but they fall short to "generalize the case study." They share the problem of "strong theoretical foundation yet weak generalization." Cases cannot answer questions by themselves. There is a leap to be made from the case study to the knowledge of the real world – that is, to generalize case studies. That is why "the economics in the real world" is also "economics of transcending empiricism." There are three keywords in its methodology: real world, cases, and the generalization of case studies.

My efforts to construct the ideal type of "Yangcheng village" is also for the sake of "sociology of transcending empiricism" and for that matter in the hope to "generalize" the case study and to realize, as I mentioned before, "a wider applicability and a more extensive dialogue ability." Moreover, for me the "Yangcheng village" is not merely "a general village" in the case study, but it is also an enterprise, a special kind of economic organization of the village and the enterprise. This kind of economic organization, which is deeply embedded in the social network of the village, provides us with a good example to explain the real economic organization and its operation rules. It enables us to observe the formation and fission of the enterprise in its natural state. Between the two ideal poles of the market and the enterprise, there is a continuous spectrum of morphs, which has diverse variations in reality and "Yangcheng village" is one of them. We are almost always able to discover the keys to "universal rules" from certain exceptional examples in reality. In scientific research, "exception" never negates the "universal rule" but amends and expands the boundary of the "universal rule."

With regard to writing style and the analytical focus, I give credit to two books. The first one is *The Economics of Life* by the Beckers, Gary S. Becker and Guity Nashat Becker, which is a collection of column essays written by Gary S. Becker – the authoritative figure in the school of the rational choice – for *BusinessWeek* from 1985 to 1995. Gary S. Becker, known for his pulling economics out of "the blackboard economics" and stepping outside "the ivory tower," was awarded the Nobel Prize in Economics in 1992 for his achievement in applying the economic analysis to social problems. In the letters to the readers, he examined a wind range of phenomena in the real world in plain language and by straightforward theory, from crime, immigration, discrimination, labor, education, drug abuse, marriage, the status of women, and tobacco sales, to the tax system, government regulation, interest groups, international trade, stock market, and economic recession. His language is simple but each word is a gem permeated with insights. Reading his articles makes me even more sick and tired of obscure, esoteric, and pretentious style. A few colleagues from the academics who were once in the rural region, found themselves overwhelmed with all sorts of feelings after listening to the insights on living from an elderly farmer. They said in a self-deprecating manner that while the learned academic predecessors in the past were particularly skilled at explaining profound knowledge in the language as accessible as the elderly farmer's story, our generation of scholars seem to be specialized in creating vague and aloof concepts to explain the commonsense. Therefore, for the narrative in this book, I painstakingly warn against being pedantic.

Another book that affects the focus of my writing is *Sociology of Economic Life* edited by Mark Granovetter and Richard Swedberg in 1992. They selected 15 articles by prestigious sociologists, economists, and anthropologists, which take historical, comparative, and sociological perspectives to explore economic life, economic organization, and economic institutions. The authors may vary in their choices of theories among the sociology of rational choice, new economic sociology, social economics, and transaction costs economics, and the economics of psycho-socio-anthropology. However, their common interest is the problems at the intersection of economy and society. They emphasize that economic action is social action, which is embedded in the social situation, and the economic institution is a social construct. This constitutes the main assumption for my book in which I would search for the social rules in economic life.

This book writes about the end of village, and its rudimental conclusions and contributions are as follows. First, the end of the village is not necessarily identical to the end of farmers, which cannot be solved by nonagriculturalization, industrialization, or reforming the household registration system. The process in which the village comes to an end is more formidable and takes longer period of time. Attempts to reach the goal overnight will definitively rip the social apart. Second, as the village comes to an end, the property rights and social networks are facing restructuring. Meanwhile, the process must be accompanied by fierce interest and value conflicts. A new cooperative and integrated mechanism that transcends "zero sum game" is in bad demand. Third, the traditional local resources of the village organization are not completely the opposite of the modernity, but they can also be incorporated into or constitutive of new modern traditions. Between what seemingly two opposite poles there is always a continuous spectrum of transition and diversity. Fourth, the "urban village" plays dual roles in the process of urbanization. It is both the alienated fringe of the urban center and the cradle and the springboard, the substitute of slums, for migrant workers to blend into the cities as new urban citizens. Fifth, studies on "urban villages" pave the way for us to reveal the ultimate transformation logic from village nonagriculturalization, industrialization, and de-industrialization to urbanization and the end of the village.

Note

This chapter was originally published in *The Ideological Front*, 2004, issue 1.

1   The chapter appeared under the title "The Entry and Methodology of the Village" in the book titled *The End of Village* published by the Commercial Press. At the time of writing, the editor came up with this new title, and the author adapted the chapter for the inclusion in this collection.

References

Anderson, B. (1983). *Imagined Communities*. London: Verso.

Becker, G. S., & Becker, G. N. (1997/2000). *The Economics of Life* (D. Xue, Trans.). Beijing: Huaxia Press.

Bell, D. (1973/1997). *The Coming of Post-Industrial Society: A Venture in Social Forecasting* (X. Gao, Trans.). Beijing: Xinhua Press.

Burns, J. P. (1988). *Political Participation in Rural China*. New Haven: Yale University Press.

Cao, Q. (2000). *China along the Yellow River: Reflections on Rural Society*. Shanghai: Shanghai Literature and Art Publishing House.

Cao, Q., Zhang, L., & Chen, Z. (1995/2001). *Contemporary Social and Cultural Changes in Rural Areas in North Zhejiang Province*. Shanghai: Shanghai Far East Publishers.

Chan, A., Madsen, R., & Unger, J. (1992). *Chen Village under Mao and Deng*. Berkeley: University of California Press.

Chayanov. A. V. (1925/1986). *The Theory of Peasant Economy*. Madison: University of Wisconsin Press.

Chen, J. (1998). *Relation Resources and Nonagriculturalization of Peasants: An Empirical Study on the Village of East Zhejiang Province*. Beijing: China Social Sciences Press.

Cheung, S. N. (1969/2000). *The Theory of Share Tenancy: Agriculture in Asia and Land Reform in Taiwan*. Shanghai: The Commercial Press.

Deng, Y., Cui, Z., & Miao, Z. (1996). *Nanjie Village*. Beijing: Contemporary China Publishing House.

Duara, P. (1988/1994). *Culture, Power, and the State: Rural North China, 1900–1942* (F. Wang, Trans.). Nanjing: Jiangshu People's Publishing House.

Durkheim, E. (1901/1950). *The Rules of Sociological Method*. Glencoe: Free Press.

Fei, X. (1943/1985). *From the Soil: The Foundations of Chinese Society*. Hong Kong: SDX Joint Publishing Company.

Fei, X. (1943/1999). "Cultivated Land in Lv Village." In X. Fei & C. Chang (Eds.), *Earthbound China: A Study of Rural Economy in Yunnan*. Tianjin: Tianjin People's Publishing House.

Fei, X. (1999). "Jiang Village Economy." In *Collected Works of Fei Xiaotong*. Vol. 2 (K. Dai, Trans.). Beijing: Qun Yan Publishing House.

Feng, E. (1994). *Chinese Lineage Society*. Hangzhou: Zhejiang People's Publishing House.

Freedman, M. (1958). *Lineage Organization in South China*. London: Athlone.

Freedman, M. (1966). *Chinese Lineage and Society: Fukien and Kwangtung*. New York: Humanities Press.

Friedman, E., Pickowicz, P. G., Selden, M., & Johnson, K. A. (1991). *Chinese Village, Socialist State*. New Haven: Yale University Press.

Geertz, C. (1973). *The Interpretation of Cultures*. New York: Basic Books.

Geertz, C. (1983/1999). *Local Knowledge* (H. Wang & J. Zhang, Trans.). Beijing: Central Party Literature Press.

Granovetter, M., & Swedberg, R. (Eds.). (1992). *The Sociology of Economic Life*. Boulder, CO: Westview Press.

Guo, Y. (1996). "Traditional Affinity Relationship in the Rural Modernization." *Sociological Research, 6.*

Guo, Z. (1999). *Chinese Village System: China Federation of Literary and Art Circles.* Beijing: People's Publishing House.

He, X., & Tong, Z. (2002). "On Social Solidarity of Villages – Also on the Social Basis of Village Order." *Social Sciences in China, 3.*

He, X., & Xiao, T. (1999). "Stratification and Its Deepening of the Study of the Village Society." *Social Sciences in China (Hong Kong), 25.*

Hu, B. (1996). *Institutional Change and Power Allocation in Chinese Villages.* Xi'an: Shanxi Economic Publishing House.

Huang, P. (1986). *The Peasant Economy and Social Change in North China.* Beijing: Zhong Hua Book Company.

Huang, P. (1990). *The Peasant Family and Rural Development in the Yangzi Delta, 1350– 1988.* Beijing: Zhong Hua Book Company.

Huang, P. (1992). *Ultra-density in Chinese Village and Modernization: Crisis in Normative Perception and Its Solution.* Shanghai: Shanghai People's Publishing House.

Huang, P. (Ed.). (1997). *In Search for Survival: A Sociological Study of Contemporary Migration Population from Rural China.* Kunming: Yun'nan People's Publishing House.

Huang, S. (1994). *The Story of Lin Village: The Rural Reform in China after 1949.* Shanghai: SDX Joint Publishing Company.

Jiang, Z. (1998). "The Analysis of the Authority Structure of the Village Family and the Mainland Rural Community." *Mainland China Studies (Taipei), 41.*

Jin, Y., & Qin, H. (1996). *Rural Commune, Reform and Revolution – The Tradition of the Village Society and the Modernization of Russia.* Beijing: Central Compilation & Translation Press.

Kuhn, P. A. (1970). *Rebellion and Its Enemies in Late Imperial China: Militarization and Social Structure 1796–1864.* Cambridge, MA: Harvard University Press.

Lan, Y. (2003). *Urban village: Fieldwork on a "New Village Community."* Dissertation. Beijing: Graduate School of the Chinese Academy of Social Sciences.

Li, P. (2002). "Tremendous Changes: The End of Villages-A Study of Villages in the Center of Guangzhou City." *Social Sciences in China, 1.*

Li, P. (Ed.). (2003). *Migrant Workers: An Economic and Social Analysis of Rural Migrant Workers in China.* Beijing: Social Science Academic Press.

Lin, Y. (1935/2000). *Studies on the Lineage in Yixu.* Shanghai: SDX Joint Publishing Company.

Lin, Y. (1944/1989). *Golden Wing: A Family Chronicle* (K. Zhuang & Z. Lin, Trans.). Hong Kong: SDX Joint Publishing Company.

Lipman, J. N., & Harrell, S. (Eds.). (1990). *Violence in China: Essays in Culture and Counterculture.* Albany: State University of New York Press.

Little, D. (1989). *Understanding Peasant China: Case Studies in the Philosophy of Social Sciences.* New Haven: Yale University Press.

Lu, X. (Ed.). (2001). *Village with Internal Development: Xingren Village.* Beijing: Social Science Academic Press.

Lynd, R. S., & Lynd, H. M. (1929). *Middletown.* New York: Harcourt Brace Jovanovich.

Lynd, R. S., & Lynd, H. M. (1937). *Middletown in Transition*. New York: Harcourt Brace Jovanovich.

Madsen, R. (1984). *Morality and Power in a Chinese Village*. Berkeley: University of California Press.

Malinowski, B. (1922). *Argonauts of the Western Pacific: An Account of Native Enterprise and Adventure in the Archipelagoes of Melanesian New Guinea*. London: Routledge and Kegan Paul.

Mao, D. (2000). *History of a Village Community*. Beijing: Xue Lin Publishing House.

Marks, R. B. (1984). *Rural Revolution in South China: Peasants and the Making of History in Haifeng County 1570–1930*. Wisconsin: University of Wisconsin Press.

Mendras, H. (1984/2005). *La Fin Des Paysans* (P. Li, Trans.). Beijing: Social Science Academic Press.

Myers, R. (1970/1999). *Chinese Peasant Economy: Agricultural Development in Hopei and Shantung, 1890–1949* (J. Shi, Trans.). Nanjing: Jiangsu People's Publishing House.

Nolan, P. (1988). *The Political Economy of Collective Farms: An Analysis of China's Post-Mao Rural Reforms*. Boulder, CO: Westview Press.

Oi, J. C. (1989). *State and Peasant in Contemporary China: The Political Economy of Village Government*. Berkeley: University of California Press.

Parish, W. L. (Ed.). (1985). *Chinese Rural Development: The Great Transformation*. New York: Routledge.

Polanyi, K. (1985). *The Great Transformation*. Boston: Beacon Press.

Popkin, S. L. (1979). *The Rational Peasant: The Political Economy of Rural Society in Vietnam*. Berkeley: University of California Press.

Potter, S. H., & Potter, J. M. (1990). *China's Peasant: The Anthropology of a Revolution*. Cambridge: Cambridge University Press.

Qian, H., & Xie, W. (1995). *Tradition and Transformation: The Rural Clan Order in Taihe, Jiangxi*. Shanghai: Shanghai Academy of Social Sciences Press.

Redfield, R. (1956). *Peasant Society and Culture*. Chicago: The University of Chicago Press.

Saith, A. (1987). *The Re-emergence of the Chinese Peasantry: Aspects of Rural Decollectivisation*. London: Croom Helm.

Schultz, T. W. (1964). *Transforming Traditional Agriculture*. New Haven: Yale University Press.

Scott, J. C. (1976). *The Moral Economy of the Peasant: Rebellion and Subsistence in the Southeast Asia*. New Haven: Yale University Press.

Scott, J. C. (1985). *Weapons of the Weak: Everyday Forms of Peasant Resistance*. New Haven: Yale University Press.

Shen, Y. (1998). "The Rise and Fall of Village Politics and Reconstruction." *Strategy and Management, 6*.

Shue, V. (1988). *The Reach of State: Sketches of the Chinese Body Politics*. Stanford: Stanford University Press.

Skinner, G. W. (1964/1965). "Marketing and Social Structure in Rural China." *Journal of Asian Studies, 24*(1), 3–44; *24*(2), 195–228; *24*(3), 363–399.

Su, L. (2000). *Delivery Legal Knowledge to the Rural Areas*. Beijing: China University of Political Science and Law Press.

Thomas, W. I., & Znaniecki, F. (1984/2000). *The Polish Peasant in Europe and America* (Y. Zhang, Trans.). Nanjing: Yilin Press.

Vermeer, E. B., Pieke, F. N., & Chong, W. L. (1998). *Cooperative and Collective in China's Rural Development: Between State and Private Interests*. New York: Sharpe.

Walder, A. G. (1998). *Zouping in Transition: The Process of Reform in Rural China*. Cambridge, MA: Harvard University Press.

Wang, C. (1995). *Social Mobility and Restructuring: A Study on the "Zhejiang Village" in the National Capital*. Hangzhou: Zhejiang People's Publishing House.

Wang, H. (1991). *Contemporary Rural Community and Clan Culture in China*. Shanghai: Shanghai People's Publishing House.

Wang, H., Liu, S., Sun, L., & Xiang, B. (1997). "'Zhejiang Village': A Special Way for Chinese Farmers to Blend into the City." *Sociological Research, 1*.

Wang, H., Yan, X., Cheng, W., & Yang, W. (1990). "Industrialization and Social Differentiation: Social Structural Changes of Chinese Villages since the Reform." *Rural Economy and Society, 4*.

Wang, M. (1997). *Culture and Power from the View of the Village: Investigations into Three Villages in South Fujian Province*. Shanghai: SDX Joint Publishing Company.

Wang, X. (1991). "The Differentiation and Integration of the Rural Society." *Sociology and Social Survey, 2*.

Wang, X., & Zhu, C. (1996). *Private-Owned Enterprise and Family Economy in Chinese Rural Areas*. Xi'an: Shanxi Economic Publishing House.

Wang, Y. (1996). *New Collectivism: Re-organization of the Rural Society*. Beijing: Economic Management Publishing House.

Ware, C. F. (1935/1977). *Greenwich Village: 1920–1930*. New York: Octagon Books.

Wen, T. (1999). "The History of Rural System over the Half of a Century." *Strategy and Management, 6*.

Whyte, W. F. (1943/1994). *Street Corner Society: The Social Structure of an Italian Slum*. Shanghai: The Commercial Press.

Wu, Y. (2002). *Authority and Order in Village Governance Change: Expressions of the Two Villages in the East of Sichuan Province in 20th century*. Beijing: China Social Sciences Press.

Xiang, B. (2000). *Communities across Borders: Life History of the "Zhejiang Village" in Beijing*. Shanghai: SDX Joint Publishing Company.

Xiang, J. (2002). *Rural Governance in the Context of Collective Economy*. Wuhan: Central China Normal University Press.

Xiao, T. (2001). *Clan in the Village Governance: Investigation and Study on Nine Villages*. Shanghai: Shanghai Bookstore Publishing House.

Yan, Y. (1996/2000). *The Flow of Gifts: The Principle of Reciprocity and Social Networks in a Chinese Village* (F. Li & Y. Liu, Trans.). Shanghai: Shanghai People's Publishing House.

Yang, M. C. (1984). *The Evolution of Rural Society in China*. Taipei: Taiwan River Books Inc.

Yu, J. (2001). *Politics in Yue Village*. Shanghai: The Commercial Press.

Zhang, L. (1998). *Farewell to the Ideal: A Study on People's Commune System*. Taipei: Oriental Publishing Center.

Zhao, X. (1998). *Chinese Village System*. Beijing: Social Science Academic Press.

Zhe, X. (1996). "Diversification of the Village Boundaries: The Conflict between and the Symbiosis of the Open-border Economy and the Closed Society." *Social Sciences in China, 3*.

Zhe, X. (1997). *The Reconstruction of the Village – Social Change of a "Super Village."* Beijing: China Social Sciences Press.

Zhou, Q. (1999). "Studying Economics in the Real World." In S. Zhang (Ed.), *Case Studies in China's Institutional Change*. Beijing: China Financial and Economic Publishing House.

Zhou, X. (1998). *Tradition and Transformation – Social Psychology of Peasants in Jiangsu and Zhejiang Provinces and Its Evolution since the Modern Era*. Shanghai: SDX Joint Publishing Company.

Zhuang, K. (1999). *Silver Wing – Local Culture and Cultural Changes of China*. Shanghai: SDX Joint Publishing Company.

Zweig, D. (1997). *Freeing China's Farmers: Rural Restructuring in the Reform Era*. London: Sharpe.

Note on Romanization and translations

The text throughout the book uses current Hanyu Pinyin system for Romanization of Chinese characters, including names, locations, agencies, titles, positions, and so on, unless otherwise noted in the parentheses. Exceptions are made for widely acknowledged and accepted names or terms, such as Sun Yat-sen, Yung Wing, or Tao. The translator keeps the original order of the family name and given name as the Chinese name appears. In translation of technical terms, the translator keep Chinese Pinyin in one of the following two situations. First, the Pinyin of core concepts from the author's theory is maintained when the terms lack precise English translations or their meanings are so complicated and nuanced that they can only be conveyed by paraphrasing in English. Under this circumstance, the translator would put a note of explanation. Second, the Pinyin is maintained when the terms in question are well-known to English readers, most of which are ancient Chinese philosophical notions like *ren* (benevolence) and *yi* (righteousness).

Index

For Product Safety Concerns and Information please contact our EU
representative GPSR@taylorandfrancis.com
Taylor & Francis Verlag GmbH, Kaufingerstraße 24, 80331 München, Germany

www.ingramcontent.com/pod-product-compliance
Ingram Content Group UK Ltd.
Pitfield, Milton Keynes, MK11 3LW, UK
UKHW021002180425
457613UK00019B/779